The Quest for
Global Quality

The Quest for Global Quality
A Manifestation of Total Quality Management by Singapore Airlines

Chang Zeph Yun
Yeong Wee Yong
Lawrence Loh
Faculty of Business Administration
National University of Singapore

Cover design and illustrated by Michael Chan Chian Fu, Singapore
Text design by Lesley Stewart
Typeset by JTS Multi-lingual Pte Ltd
Printed in Singapore

First printed in 1996.

Library of Congress Cataloging in Publication Data

Chang, Zeph Yun
  The quest for global quality : a manifestation of total quality management by Singapore airlines / Chang Zeph Yun, Yeong Wee Yong, Lawrence Loh
  p.   cm.
  Includes bibliographical references and index.
  ISBN 0-201-42087-2
  1. Singapore Airlines — Management. 2. Aeronautics, Commercial — Singapore — Management. 3. Airlines — Singapore — Management.

  4. Total quality management — Singapore. I. Chang, Zeph Yun. II. Yeong Wee Yeong. III. Loh, Lawrence. IV. Title
  HE9874.A4Y46 1996
  387.7'06'55957—dc20   96-15982
                                                                CIP

Preface

This book was written to cater to a spectrum of readers.

The myriad definitions for TQM has often left many confounded; the authors included. It was this shroud of ambiguity over what might easily be THE management concept of the century that prompted the authors to attempt giving TQM a worthy description/definition.

Anyone who has been in the fraternity of TQM practitioners long enough will agree that this is no mean feat. Many painstaking hours have been devoted to traditional research methods such as extensive/ intensive literature review to coalesce the different definitions into one universal all-encompassing definition. In addition, we feel it is necessary to support this definition with a true to life case study; for a number of reasons. Firstly, to further shed light on TQM, and secondly, to inject realism to the whole concept of TQM.

This is a casebook for TQM; catering to those involved in expounding TQM concepts. As this book was written based on the experience and methods of an actual industry giant, it offers a lucid demonstration of TQM in practice and will definitely prove useful and interesting to educators in this area.

Present practitioners of TQM will also find this book enlightening as it presents Singapore Airlines' (SIA) unique TQM approach. From this book, certain useful tips to fine-tune their own existing practice might be picked up.

Time and again, we are baffled by the sheer number of people and amount of effort in planning and coordination needed to make a trip trouble-free. Hopefully, readers will find this book useful as it also offers some invaluable troubleshooting tips for those who encounter difficulties along their journey.

Throughout the years, SIA has earned a reputation that transcends boundaries. It is our hope that by writing this book, many ardent 'SIA Fans' may have a glimpse of the meticulous work the SIA people put in to deliver the quality service that they appreciate so much.

This book is a tribute to the concept of TQM and its realization in SIA.

Foreword

Singapore Airlines is honoured to have been selected by the Faculty of Business Administration, National University of Singapore, for in-depth research, culminating in this book on total quality management.

We have always striven for quality and excellence in everything we do. Our reputation for product innovation, high-quality inflight and ground services, investment in advanced technology and human resource development, far-sighted planning and prudent financial management are evidence of this corporate philosophy.

Success did not come to us by accident. Our orientation to quality has been our main driving force. Although we have done well so far, we do not intend to rest on our laurels. In the increasingly competitive global economy of today, we will continue to set the lead in product and service, while striving to improve productivity.

We appreciate this opportunity to share with you our experiences, and hope that readers of this book will benefit from this research.

Dr Cheong Choong Kong
Managing Director
Singapore Airlines

In recent times, we are witnessing a total revamp in the perception of quality management and its strategic significance in business. From a defensive approach, many business leaders are now convinced of the efficacy of quality as a competitive weapon.

The Faculty of Business Administration at the National University of Singapore is committed to the research and promotion of the most current management/business theories, especially in the Asian context. We hold the view that, Singapore, being at the crossroads of the East and West can be instrumental in the 'Asianization' of many Western-conceived business theories and vice versa. Total quality management (TQM) and its implementation at Singapore Airlines (SIA) is one such excellent example.

Microsoft, Coca-Cola etc., are easily identified as American businesses. Indeed, these brands are 'Business Ambassadors' of the United States. What qualifies as Singapore's 'Business Ambassador'? The irrefutable choice is SIA.

SIA is significant and noteworthy for many reasons. Firstly, it is Singapore's premier business and one of a few, if not the only globally-recognized Singapore business. Secondly, through the implementation of TQM, SIA has lent impetus to the thesis that 'Asianized' Western business concepts extract the best from both the East and the West. This is substantiated by SIA's unblemished track record. Thirdly, SIA's unequivocal success amply attests to the tremendous promise TQM holds.

I am pleased that the significant implications in the "SIA Story" can be brought to the public through this book.

Professor Wee Chow Hou, Ph.D, PPA
Dean
Faculty of Business Administration
National University of Singapore

Acknowledgements

We would like to express our special thanks to Dr Cheong Choong Kong, Managing Director of SIA, for agreeing to pen the Foreword of this book.

We are also deeply indebted to Mr Karmjit Singh, Assistant Director for Corporate Affairs, SIA for his unceasing support and help. The many interviews and information this book was based on were possible only because of his generous assistance.

The staff at SIA were particularly helpful and generous for taking the time to grant us interviews and provide valuable information. These gave us the much needed insight into the mechanics of SIA's success. We would like to record our thanks to these individuals. They are:

> Captain Maurice de Vaz, Director of Flight Operations
> Mr Yap Kim Wah, Chief Executive, SATS Catering
> Mr Michael Loong, Assistant Director of Engineering Company
> Mr Raja Segran, Senior Manager, Ground Services
> Mr George Lee, Senior Manager, Inflight Services
> Dr Lor Kim Loon, Food Research & Development Manager, SATS Catering
> Mr Chew Tai Lu, Cabin Crew Manager (Crew Performance)
> Mr Lim Soon Leng, Cabin Crew Manager (Service Development)
> Mr Pritam Singh, Head Customer Relations
> Mdm Katherine C. Y. Chen, Personnel Training Executive, Management Development Center

We also wish to express our appreciation to the staff of Management

Services Division & SIA Library who have contributed in one way or another in providing information for this book.

A book on SIA would only have added meaning if its contents were authenticated by those who made up SIA. We believe it is a strong sense of loyalty, coupled with responsibility in ensuring that a true picture of SIA is presented, that motivated those at SIA to take on the tedious and time-consuming task of vetting the contents.

We hope the book will be a worthy tribute to the tireless efforts of the SIA staff in being the best.

Finally, our thanks must go to Ms Lynn Y. Kuah, Marketing Executive, Addison Wesley Singapore Pte. Ltd. The release of this book is the result of her professionalism, perseverence and patience.

Dr Chang Zeph Yun
Dr Yeong Wee Yong
Dr Lawrence Loh

Contents

Preface   **v**

Foreword   **vii**

Acknowledgements   **ix**

**1. Introduction: A Manifestation of Total
     Quality Management by Singapore Airlines**   **1**
   1.1 Introduction   1
   1.2 TQM as an Evolving Concept   1
   1.3 TQM as a People-Focused Management System   2
   1.4 TQM as a Time-Oriented Program   2
   1.5 TQM Under ISO 9000 Series of Standards   3
   1.6 How Does a Company Qualify as a TQM Company?   4
   1.7 A Refreshing Manifestation of TQM by SIA   5
        References   6

2. The Prelude to Success   **7**
   2.1 Introduction   7
   2.2 The Early History of Singapore Airlines   7
   2.3 Talent and Expertise   7
   2.4 Political Changes and the Separation of Singapore
        from the Federation: A Fresh Start   8
   2.5 'We Were on Our Own'   9
   2.6 The Fight for Traffic Rights   11
   2.7 Hit by the Oil Crisis   12
   2.8 The Concorde Saga   13
   2.9 Modernization of the Fleet   14
   2.10 Conclusion   15

3.   The Airline and its Global Service Quality   17
3.1   The National Analogy   17
3.2   The Global Service Quality   18
3.3   The Turbulent Business Environment   21
3.4   The Challenges   21
3.5   Commitment to Total Quality Management: Key
        Principles of SIA's TQM Initiative   22
      References   27

4.   The SIA-TQM Approach   29
4.1   The Era of Total Quality Management   29
4.2   Definitions of Quality   29
4.3   Service Quality   32
4.4   Total Quality Management (TQM)   36
4.5   Developing a TQM System   36
4.6   SIA's TQM Approach   38
4.7   The SIA-TQM System   40
      References   41

5.   Strategic Quality Management   43
5.1   The Need for Strategic Quality Management   43
5.2   Framework of Strategic Quality Management   43
5.3   Mission Statement   46
5.4   Goal   46
5.5   Competitive Strategies   47
5.6   Quality Objective and Performance Measures   51
5.7   Organization for Quality   55
5.8   Quality Policies   57
5.9   Planning for Quality   57
5.10 The SQM Cycle and Strategic Alignment   60
      References   61

6.   Management of Market Quality   63
6.1   Elements of Market Quality Management   63
6.2   Concepts of Market Quality   63
6.3   Marketing Functions in Quality Management   66
6.4   Design of Market Quality   67
6.5   SIA's Design of Total Product   69
      References   75

7.	**Management of Airworthiness: Safety and Reliability**	**77**
	7.1 Introduction	77
	7.2 SIA's 'Beyond Airworthiness' Aircraft Fleet	77
	7.3 Auditing New Aircraft in Production	78
	7.4 Organizing for Aircraft Quality	79
	7.5 Aircraft Quality	80
	7.6 Control for Airworthiness	82
	7.7 Management of Line Stations	92
	References	94

8.	**Management of Flight Operations**	**95**
	8.1 Excellence in Technical Operations	95
	8.2 Goals of Flight Operations Management	95
	8.3 The Importance of Competent Pilots	95
	8.4 Pilot Training	96
	8.5 The Flight Crew Training Center	97
	8.6 The Human Aspects of Flight Operations Management	98
	8.7 Strategic Information Systems for Flight Operations	100
	References	102

9.	**Managing Key Airline Business Operations: The Use of Customer Focused Technology**	**103**
	9.1 Introduction	103
	9.2 Strategic Information Systems	103
	9.3 Abacus Computer Reservation Operations	105
	9.4 Schedule and Computerized Route Planning	107
	9.5 Departure Control Systems	114
	9.6 Arrival Control Systems	116
	9.7 Quality Measures of Airline Operations	117
	9.8 Station Crisis and Delay	121
	References	127

10.	**Management of Customer Services**	**129**
	10.1 Customer Service and the Spiral of Quality Progress	129
	10.2 Definition of Customer Service	129
	10.3 Strategic Issues of Customer Service Management	130
	10.4 Importance of Customer Service	131
	10.5 SIA's Three Levels of Customer Satisfaction	132

10.6 Types of Customer Service   133
10.7 Critical Quality Factors of Customer Services   133
10.8 SIA's Principles on Extreme Customer Service   137
References   139

11. Towards a Total Customer Service System   **141**
11.1 SIA's Principle on Customer Services   141
11.2 SIA's Total Transactional Customer Services   141
11.3 SIA's Approach Towards Quality Customer
      Services   142
11.4 SIA's Preflight Customer Services   146
11.5 SIA's Airport Ground Customer Services   151
11.6 SIA's Postflight Customer Services   163
References   166

12. Essence of Outstanding Ground Services   **167**
12.1 Paradigm Shift of Competition   167
12.2 Benchmarking Airline Ground Services   167
12.3 Airline's Management of Strategic Partners: The
      Handling Agents   170
12.4 The Handling Company's Management of
      Ground Services   172
References   177

13. Management of Inflight Service Quality   **179**
13.1 Introduction   179
13.2 SIA's Commitment to Inflight Service Quality   179
13.3 Management of Cabin Crew   185
13.4 Seamless Inflight Services   193
References   195

14. Management of Inflight Catering   **197**
14.1 Managing Inflight Food and Beverages   197
14.2 Design of Market Quality for Inflight Meal
      Product   200
14.3 SATS Inflight Kitchen as a Production Center
      for Inflight Meals   203
14.4 Culinary Standards of SATS Catering   206
14.5 Maintenance of Food Quality   207

14.6 Quality Assurance: The ISO 9002 Certification 210
References 211

15. The Human Dimension of SIA's Success 213
15.1 The Vital Role of Human Behavior in Service
Quality 213
15.2 Characteristics of SIA's Quality Leadership 213
15.3 Management's Commitment 215
15.4 Total Participation 220
15.5 Teamwork and Networking 221
References 227

16. Training and Development: The MDC Approach 229
16.1 Introduction 229
16.2 Training Philosophy 229
16.3 Training Expenses 230
16.4 Training Facility: The SIA Training Center 230
16.5 Management Developement: The MDC Approach 230
16.6 Service Training for Clients: The SQ Center 234
16.7 The Training Award 235
Reference 235

17. Epilogue: Towards the State of 'Beyond TQM' in SIA 237
17.1 State of TQM Normalcy 237
17.2 State of Beyond TQM 237
17.3 A Realization of the Normalcy of TQM in SIA 238
Reference 238

Appendix 239

Index 265

CHAPTER ONE

Introduction: A Manifestation of Total Quality Management by Singapore Airlines

1.1 Introduction

Quality has evolved from a discipline relegated to inspectors and technicians to a strategic focus and a process-oriented approach to management that commands the attention of all employees, from chief executive officers and presidents to frontline workers(Bounds *et al*, 1994). Total quality management (TQM) is a concept currently being zealously pursued in business and academic circles. Business managers are eager to get information on how to apply the concept of TQM while academics are trying to determine what TQM really is all about.

1.2 TQM as an Evolving Concept

The term TQM conveys the comprehensive nature of management in the context of different organizations in different industries. With the emphasis on the word 'total' together with the broad definition of 'quality', there is however no uniformity in the various approaches that go by the name. The only thing that business managers and academics have in common is that neither can reach a consensus on either the definition or actual practice of TQM. The rift that exists between the theorists and the practitioners of TQM has inevitably created a shroud of ambiguity on what really constitutes TQM. It is hoped that this chapter will clear up some, if not all, of these ambiguities before embarking on the study of a manifesto for TQM. The following describe a variety of approaches to TQM postulated by TQM experts.

1.3 TQM as a People-Focused Management System

Some believe that TQM encompasses customer focus, continuous improvement, employee empowerment, teamwork and total participation, among other things. This view seems too simple and places too much emphasis on the human aspects of quality management. It ignores the totality of TQM concepts; namely, the technological, operational and the marketing aspects of quality management.

TQM, as its name suggests, is an approach to improving the effectiveness and flexibility of a business as a whole, centered around quality. It is essentially a way of organizing and involving the whole organization—every department, every activity, and every individual at every level—in the attainment of quality. The strategic issues, the marketing issues, the technical aspects of the operations all have to be addressed along with the human aspects of the organization. A narrow perspective is counteractive to TQM.

1.4 TQM as a Time-Oriented Program

Another misconception is that TQM is often associated with the 'program mentality', and that it should be implemented in the form of a time-phased program. This concept restricts TQM to a set program that must be implemented over a fixed-time span, with a marked beginning and end.

This concept is contradictory to actual business practices. In the United States, TQM is often used to refer to the management approaches being developed in the current era of strategic quality management (SQM). Ideally, SQM managers should consider TQM more than a program (Bounds *et al*, 1994).

In general, several points should be taken into account while establishing a TQM system:

1. Quality concerns both short-term and long-term issues.
2. Although quality concerns both the short-term and long-term

issues, it does not come about through piecemeal efforts or through a single quality improvement program. It is the result of a totally integrated set of actions with a long-term commitment. Quality is more a long-term focus than a short-term function.

3. TQM is a continuous effort beyond the time horizon. A time-marked program is not essential.

1.5 TQM Under ISO 9000 Series of Standards

Although previously mentioned TQM concepts have been comprehensive, it is appropriate to review the definition of TQM as stated in the International Standard ISO/DIS 8402 as follows:

'TQM is the management approach of an organization, centered on quality, based on the participation of all its members and aiming at long-term success through customer satisfaction, and benefits to the members of the organization and to the society.'

In this context, the word 'total' conveys the idea that all employees, functioning at every level of an organization, pursue quality. This begins with strategic quality management and extends through product core-quality design, product market-quality design, manufacturing, marketing, customer services, and so on. Of the many different definitions of TQM, the ISO one is by far the most appropriate.

In his book, Total Quality Management in Government (1993), Columbia University's Steven Cohen, recipient of the Environmental Protection Agency's Gold Medal for his demonstrated leadership in TQM, defined TQM in consonance with the ISO definition as follows:

1. **Total** implies applying the search for quality to every aspect of work, from identifying customer needs to aggressively evaluating whether the customer is satisfied.
2. **Quality** means meeting and exceeding customer expectations.
3. **Management** means developing and maintaining the organizational capacity to constantly improve quality.

Puri (1992) defined a TQM system as one that comprises all

aspects of management, systems, procedures, processes and methodologies properly coordinated, with an absolute focus on customer satisfaction.

Others may define TQM differently, but our research as presented in this book is based on definitions of the ISO, Cohen and Puri.

1.6 How Does a Company Qualify as a TQM Company ?

1. It is imperative that any company truly committed to the concept of TQM must first seek to establish quality management systems. These must be relevant to all the activities and tasks that must be performed to attain fitness for purpose or use, instead of a 'quality program' aimed at achieving some particular quality objective or desire of management over a period of time.

2. With this in mind, it becomes clear that the management of quality has evolved beyond the level of inspectors and technical experts and literally permeate the entire organization. To further substantiate this concept, if a particular company, for example, an aerospace company, reports that it has successfully improved the efficiency and quality of not one, but several, aspects of its aircraft components repair processes and now claims to be a successful TQM company, does this company truly qualify?

   While the company cited here has managed to spruce up its operations, if it fails to address the issues of totality, such as its mission, its overall quality objectives, its policy towards customer service, etc., it can hardly qualify as a TQM company.

3. In short, a company that adopts the TQM approach must seek improvement in all 'improvable' areas. It is not enough to improve, for instance, just the product-centered aspects and neglect the service-related areas or vice versa. In TQM, a company can ill afford to 'leave any stones unturned'.

4. A company adopting the TQM approach must realize that it is an on-going process of refinement: it is continuous and not simply a quality improvement program with a fixed time-span. Indeed, it is absurd if a company boasts of attaining TQM-status through a single, discrete program by a certain target date: unless the company is claiming that it has implemented a universal program which addresses every single problem it faces now or will face in the

future. It must be understood that fulfillment of certain targets is merely a step towards TQM, since no one single program or target achieved within a specific timeframe can adequately satisfy the requirements of TQM.

The discussion above is but a guideline. There is truly no hard and fast rule or model for a company to follow in carrying out TQM, although certain basic requirements must be present. TQM is a dynamic approach and every company has different circumstances and different problems and therefore different solutions. However, all must share one thing in common: a desire for quality that borders on obsession, with attention to meticulous details and intricacies in all the functional areas within an organization. That, perhaps, is the trademark of a TQM company.

In the course of the research for this book, an exhaustive search and study of many companies was made to identify a company that adequately typifies the TQM approach. The search ended with such a company, Singapore Airlines (SIA).

1.7 A Refreshing Manifestation of TQM by SIA

Because of the volatile nature of the airline industry, SIA's management is shaped by its flexibility, adaptability and dexterity. Its dedicated and unceasing effort towards striving for excellent quality is shown by the details presented in this book.

SIA lucidly demonstrates that the TQM approach is not a rigid framework. TQM is an on-going, well-thought-out approach that has no end and is constantly updated, enhanced and rejuvenated.

Based on what is presented in this book, it suffices to say that SIA's management approach is a refreshing manifestation of TQM. It is dynamic and versatile, with no specific beginning or end, with no boundaries or restrictions; just a strong desire to be the best and a devotion to upgrading that is unceasing and continuous. This meticulous approach is what makes SIA successful. Every aspect of its operation is involved in TQM, not just those that have been involved with a program of upgrading of human skills.

References

1. Bounds G., *et al* (1994).*Total Quality Management: Towards The Emerging Paradigm.* New York: McGraw-Hill
2. Cohen, S. (1993). *Total Quality Management in Government.* San Francisco: Jossey-Bass Inc.
3. Puri, S. C. (1992). *ISO 9000 and Total Quality Management.* Ottawa and Washington, D.C.: Standards-Quality Management Group

CHAPTER TWO

The Prelude To Success

2.1 Introduction

Success. Difficult beginnings. Of the two, the more glamorous would quite obviously be **success**. All too often, people are preoccupied with the extent of a person's or business' success. We are too focused on **how** successful the business is, not why it is successful.

The essence of any success story, the elements that make it a worthy case study, are the tribulations that the business encountered during its creation, and the efforts made to mount the apparently insurmountable.

Lest people go away with the idea that SIA was an overnight success this chapter will briefly trace the early difficulties SIA faced.

2.2 The Early History of Singapore Airlines

SIA began as Malayan Airways Limited (MAL). It was incorporated in Singapore on 21 October 1937, when Singapore was still part of the Malaya Federation.

On 16 September 1963, the new Federation of Malaysia was officially born, rendering the name 'Malayan Airways' obsolete. Consequently, the airline was renamed: Malaysian Airways Limited, still (MAL).

2.3 Talent and Expertise

Just as an aircraft needs a crew to fly, Malayan Airways (MAL) needed pioneers to take on the arduous task of steering the future course of the airline.

Lim Chin Beng, an economist by training, was one such pioneer who joined MAL in June 1960. The airline business has always been riddled with its own peculiarities in terms of economics and finance and Lim Chin Beng took on the arduous task of learning and familiarizing himself with these peculiarities, eventually going on to play an instrumental role in the growth of the airline.

Another early figure in the history of the airline was Keith Hamilton who took on the appointment of General Manager when he was only thirty-five years of age. He worked tirelessly, demanding high aircraft utilization and the highest share of traffic possible.

These two early leaders of the airline possessed the attributes of all subsequent leaders of SIA: Mr Lim Chin Beng demonstrated unfaltering and unyielding determination in the face of difficulties, always more concerned about solving the problem than allowing it to weigh him down or impede the airline's growth; Hamilton had exacting standards, expecting maximum share of the business and utilization of aircraft. As a result, Malaysian Airways expanded steadily, eventually serving twenty destinations. A major success in those days. It is interesting to note how the likes of Mr J Y Pillay and Dr Cheong Choong Kong (who subsequently became Chairman and Managing Director, respectively, of SIA), held similar convictions.

It is also necessary to recognize that owing to the uniqueness of the business, it was then and still is a major challenge to find persons of the right calibre and fortitude to chart the path of the business. This was especially true in the early days. If the airline had, at any point in its history, leaders of less mettle than those cited above, the airline would not have been able to survive the numerous difficulties it faced.

2.4 Political Changes and the Separation of Singapore from the Federation: A Fresh Start

MAL continued to be highly profitable through 1965/66, proof of which could be found in a note in *The Malay Mail*: 'Work is shortly to begin on the foundations for a fifteen-storey, $11million new headquarters building for the airline, to be built in Robinson Road.' However, MAL was not to exist for long because the political changes that were to unfold later would mean a sad and untimely division of the airline.

The political changes were significant for the then Malaysian Airlines. In August 1965, Singapore was separated from the Federation of Malaysia.

The first significant change for the airline was one of ownership. Up till then, the majority shareholders had been BOAC and Qantas, with the Malaysian and Singapore Governments holding minority shares. Following the political split of the two countries, an injection of additional capital was made by each country in May 1966. This effectively meant that the stakes each country held in the airline was boosted to 42.79% each with the rest collectively held by the Brunei Government, BOAC, Qantas and the Straits Steamship and Ocean Steam Ship companies.

Each country, with their raised equity, was anxious to see its equal partnership status reflected in the name of the joint airline, so MAL became Malaysia-Singapore Airlines, or MSA It was agreed that the airline should be known by that name from 1 January 1967.

As it turned out, MSA proved hugely successful. It was presenting a smart image to the world and creating a name for itself. In short, something of a niche had evolved.

In April 1971, Malaysia's Deputy Prime Minister announced that the alliance would cease and that its own national airline named Malaysian Airline System (MAS) would be formed. This sad state of affairs arose mainly because the Singapore and Malaysian Governments could not agree on the focus of the combined airlines' services. Singapore was keen on international services but Malaysia wanted to operate more domestic and regional routes.

A new day was about to dawn.

The airline was dissolved. Assets were equitably divided, including all land, buildings, vehicles, equipment, and the twenty-four aircraft, A division when business was brisk and a lot of goodwill had been established was something of a setback, to say the least. After twenty-five years of painstaking work, Singapore's new fleet now had no name at all.

In the course of the search for a name, a Government official with unarguable logic enthused: 'Why not simply Singapore Airlines Limited?', and so it became. On 30 June 1972, Singapore's national carrier was named Singapore Airlines, or SIA.

2.5 'We were on our own'

'We were on our own,' recalled Mr J Y Pillay, who was still Chairman in the airline's 40th anniversary year.

SIA was in its infancy then, but spoon-feeding was never part of the plan for SIA because, as the Chairman went on to say, '... the Government made that patently clear. The Government provided no budget for the start of operations, nor did it make an advance of any kind. But neither did it insist on our earning profits from the outset. It simply wanted to see in due course a successful international airline which represented Singapore and paid its due course a successful international airline which represented Singapore and paid its way.'

With no sign of a Government backed start-up in sight, the leaders of SIA took a substantial risk three months before taking to the skies by signing a contract with Boeing Company for the purchase of two B747-200s, with an option for two more. This bold order made SIA the first airline in Southeast Asia to order jumbo jets, Such a decision could only have been made by a team of leaders who had vision, optimism, initiative and, most certainly, courage.

A bold step had been taken, but SIA was not taking an uncalculated risk. In fact a very cautionary attitude had been adopted. The leaders of SIA were prepared to fill the huge hole in the airlines' coffers 'by increasing the payloads and cutting costs to the bone' as Pillay put it. This was major challenge faced by the airline. The sales figure for the first six months suggested that there would be no fall in sales from the previous six months, when there was an MSA overlap. However, recognized it was that it would be increasingly difficult to maintain the margin of profits.

However profit it did! Shortly after starting operations, SIA registered a ten-percent dividend on the airlines' capital.

The Singapore Government had laid the ground rules: it would not allow Singapore the luxury of an airline which did not justify its existence. SIA had earned its right to exist, albeit after some necessary and crucial, risk-taking decisions.

Other problems lurked. Singapore Airlines was a new name on the aviation scene. There was the issue of establishing the name Singapore Airlines and its abbreviation SIA. This was a task to be reckoned with by sales managers and others. Fear of business failure with the introduction of a new name was rife. The fears were eventually dissipated by an aggressive publicity effort and promotional campaign, but concern over sales persisted for some time, until 'Singapore Airlines' was established with the flying public.

SIA overcame these difficulties and succeeded. It is noteworthy that from the outset , SIA has never operated at a loss. This of course, was helped by the stable political and economic conditions created by the Singapore Government. Consequently, Singapore became an "airfaring" city with passengers leaving and entering on a daily basis which had a positive impact on SIA.

2.6 The Fight for Traffic Rights

Traffic rights are instrumental to an airline's existence. It is a case of 'No Rights, No Flights'.

SIA and the Singapore Government were both resolute believers of the free market. They had an uncomplicated attitude towards airline operations. They believed that the world was a marketplace and that airlines should be permitted to go about their business of carrying those passengers who wished to fly with them to anywhere in the world; unfettered.

SIA was fortunate to have been endowed with a staff that was loyal and enthusiastic. SIA also enjoyed the goodwill and support of a good number of people in the aviation fraternity worldwide; but it was far from a level playing field for SIA. Stone-walling by others, governments among them, was not uncommon. The problem was a pervading sense of protectionism. Many felt that the airline industry was already getting cramped and that there was no room for yet another new national carrier, requesting traffic rights to their capital cities. To the nay saying, SIA was a serious competitive threat.

A distinctive characteristic of SIA, which probably embodies the national attitude, was a willingness, even eagerness to embrace competition provided, it was conducted within the regulatory framework of international air transport. Foreign carriers were always welcome to Singapore, as long as SIA was granted reciprocal landing or operating rights. It did not matter that SIA may not have been in a position to take up those operating rights, it was a matter of principle.

Not all shared this open view. Singapore Airlines made formal applications for traffic rights and Civil Aviation Department representatives presented proposals for bilateral air service agreements. An ominous silence was the answer from several quarters. SIA was faced with the harsh reality that some of the most important world markets might remain closed to SIA. The United States was one such unresponsive party, not wishing to grant rights to SIA, Other countries made it quite clear that they saw no reason to grant them either.

This barrage of obstacles did turn up one good thing for SIA. It taught those at SIA the art of lobbying. Hard fights were fought and patience stretched before operating authority to certain cities was granted, sometimes with mediocre initial frequencies. It made no difference that Singapore welcomed other national carriers and often SIA was left with no alternative but to argue and regularly re-present its case.

As the company was set upon substantial expansion from the start, Singapore Airlines battled with the British over an increase in air frequencies, and the Australians over routes, their operations and frequencies. The Germans, perceiving some threat to Lufthansa, were hostile, and frictions with the Italians led to the termination of the bilateral service agreement with Singapore.

Talks were carried out with the United States of America over 1974-1975. However it was only in September 1977 that an agreement was signed, allowing SIA to fly to San Francisco via Hong Kong, Guam and Honolulu.

2.7 Hit by the Oil Crisis

Oil has always been the life-blood of transport.

The Oil Crisis could not have come at a worse time. Only a few years into its operations, SIA had to grapple with the problem of a disastrous oil crisis

Fuel prices soared. Operating costs became astronomical. In a short span of a few months, fuel costs made presence felt by surging from eight to twenty-five percent of total operating costs. As if this was not enough, the problem was compounded by the lack of availability. In major locations where refueling was performed there was not enough fuel to go around.

Singapore Airlines countered this problem by attempting to economise wherever possible. Inadvertently, this meant some restrictions on flights because of the fuel availability problem, but for the most part schedules were maintained, Fortunately, by this time SIA had a stable of loyal passengers who continued to fly with the airline and were able to survive.

The crisis became a thing of the past and damage control was good but SIA was determined to prepare for future crisis. A fuel savings committee was set up to study programs aimed at reducing fuel burn.

Aircraft acquisition policy was restructured. Only the latest and best aircraft were purchased, it was imperative that only the most fuel-efficient and economical aircraft were purchased.

2.8 The Concorde Saga

In mid-1977, things began to look up for SIA as the short-term outlook pointed to favorable economic conditions and SIA began to make plans for a new, bold step that would surprise the international aviation world. SIA was gearing up for a Concorde service for its prestige and publicity value. The prospect of additional premium class traffic lent extra impetus to the whole campaign for a Concorde service.

British Airways (BA) owned the Concorde and for SIA to operate a Concorde service, it was necessary to enter into an agreement with the company at that time, BA was anxious to operate Concorde services to Singapore as part of its master plan to take the supersonic airliner to Australia and so an agreement was signed for the joint operation of Concorde services between London and Singapore starting December 1977. The single aircraft used had the British Airways colours on one side and Singapore Airlines on the other. The joint Concorde service made its maiden flight from London on 9 December 1977, straight into trouble.

At the eleventh hour, Malaysian authorities denied use of Malaysian controlled airspace on environmental grounds. Reassurances were given that the aircraft would not fly at supersonic speed when along the Malacca Straits but at subsonic speed instead. Eventually, despite all these reassurances, BA and SIA were granted only three return flights between London and Singapore. Subsequently, the service was tentatively halted pending negotiations between the British and Malaysian Governments.

Thirteen months later, on 24 January 1979, the BA-SIA Concorde service resumed on a thrice-weekly frequency. This was a marketing triumph for SIA but it was to last for only another twenty-one months.

BA and SIA had both been hopeful of the prospect of profits arising from fully exploiting the potential of the Concorde service By a twist of fate, the interruption in its service diminished, considerably, the impact of the Concorde. The exorbitant operating costs, and a lack of correspondingly high load factors made it increasingly doubtful that the supersonic partnership could be sustained for much longer.

However, SIA's Planning Director, Peter Lai Kwok Chiew, had this to say of the Concorde service. 'We never made any money on the service, but we never lost any either, and it did us a lot of good indirectly.' It certainly did. For by embarking on the joint Concorde service, Singapore Airlines enjoyed the distinction of being one of only four airlines in the world to have used the supersonic airliner.

For the passengers who flew on the BA-SIA Concorde flights, the service was something of an experience. Businessmen and other passengers forked out S$12,000 for their return flight. In return, they were raced across the heavens in confined comfort, cutting the normal eighteen-hour subsonic B747 journey by half.

The service was never destined for permanence and the agreement was terminated on 31 October 1980.

2.9 Modernization of the Fleet

The Concorde service was a glamor shot for SIA, but the airline had always been pragmatic and other serious work was being carried out on a different front. SIA had begun work on modernizing and equipping itself for future expansion.

A fleet of eight Airbus A300-B4s had been ordered at a cost of US$300 million, and new services had commenced — to Brussels, Honolulu, San Francisco, Dhahran in Saudi Arabia and Abu Dhabi.

In 1980, an order for nineteen aircraft from the Boeing Company. It was the largest single order ever placed with Boeing. Expansion and fleet modernisation determined the nineteen-aircraft order. Under an agreement with Boeing, SIA ordered thirteen B747s — ten firm and options on three — and six B727s, four firm orders and two on option. This order facilitated the replacement of four of the existing fleet of B747s with new, more powerful modern aircraft.

How did SIA finance the purchase? SIA had by now become financially-sound and on the strength of an optimistic outlook, the airline had borrowed substantially against future earnings — a bold move for any airline. Fifty percent of the total purchase cost was funded by borrowing.

Some critics voiced grave doubts and felt that the sheer magnitude of the purchases posed unjustifiable risks. However, time has proven that SIA's performance justified the deals and represented good economic sense. The May 1983 deal involved a total of US$1.4 billion, once again sending tremors through the airline world. By February 1986, when SIA made another order for US$3.3 billion worth of twenty Boeing 747-400s, the world had grown accustomed to these astronomical figures. The orders implicitly demonstrated SIA's unshakeable self-confidence. Prompted by the first fuel crisis, the fleet renewal policy was deemed a master stroke.

More recently, SIA placed order for fifty-two aircraft (twenty-two Boeing 747s and thirty Airbus A340s) worth US$10.3 billion in June 1994, and seventy-seven Boeing 777s worth $12.7 billion in November 1995. In the later case, sixteen of the B777s are intended for SIA's Singapore-based aircraft learning associate, Singapore Aircraft Learning Enterprise (SALE).

2.10 Conclusion

Now, SIA has firmly rooted itself as an industry giant and is considered a major asset to Singapore in terms of its economic contribution, At on point in its history has Singapore Airlines ever posted a loss.

With a staff of twenty-seven thousand and passengers exceeding eleven million per annum, SIA has added responsibilities. To the nation, it has grown from a small outfit, to emerge as Singapore's largest single employer. The SIA Group's value added to the economy was S$3,200 million in 1995.

SIA's fortune is closely linked with the Republic. SIA has grown in tandem with the country's economic growth; indeed, the leaders of SIA are aware that SIA's growth has been largely due to its stable and economically vibrant home base.

Is it possible to pin SIA's early success to one single factor? Yes. SIA's ethos has always been be ever alert to customer needs and this has dictated why certain decisions were made and certain things done.

Late in 1985 SIA was poised for the next step in its growth as a company. It would mean SIA would have to be leaner and even more competitive. The then Chairman, J Y Pillay, summed it up most aptly:

On 18 December 1985, SIA obtained a public listing. This had new implications. The foundations had been laid and SIA had gone public with good fundamentals previously established, but the future needed a new set of goals and policies. This chapter has traced the groundwork done during SIA's early history. The subsequent chapters will detail SIA's important achievements and its management of service quality in almost every aspect of the airline business.

'What does it all mean? The issued capital is six hundred and twenty million shares, and we have deemed fit to set an issue price of S$5 a share. It makes for a total market capitalization of S$3.1 billion. We must aim for a ten percent return, which means S$310 million for the ensuing year. If the share price rises, profit expectations will go up accordingly, If it falls with declining profits, we are all in the dock. There is no escape from the treadmill. We have new responsibilities as a listed company. The goals of the past still remain, but the age of innocence has ended.'

CHAPTER THREE

The Airline and its Global Service Quality

3.1 The National Analogy

Singapore Airlines (SIA), since its split from the Malaysian Airline System (MAS) in 1972, has been a microcosm of the nation. It is indeed easy to draw a parallel between SIA and Singapore (SIA, 1985).

SIA's commitment to meritocracy as expressed by then- Prime Minister Lee Kuan Yew (SIA, 1977):

> 'when I get on board an SIA aircraft, I shall see and feel a representative flavor of Singapore. It is important that our multi-racial society be fairly reflected. SIA should be a representative of what Singapore is, a society based on a man or woman's worth and performance, qualities which have nothing to do with a person's race, language, religion, or family status, or connections'.

Both Singapore and SIA are beneficiaries of geography. This is highlighted by the fact that SIA's revenue sources are fairly uniformly distributed between diverse parts of the world—the Orient, West Asia, Europe, the United States and Southwest Pacific.

The link between the state and the airline has been significantly strong. Temasek Holdings (a Singapore Government Investment holding company) holds a 53.8% stake in the airline, the remainder being held by the public. The airline has consistently contributed 3% – 4% of the nation's gross domestic product, and the return on shareholders' funds between 1989 to 1993 has been 25.5% – 11.5% (SIA, 1992 – 93). Other contributions to the national economy include payments to the government, statutory boards and wholly-owned government companies, and foreign-exchange earnings. The extent of SIA's influence is evident from the company's facts and figures (listed in Appendix 1), and also from the number of businesses in various sectors which form its group of companies (listed in Appendix 2).

In 1994–95, SIA's capacity grew 10.0% to 11,167 million tonne-kilometres as a result of higher number of flights, and the overall load factor gained 0.3% point to 69.8%. In general, SIA's overall capacity is expected to grow by 9%, with available seat kilometres rising 6% and available cargo capacity 12% (SIA,1995b).

SIA employed 13,280 employees in May 1996. Staff productivity, measured by the changes in capacity produced, load carried, revenue earned, and value added per employee, improved 8% over 1993-94.

Since 1972, the same work ethos that has made Singapore successful has propelled SIA to become a major player in the aviation industry. Like the rest of the country, SIA is well aware that it must be independent, never expecting favors and that nobody owes it a living. Both the nation and the airline are highly visible and vociferous in decrying protectionism. The airline and nation together strongly endorse free enterprise and free competition.

To date, SIA can be proudly acknowledged as the flag carrier of the country. SIA has continually kept travelers talking about the airline and in so doing, enhanced its own reputation and that of the country.

3.2 The Global Service Quality

The years 1989-90 saw commercial aviation struggling through one of the most difficult periods in its history. The world's top one hundred airlines recorded a US$6.7 billion (S$11.2 billion) deterioration in net results for 1990 over the previous year. In 1989, they earned US$4 billion profit. In 1990, they lost US$2.7 billion, and that was before the worst of the turndown in the Persian Gulf. Despite such disadvantageous circumstances, SIA remained at the top of the *Airline Business* ranking in terms of profitability for 1990 (SIA, 1992a).

SIA's dedication to service quality has gained international recognition, and this has been the major factor in its success in business performance. In an age where information and technology are widely accessible, product knowhow is no longer the exclusive privilege of a select few. This and globalization have made it increasingly difficult to achieve any significant product differentiation. To gain a competitive edge, many companies have turned to service quality as the crucial 'X- factor'.

When SIA first sought to establish itself in the aviation world twenty-four years ago, it embraced the concept of service quality as its corporate creed. In fact, service excellence has been the cornerstone upon which the airline has built its reputation and thus achieved its performance. SIA has consistently won world's best airline awards in surveys conducted by reputable travel magazines, such as *Air Transport World* and *Conde Nast Traveler*.

3.2.1 Honors for SIA from *Air Transport World*

In February 1994, the leading international aviation journal *Air Transport World* (ATW) presented SIA with an award for International Service at its special Twenty Years of Excellence Awards with a citation that read: 'the most successful and profitable airline in the world over the past two decades.'

'Passenger service, financial planning, marketing, technical and fleet strategy and maintenance are all exemplary at Singapore Airlines', said ATW in a salute to SIA in its February 1994 issue (SIA, 1994a). The article continued:

> 'Singapore Airlines began offering free drinks, a choice of meals, and free headsets back in 1970s, when the IATA (International Air Transport Association) carriers required a charge. Lately, it has installed personal videos at each seat and has been a leader in offering satellite-based inflight telephone service anywhere in the world... Singapore Airlines is the measure by which others are judged.'

3.2.2 The Conde Nast Award for the Seventh Year

Other global measures of SIA's excellent service quality include the 'best airline award' for the seventh consecutive year from the prestigious travel magazine *Conde' Nast Traveler* in October 1995. This US-based magazine's annual Readers' Choice survey drew responses from thirty thousand subscribers. Airlines were rated on their

- scheduling
- punctuality
- cabin comfort and service
- food and
- baggage handling.

SIA scored 79.8 points and walked away with the Best Airline Award while Swissair came in second with 75.6, and the Australian national carrier Qantas was third with 72.4 points.

The magazine observed that SIA's shrewd planning, technological expertise and 'panache' have taken the airline considerably beyond its initial reputation for superb service. 'The airline also has the re-markable ability to capture the allure of the Orient while reflecting the attention to detail for which the region has become known,' it stated. The magazine also attributed SIA's service record to its young aircraft fleet, stellar safety record and efficient home base at Changi Airport (SIA, 1992c).

3.2.3 The Boeing Punctuality Award

For a period of twenty months from August 1990 to April 1992, SilkAir, a subsidiary of SIA, achieved a technical dispatch reliability of 99.6 % for its Boeing 737-300 aircraft fleet of three. These aircraft operate to nine regional destinations averaging four hundred and seventy flight sectors a month with an average utilization of over nine block hours per aircraft a day. Commending SIA's achievement of excellent punctuality, the Boeing Everett's vice president/general manager presented a plaque to the airline, not the first time that SIA has gained recognition for the global service quality it has rendered (SIA, 1995b).

3.2.4 Singapore Airlines: The Winning Streak

SIA has won a string of accolades. It was voted both Best Airline for In-ternational Business Travel (for the fifth successive year) and Best Trans-pacific Airline in the US-based Business Travel International magazine's 1993 reader survey. SIA has also won the Best Airline to Asia in the 1994 Travel Industry Globe Awards, organized by the United Kingdom travel trade newspaper *Travel Weekly* (SIA, 1994b). (See Appendix 3 for a list of prestigious awards won by SIA in 1993–94.)

3.3 The Turbulent Business Environment

For nearly half a century, the world airline industry operated in a highly regulated environment. Through a host of international conventions and bilateral agreements, restrictions were placed on the number of participants in the market, the capacity to be offered and the traffic rights to be exercised (SIA,1984).

Although the system of bilateral agreements between countries did not attempt to regulate pricing, a unique system exists that allowed fares to be set through IATA in accordance with the interests of the least efficient international carrier. Government merely rubber-stamped the IATA 'consensus'. It is always all too easy for governments to look for protectionist solutions when their carriers are in trouble, to the detriment of consumers. A striking example is the termination of the landing rights agreement between Canada and SIA well before the expiration of the agreement (SIA, 1992a). This apparent act of protectionism highlights the difficulty that exists in the aviation industry.

Progress towards a multilateral regime can be assessed on two levels. At the official level, direct government negotiations on the subject remain limited. At the unofficial level, debate within the industry and informal statements by regulators have resulted in some positive progress.

Competition has also been intensified by American and European carriers buying smaller airlines in an effort to expand business to the Asiatic region thereby creating 'megacarriers'. Despite this highly competitive and sometimes even hostile business environment, SIA has managed to forge ahead.

3.4 The Challenges

SIA is expected to operate to all six continents with about ninety aircraft, including full-freighters. The number of cabin crew will probably go up from the present four thousand five hundred to eight thousand, serving some thirteen million passengers a year. As indicated by its deputy managing director at the World Marketing Conference, the three challenges the airline industry will be facing are (SIA, 1992a):

1. The quality challenge—the need to ensure high quality and continued customer satisfaction despite considerable expansion.
2. The technological challenge—the impact of information technology on sales, marketing and services.

3. The 'mega' challenge—the trend towards globalization, reflected in takeovers, alliances, cross-equities and mergers, could see the successful major carriers growing from strength to strength.

SIA predicts that the overall capacity for 1995–96 is expected to grow by 9%, with available seat kilometres rising 6% and available cargo capacity 12%. To succeed as a global player, an airline must have an extensive route network, a growth market, a strong product and service culture, the latest technology, well-trained staff, prudent management and financial strength.

3.5 Commitment to Total Quality Management: Key Principles of SIA's TQM Initiative

SIA has encountered its fair share of problems but the dynamic leadership of the management has allowed it to ride them out. Ultimately, SIA's spectacular, perhaps even miraculous success story is true testimony to an attitude of striving for excellence, and commitment to TQM.

In its simplest form, TQM involves two major aspects: determining of customer requirements/expectations and organizing to deliver these requirements/expectations. It follows that the *driver* of the entire system is the customer (Ross, 1992). The following sections summarize SIA's key principles of TQM commitment while the detailed practices will be presented in subsequent chapters of this book.

3.5.1 Commitment to Customers

Customer Focus

At SIA, the importance of customer focus has been reiterated incessantly. The most recent affirmation of this was made by the airline's managing director when receiving *Air Transport World*'s award for international service in 1994. At the award presentation banquet, the managing director paid tribute to SIA's passengers. He stated that passengers are their '*raison d'etre*'; they are what the whole, bewildering business is all about; and that if SIA is successful it is largely because the airline never forgot that all-important fact [10].

This is the type of mindset the SIA staff has been imbued with since its establishment. The airline has clearly stated that a sound philosophy is essential to quality management. SIA's corporate goal is *to deliver the highest quality of customer service that is safe, reliable and economical. The 'Customer First' approach has been one of the key ingredients in SIA's success*, and this is clearly understood from top management down (SIA, 1988).

The 'Customer First' Approach

Some examples of SIA's Customer First Approach are presented below.

Passenger Opinion Surveys

Understanding customers' needs is the first step towards maximizing customer satisfaction. Apart from informal channels of communication, SIA also conducts regular passenger opinion surveys to monitor the quality of its services. Passengers are asked to rate the quality of SIA's inflight service, food and beverages, inflight entertainment, aircraft interior, airport operations, reservations and ticket office operations. Under each of these service categories, the passenger's feedback is sought on matters ranging from prompt and friendly service to the taste and flavour of the coffee served. Even the survey forms take a customer focus. They are written in clear and simple language and designed to take only about five minutes of the passenger's time to complete. The forms are printed in five different languages to cover the widest spectrum of passengers.

Service and Performance Index (SPI)

The survey results are analyzed and a quarterly SPI, comparing past and present performance, is distributed to key personnel in the organization. Action is taken to address areas that show a drop in ratings. The data is also useful in determining areas that require further investment. For instance, SIA's decision to invest more than US$52 million in a cabin management and interactive video system was prompted by the relatively lower ratings scored by inflight entertainment compared to other areas of inflight service (details will be presented in the chapter on inflight service).

Ratio of Compliments to Complaints

Customer feedback is also obtained from the compliments and complaints received by the airline. Prompt action is taken on every valid comment. Statistics are compiled to determine the ratio of compliments to complaints, which is tracked over time to monitor trends.

Focus Group Studies

Focus group studies are conducted regularly by the Market Research Department to predict future customer requirements.

Concept of Internal Customers

The 'Customer First' approach also applies to the airline's internal structure. SIA staff are made aware that every member within the company has a customer; that is, their colleague at the next workstation is their customer, and all the staff members are the company's internal customers. It is acknowledged that the needs, requirements and expectations of the internal customers must be met first before the organization can provide the services that satisfy its external customers. This concept of internal customers facilitates the establishment of a total customer service system whereby all service operations are connected to form a service chain. The formation of a service chain is especially crucial in a relatively large organization like SIA (SIA, 1995a).

3.5.2 Commitment to Quality

Quality as a Strategic Weapon

Service is a buzzword in today's business world. Commitment to quality is another popular phrase with companies seeking the recipe for success. The airline realized right from the beginning that it operated in an environment where other airlines offered the same type of aircraft, level of fares and frequency of flights. The way to forge ahead, therefore, has been to consistently provide the utmost in customer service with *'a little extra'* aimed at establishing its market niche.

The Competitive Approach Towards Service Quality

Meeting competition head-on has been SIA's experience since its inception. Based in one of the world's smallest countries, the airline has demonstrated that neither the size of the company nor that of its home market matters in this global economy. It quickly learnt the lesson that service quality can only be cultivated in an openly competitive environment. Protectionist measures and over-regulation hide inefficiencies, which translate into low productivity and poor quality. The following sections present SIA's competitive approach towards quality.

Systematic Processes Management

SIA achieves quality services through systematic service processes management, focusing on the critical success factors. In all key operational areas, a set of service standards is designed and measured periodically to ensure that standards are maintained. Task forces are formed to review any prevailing issues. For example, given the competitive aviation environment, SIA formed various task forces to explore ways of reducing costs. Cost deduction can be achieved through careful examination of processes. It is no longer enough to evaluate how to improve just one production process. SIA's TQM initiatives require a constant review of the necessity of all the processes.

Competitive Service Indicators

Service indicators provide useful feedback in managing the process quality. A service benchmark offers the necessary target for the achievement of service improvements. SIA subsidiary Singapore Airport Terminal Services (SATS) tracks the flight delay rate, baggage mishandling rate, cargo mishandling rate, average passenger check-in time, baggage presentation time, cargo delivery time, ground support equipment maintenance and servicing rate and microbiological tests results. Through the use of these service indicators, the causes of problems and failures to meet standards are readily identified and solutions are determined and implemented without delay.

3.5.3 Total Involvement

Total Involvement as a Management Philosophy

SIA regards its people as its most valuable resource. The airline believes in the total involvement of every employee in achieving service quality for the company. Empowering employees and motivating them to perform at their best can only be achieved when the supporting structure is in place.

Decentralized Organizational Structure

To facilitate total involvement and at the same time simplify the decision-making process, SIA practices decentralization. This brings decision-making to the lowest possible level. To promote greater autonomy in decision-making and a sharper focus on quality and customer services, SIA has formed some twenty-one subsidiaries and five associated companies. In recent years, growth rates in the subsidiaries are significant compared to overall group performance, demonstrating the benefits of organizational restructuring based on the total involvement management philosophy.

Empowerment

Empowerment through delegation of authority filters through the SIA organizational structure. SIA's management systems and training are designed to ensure that even low-level mangers are empowered and encouraged to make independent decisions according to their own judgment of the situation.

Job Rotation

SIA practises management job rotation, which moves executives between departments every few years. This not only helps young mangers to develop a thorough understanding of how the entire organization works, but also promotes a corporate outlook among staff. Sectoral interest is minimized when staff acquire a total perspective. This management practice creates an appetite for change and innovation as people constantly bring new ideas with them to new jobs. In pursuing job rotation, SIA is flexible enough to recognize that certain areas require specialization and make appropriate exceptions.

Training

Human resource development is of particular importance in a service industry such as air travel. Apart from helping employees acquire the right skills to perform their job better, training should be a motivator. SIA spends approximately US$3,200 per employee in training annually (SIA, 1995b). This figure is much higher than the national average of US$200 per worker in terms of training investment. SIA believes in continuing education and provides training throughout an employee's career.

Rewards and Recognition

These are integral to the cultivation of a strong corporate culture. SIA conducts regular reviews to ensure that its salaries are market-competitive. Under a profit-sharing scheme employees receive special bonuses based on the profitability of the company.

Communications

Effective employee communications are essential to building total service involvement. Corporate-wide business meetings and briefings are held regularly to keep staff informed of the latest developments. Corporate newsletters and circulars help promote information-sharing. Interaction between staff and management is encouraged through regular staff meetings.

While the above are the key principles of SIA's commitment to TQM, subsequent chapters of this book will cover details of its TQM systems design and control, and the organizational and behavioral aspects of TQM.

References

1. Ross, J.E. (1992). *Total Quality Management: Text, Cases and Readings*. Delray Beach: St. Lucie Press
2. SIA (1977). *Outlook*, June. Singapore: SIA
3. SIA (1984). *Outlook*, April. Singapore: SIA
4. SIA (1985). *Outlook*, May. Report of speech by Dr. Cheong Choong Kong, Managing Director, SIA, to Young President's Organization. Singapore: SIA
5. SIA (1988). *Outlook*, September. Singapore: SIA
6. SIA (1992a). *Outlook*, January. Singapore: SIA
7. SIA (1992b). *Outlook*, June. Singapore: SIA
8. SIA (1992c). *Outlook*, November. Singapore: SIA
9. SIA (1992 – 93). *Simplified Financial Report*. Singapore: SIA
10. SIA (1994a). Note to Editors, February 21. Singapore: SIA
11. SIA (1994b). Note to Editor, March 10. Singapore: SIA
12. SIA (1995a). TQM as Differentiation Strategy for Service Quality. Singapore: SIA
13. SIA (1995b). News Release, May 22. Singapore: SIA

CHAPTER FOUR

The SIA-TQM Approach

4.1 The Era of Total Quality Management

As stated by Robert C. Stampel, chairman of General Motors Corporation:

> 'the worldwide quality revolution has permanently changed the way we all do business. Where once quality was limited to technical issues, it is now a dynamic, perpetual improvement process involving people in all aspects of the business' (Ross, 1992).

Since the scientific movement begun by Frederick Taylor in 1907, no management issue has had greater impact than that of quality. US executives are in agreement in citing quality in products and services as an essential ingredient in maintaining quality and improving competitiveness in international markets. Quality expert J.M. Juran calls this movement a major phenomenon in the present age.

As indicated in Figure 4.1, one may come to the conclusion that the end of the 20th century is the era of total quality management. Today, when we talk about quality, we refer to the quality of all aspects of a business organization, such as the quality of products and services, the quality of work-life, employee involvement and empowerment, productivity improvement, competitive position and customer satisfaction.

Before embarking on any further discussion, it is critical to define quality. The word quality is widely used, and its meaning and interpretations are as many as the people who use it.

4.2 Definitions of Quality

Quality is summative in nature. It is not a discrete entity but rather a broad term covering the totality of all characteristics of a product or service that commands superiority and excellence.

Figure 4.1: Evolution of Quality Management

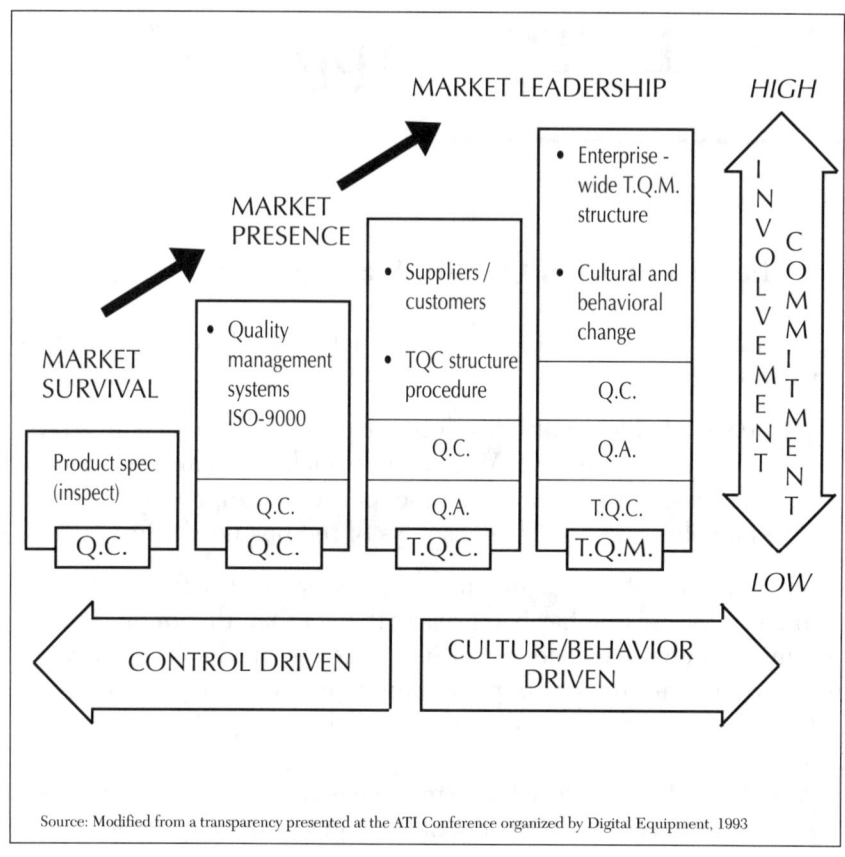

Source: Modified from a transparency presented at the ATI Conference organized by Digital Equipment, 1993

Quality can be defined in a number of ways as listed below.

I. Definitions developed by ISO (International Organization for Standardization)

   • Quality is fitness for purpose or use.
   • Quality is conformance to specifications.
   • Quality is freedom from deficiencies.
   • Quality is customer satisfaction.
   • Quality means customer value.
   • Quality means credibility.
   • Quality means pride of ownership.

II. ISO-8402 (1986): Quality Vocabulary

- Quality is the totality of features and characteristics of a product or service that bear on its ability to satisfy stated or implied needs.

III. Quality is all of the above.

4.2.1 Approaches to Defining Quality

The definitions of quality as listed in the above table appear to be too divergent and are not very useful to managers competing in a fierce international marketplace. David Garvin in his book, *Managing Quality*, described several approaches to define quality (Garvin, 1988). They are:

- Transcendent: The idea here is that quality cannot be defined, and is recognized only when it is seen.
- Product-based: Quality is based on the presence or absence of a particular product attribute.
- Manufacturing-based: This refers to the quality in manufacturing that conforms a product or service to a predetermined set of requirements.
- User-based: Quality is determined solely by the product's ability to satisfy the customers' requirements, expectations, or wants. In other words, it is fitness for use.
- Value-based: Products or services with certain characteristics have to be offered at an acceptable price for quality to be defined.

4.2.2 ASQC's Consumer Product Quality

A survey by the American Society for Quality Control (ASQC) of purchasers of consumer products summarized the following factors in decisions to purchase:

Performance	Service	Easy to use
Lasts long time	Warranty	Appearance
Easy to Repair	Price	Brand name

Recent efforts to codify the concepts of quality and provide baselines for measurement have yielded these characteristics:

Performance features	Conformance to specifications
Reliability	Serviceability
Durability	Perceived quality
Aesthetics	

4.2.3 Strategic Definition of Quality

The definitions of quality as described in the foregoing sections have been made in the pursuit of product- or user-based quality. As we moved in the 1990s to a new consumer-oriented economy, a new definition of quality that can be applied to describe the management approach for achieving the organizational objectives was required. To fulfill this requirement, Tenner and DeToro (1992) suggested a strategic definition of quality as:

'Quality: A basic business strategy that provides goods and services that completely satisfy both internal and external customers by meeting their explicit and implicit expectations.'

Furthermore, this strategy utilizes the talents of all employees to the benefit of the organization in particular and society in general, and provides a positive financial return to the shareholders.

4.3 Service Quality

The concept of quality is relevant in both a manufacturing setting and a service setting. In particular, a discussion of the notion of service quality would be useful for a better understanding of TQM in the airline context. Further, a preliminary and brief discussion of the unique context of the Singapore economy would be useful.

4.3.1 Service Industries and Service Functions

The Singapore economy is made up of various industry sectors. Figure 4.2 depicts a simplified model of the industrial structure that makes up the economy.

It is clearly evident from Figure 4.2 that with the exception of manufacturing and building construction, the rest come under the service industry sector. The following are some service industries:

- Banking
- Business services: legal, engineering, accounting, data processing, etc.
- Education
- Entertainment, recreation
- Finance
- Government: local, state, federal
- Health
- Hotels and motels
- Insurance
- Personal service: household service, beauty, cleaning, etc.
- Professional services
- Public utilities: water, gas, electricity, telephone, etc.
- Real estate
- Restaurants and cafeterias
- Retail trade
- Transportation
- Wholesale trade

Figure 4.2: Simplified Industrial Structure of Singapore Economy

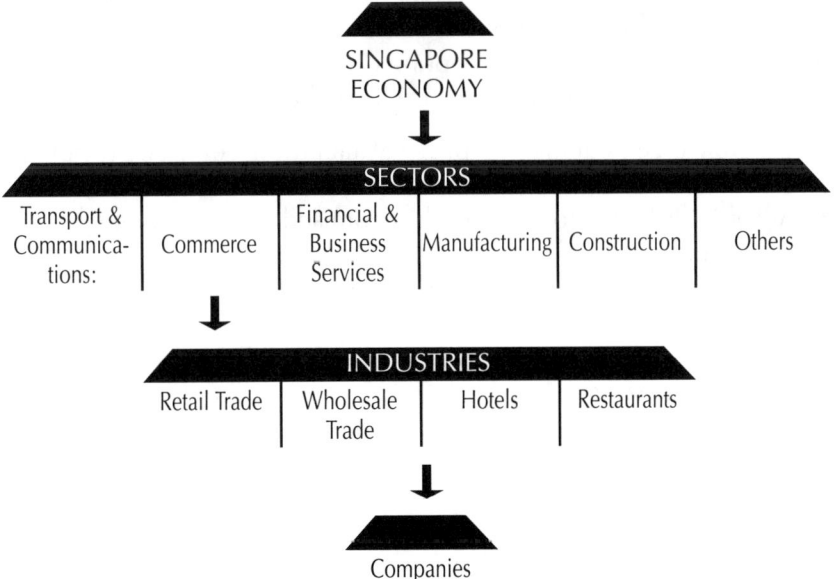

In addition to the service industries, manufacturing companies are also concerned with service functions. Overhead functions not associated with, but which are necessary for direct production, have to be taken into consideration, because these functions may account for as much as 30–35% of the total cost of doing business. They are:

auditing	accounting	purchasing	communication
legal	shipping	marketing	administrative
travel	financial	advertising	transportation
sales	training	packaging	customer service
storage	computer	personnel	receiving inspection

All these functions can be found in service companies and in manufacturing companies. Today, when we talk about service quality, we mean both the quality of the outputs of service companies and the quality of supportive services, in particular customer service. Hence, it can be seen that service quality is a central issue of all organizations. It is difficult to name even one industry for which service matters are unimportant.

4.3.2 Ten Dimensions of Service Quality

While literature on quality has been predominantly goods-oriented, Zeithaml *et al*, (1990) concluded that service quality is defined by the customers. Service quality is defined as the discrepancy between customers' expectations and perceptions. The ten dimensions of service quality as specified by Zeithaml are listed below.

- Tangibles: Appearance of physical facilities, equipment, personnel, and communication materials.
- Reliability: Ability to perform the promised service dependably and accurately.
- Responsiveness: Willingness to help customers and provide prompt service.
- Competence: Possession of the required skills and knowledge to perform the service.
- Courtesy: Politeness, respect, consideration, and friendliness of contact personnel.
- Credibility: Trustworthiness, believability, honesty of the service provider.
- Security: Freedom from danger, risk, or doubt.

- Access: Approachability and ease of contact.
- Communication: Keeping customer informed in language they can understand and listening to them.
- Understanding: Making the effort to get to know customers and their needs.

4.3.3 The Service Quality Gap

Christopher (1992) in his book, *The Customer Service Planner*, indicated that there is a gap between service performance and expectations, that is, performance does not match expectations. There is a need for management to fully understand what the main influences are both on expectations and on perceptions of performance. There are a number of factors that contribute to the expectations of the level of service, such as the nature of the service or product on offer, the needs of the customer, word-of-mouth communication, past experience, corporate image, as well as the content and process of the service experience.

4.3.4 Characteristics of Service Leaders

Service leaders may appear in all shapes and sizes (Zeithaml *et al.* 1990). Yet, there are some common characteristics they all share. These are:

- Service vision. Service leaders have the ability to see that service quality is a success key and that it is integral to the organization's future. They realize that quality of service is the foundation for competition.
- High standards. True service leaders recognize the importance of high standards and the opportunities that can be found in small actions. It can enable the customers to differentiate their organization from other organizations.
- In-the -field leadership style. A hands-on approach by service leaders is necessary to build a climate of teamwork within the organization. Service leaders must be visible to their people in order to lead effectively.
- Personal leadership and integrity. These are the essential characteristics of service leaders because they enable them to earn the trust of associates and thus makes their leadership more effective. Without them, it would be impossible to build a service-minded attitude in an organization.

4.3.5 Award of Service Quality Leadership

A significant milestone in the promulgation of service quality leadership was the introduction of the Malcolm Baldrige National Quality Award in 1987. The advent of this award provided the platform for greater recognition of excellence in quality achievement and quality management in US companies. Originally intended to be a competitive award, it has gradually evolved into a benchmark-like symbol of total quality criteria for large business organizations such as IBM and Federal Express seeking advancement in service quality.

4.4 Total Quality Management (TQM)

TQM includes all the functions of a business. It is the integration of the functions and related processes into the product life-cycle at different stages, such as design, planning, production, distribution and field service.

The definition of TQM given in the International Standards (1991) for Quality Management, ISO/DIS 8402 is:

'Total Quality Management: A management approach of an organization, centered on quality, based on the participation of all its members and aiming at long-term success through customer satisfaction, and benefits to the members of the organization and to the society.'

The measurement of the TQM success is customer satisfaction and the way to achieve it is mainly through systems design and continuous improvement.

4.5 Developing a TQM System

TQM issues as listed above can be effectively dealt with through a proper system development.

A TQM system can be developed in many ways. It can be based on the fundamental requirements outlined in ISO-9004, which is part of the set of standards laid out by the International Organization for Standardization (ISO). It can also follow approaches developed by various quality pioneers, or even follow its unique approach based on the basic principles of quality.

4.5.1 The ISO-9004 TQM System

The ISO-9004 provides guidelines for developing and implementing a TQM system. The document addresses aspects of quality management systems in relation to the need for a business to: achieve quality at optimum cost, ensure profitability, expand market share and maintain long-term survivability. The ISO-9004 TQM system typically applies to, and interacts with, all activities pertinent to the quality of a product or service (ISO Central Secretariat, 1991). It involves all phases from initial identification to final satisfaction of requirements and customer expectations. These phases and activities are as follows:

- Marketing and market research
- Design/specification engineering and product development
- Procurement
- Process planning and development
- Production
- Inspection, testing and examination
- Packaging and storage
- Sales and distribution
- Installation and operation
- Technical assistance and maintenance
- Disposal after use

4.5.2 General Approach for Developing a TQM System

Puri (1992) presented a general approach for developing a TQM system, irrespective of the various TQM philosophies. It can be modified and presented as follows:

Step 1: Establish a TQM environment by drafting a corporate vision/mission statement and determining TQM principles such as, customer focus, quality commitment, employee involvement and disciplines, etc.

Step 2: Establish supplier/customer/management relationships.

Step 3: Set up management systems for all the processes throughout the product life cycle including market research, product development, purchasing, manufacturing, testing and inspection, packaging and transportation, customer service, etc.

Step 4: Establish evaluation systems such as internal audit and quality assurance, etc.

Step 5: Continuously improve management systems.
Step 6: Review and revise the continuous improvement cycle.

4.6 SIA's TQM Approach

For an organization to effectively practice TQM in order to gain success through customer satisfaction, it needs a proper TQM approach. There are three elements in a TQM approach; organizational responsibilities/objectives, management leadership and principles, and management functions. SIA's TQM approach is summarized in a matrix as shown in Figure 4.3.

4.6.1 Corporate Responsibilities

As stated in its *Perspectives* (SIA, 1988), the foremost responsibility of SIA is to its customers. SIA is committed to providing customers with the highest standard of service that is safe, reliable and economical.

The airline's second responsibility is to its employees. Management does not treat the employees as mere economic digits. Management's objectives are to enable employees to develop, through training and career development, to their full potential, and to reward them adequately. It also has its responsibilities to the public, to the government, to the shareholders and to the company itself in generating reasonable profits as a competitive enterprise.

The ultimate objective is of course to generate the right products at the right price levels in order to generate the targeted level of profitability as indicated in the last column of Figure 4.3.

In order to achieve its corporate objective, the organization needs to acquire the right people with right mindset and leadership traits so that the quality of management is there and the right management principles are applied to various management functions.

4.6.2 Management Leadership and Commitment

SIA's quality leadership and management commitment is demonstrated by its strategic management of a well-defined corporate mission, goals and objectives. This is manifested on two fronts; through the planning function and through its implementation of control functions in the form of well-designed competitive strategies using new aircraft and a well-facilitated airport.

Figure 4.3: SIA's TQM Approach

Total Quality Management Approach				
Quality Mgmt. Mgmt. Mgmt. & Philo. Functions	Leadership and Commitments	Customer Focus	Total Participation	Corporate Responsibilities/ Objectives
Planning	Strategic Quality Management – Mission – Goals – Objectives	Market Quality Management – Customers – Customer requirements – Benchmarking	Human Resource Management – Organizations – Shared vision – Shared plans	Responsibilities to – Customers – Employees – Share holders
Design	Strategies – Infrastructure – Aircraft, etc.	Business Operations Services Ground services Inflight services	Human Resource Management Systems – Payment – Training	Right Products – Safety and Reliability – Availability
Implementing and Control	Investments – Airport – Aircraft, etc.	Flight Operations	Networking	Right Profits – Right productivity – Right price
Success Through Customer Satisfaction				

4.6.3 Customer Focus

SIA has very strict standards of service and its 'customer first' approach is strictly adhered to by management and staff. All customer complaints are dealt with personally by management. SIA's customer focus has been realized through the planning, design, implementation and control of its various quality management systems, details of which are presented in subsequent chapters of this book.

4.6.4 Total Participation

SIA strongly believes in the involvement by employees at all levels of the organization. Section 15.4 provides more details of this involvement.

Figure 4.4: The SIA-TQM Systems

Systems Planning, Design, Implementation & Control

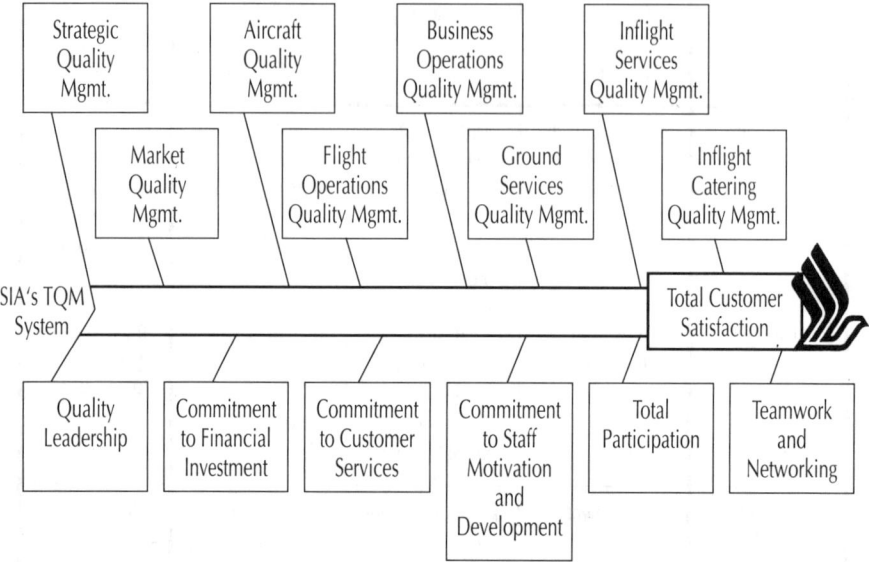

Organizational Behavior & Culture

4.6.5 Management Functions: Planning, Design, Implementation and Control

An organization should plan what it intends to fulfill as its responsibilities and what it intends to achieve as its objectives as indicated in Figure 4.3. The design of quality management systems aims at generating products of infallible quality. It is only after proper implementation and control that the end-products will contribute to corporate profitability.

4.7 The SIA-TQM System

Figure 4.4 provides a summary of SIA's TQM System. The ultimate purpose of the system is to achieve global service quality through total customer satisfaction. The two basic elements are: systems planning, design, implementation and control, and organizational behavior and culture as depicted in Figure 4.4.

References

1. ATI Conference (1993). *Effective Integration of ISO 9000, TQM and Quality Strategy*, June. Organized by Digital Equipment.
2. Christopher M. (1992). *The Customer Service Planner*. Oxford: Butterworth-Heinemann.
3. Garvin A.D. (1988). *Managing Quality*. Toronto: The Free Press.
4. ISO Central Secretariat (1991). *ISO 9000 International Standards for Quality Management*. Geneva: ISO Central Secretariat.
5. Puri S.C. (1992). *ISO 9000 Certification and Total Quality Management*. Ottawa and Washington, D.C.: Standards-Quality Management Group.
6. Ross J.E. (1992). *Total Quality Management: Text, Cases and Readings*. Delray Beach: St. Lucie's Press.
7. SIA (1988). *Perspectives*, December. Singapore: SIA.
8. Tenner A.R. and Toro I.J. (1992). *Total Quality Management: Three Steps to Continuous Improvement*. Reading: Addison-Wesley.
9. Zeithaml V.A. *et al.* (1990). *Delivering Quality Service: Balancing Customer Perceptions and Expectations*. Toronto: The Free Press.

CHAPTER FIVE
Strategic Quality Management

5.1 The Need for Strategic Quality Management

Quality is a broad term that finds its application in every aspect of production, be it the quality of products and services, the quality of work-life, employee involvement and empowerment, productivity improvement, competitive position, customer satisfaction etc.

Pressure for quality improvement is met with different reactions from various organizations. Those in the reactive mode have generally a short-term focus and consequently, their efforts are limited to quality control and quality assurance activities to improve the excellence of their products and services. This is in contrast to proactive organizations that operate on long-term goals. The emphasis of these companies is on improvement in the quality of all aspects of product life to achieve total customer satisfaction. While ensuring continuous quality improvement of their products and services, these companies are also concerned about the welfare of their employees, partnership with their suppliers/subcontractors, and service to society in general.

Quality improvement is an on-going process that cannot be realized through a single quality improvement program, procedure or process. It is a result of a totally integrated set of actions with a long-term commitment and it can never be a short-term function.

Quality management is a strategic issue. To be successful, quality issues should be identified and integrated into a company's strategic management process.

5.2 Framework of Strategic Quality Management

Glueck and Jauch (1984) define strategic management as '*a stream of decisions and actions which leads to the development of an effective strategy or strategies to help achieve corporate objectives'*. Juran and Gryna (1993) define strategic quality management (SQM) as *'a process of establishing long-range quality goals and defining the approach to meeting these goals by upper management'*. Delaplane (1987) discusses integrating quality into strategic planning of an organization. Even quality management guru Juran recognizes that specific approaches to strategic quality management are still evolving. This suggests that management would have to review the basic elements of strategic management and then address the general approaches on how a quality parameter can be integrated.

5.2.1 Elements of Strategic Quality Management

Although Juran recognizes the deficiencies in the development of strategic quality management, he identifies some of the basic elements as stated below (Juran and Gryna, 1993):

- Define mission
- Develop goals
- Select strategies
- Formulate quality objectives and policies
- Organizing for quality
- Planning for quality
- Monitoring performance and review

5.2.2 Approaches to Integrating Quality into Strategic Management

The General Approach

The corporation should have a structured process for strategic planning to which the business units are required to adhere. By this process, a five-year strategic plan may be developed in broad terms with the first year specified in greater detail. The process is to be repeated annually.

It is necessary for members of the business team to learn about specific concepts such as how quality factors influence purchasing decisions, extra costs associated with poor quality, market research for quality, quality goals, quality processes, etc., and to be able to assess the relevance of these concepts to the company's products or services.

Quality-related issues considered worthy to be included in the overall planning process have to be identified and studied further after the concepts learning process. For example, product planning by the management team of a company should place more emphasis on value, the combination of quality and price rather than on quality alone. A product quality plan would therefore be drafted to keep future development in line with these general guidelines.

The Brainstorming Approach

Allen and Bailes (1988) propose a brainstorming approach for SQM. Using this approach, middle managers become the source of input when developing a strategy. A series of meetings are held to identify critical issues that act as obstacles to quality. The most important issues are singled out and more meetings are held to develop goals to address the issues. The goals are then grouped into macro strategies. For each of the macro strategies, brainstorming sessions are employed to identify action items. The action items provide a framework for each strategy and lead to the development of a five-year plan for quality.

The Profit-Quality Approach

The case of General Electric (Utzig, 1980) serves as a general model which can be applied to a specific product or product line of a company. The GE approach involves deliberations such as:

- financial goals for a particular product/product-line,
- key quality factors that influence customers' purchase decisions,
- the competitive analysis of key quality factors,
- current quality goals and internal results quality,
- alternative quality goals with respect to competition,
- departmental goals needed to achieve changes of level in key quality factors, and
- departmental plans and resources required.

The driving force of this approach is the integration of financial goals with quality goals.

Implementation of SQM

Implementation of SQM requires upper management's support and an infrastructure for quality. In some situations, management would have to start SQM small and learn from pilot activities. A small number of pilot projects, with their scope carefully defined would be more effective than omitting the pilot phase to achieve results more rapidly.

In general, any new attempt at implementing SQM would involve the lessons of success and failure encountered by other organizations.

5.3 Mission Statement

Strategic management starts off with the mission, primary overall purpose of the organization and its expressed cause for existence. Ideally a corporate mission statement should be an expression of the *vision*, the *culture* and the *shared values* of the organization as well as a definition of the boundaries or scope of the business.

The process of defining the mission statement will itself be a valuable exercise because it will involve the top management of the organization and also draw upon the views of those responsible for the development of the detailed implementation of the programs. The last thing that any company needs is another set of platitudes, issued from the top, that embodies fine-sounding rhetoric but does not carry any commitment.

For a service organization, the most important function that a mission statement can provide is underlining the service dimension of the organization's intended strategic positioning.

It should be noted that the mission statement should be treated as a living thing. It needs to be reviewed periodically and adjusted to reflect changes in the marketing environment and the company's response to that environment.

5.3.1 SIA's Corporate Mission

SIA's official statement of mission is:

> 'Singapore Airlines is engaged in air transportation and related businesses. It operates worldwide as the flag carrier of the Republic of Singapore, aiming to provide services of the highest quality at reasonable prices for customers and a profit for the Company.'

5.4 Goal

A *goal* is a statement of the prime reason for the initial setup of a business. A business without a goal is unlikely to succeed and the resources it uses could be probably be put to better use elsewhere in the economy. A business must be goal-oriented, as only by this means can it be ensured that it can achieve what it has stated in its mission statement.

A goal is a desired value. It is different from an objective in that it does not indicate a quantitative result to be achieved within a specific period of time. For example, the goal of a purchasing system is to obtain all parts, materials and equipment for the business, while the objective of the system is to obtain supplies at the most economical prices, of the right quality and at the right time. In other words, a goal is a qualitative result a company intends to achieve through its business operations. More often than not, it is of a strategic long-range nature.

Goals may be created for providing strategic direction or for break-through.

5.4.1 SIA's Corporate Goals

SIA's corporate goals are:

- To deliver the highest quality of customer service that is safe, reliable and economical.
- To generate earnings that provide sufficient resources for investment and satisfactory returns to shareholders.
- To adopt human resource management practices companywide that attract, develop, motivate and retain employees who contribute to the company's objectives.
- To maximize the utilization and productivity of all resources.

5.5 Competitive Strategies

Strategies may be viewed as specific major actions or patterns of action for attaining goals or objectives (Paine and Naumes, 1982). For an organization, a whole series of strategy decisions must be made for various functions, such as finance and control, operations, research and development, procurement and marketing mix. For example, the marketing strategy would involve the combination of product policy, promotion, packaging, advertising, and distribution channels. The marketing strategy chosen could then be one way of using technology to satisfy customers' or clients' needs for information, convenience, reassurance of service and availability. An overall strategy, then, is the total sum or pattern of past and present actions or decisions.

5.5.1 SIA's Corporate Strategies

The elements that contribute to SIA's success as a major international airline include its excellent service, steady growth, commitment to free enterprise and willingness to make bold, judicious investments (SIA, 1985).

Thus, the first strategic decision was made, that of market development. SIA decided that its market was in international routes, which largely differed from that of the Malaysia-Singapore Airlines, leading to their parting in 1972. This was to trigger off a tradition of bold but strategic decision-making that was to form the mainstay of SIA's success. All this has culminated in the six main strategies detailed below that orchestrate SIA's operations.

Strategy I: New Aircraft Technology

Sustained growth can be achieved only through innovation, imagination, prudent risk-taking and the entrepreneurial drive. With these prerequisites in mind, SIA aims to stay competitive by keeping abreast of the latest in technology and by providing outstanding service at the lowest operating cost, without sacrificing safety standards.

Fleet acquisition is an area in which SIA has demonstrated its boldness in risk-taking for making long-term commitments. In 1973, barely one year after separating from Malaysia-Singapore Airlines, SIA took possession of two 400-seat Boeing 747s, and became the third carrier in Asia, after Japan Airlines and Air-India, to operate this type of aircraft.

In March 1995, SIA's fleet comprised sixty-six aircraft: twenty-eight Megatop 747s, seven Boeing B747-300s (Big Top 747s), three B747-300 Combis, two B747-200s, seventeen Airbus A310-300s, four A310-200s, three Mega Ark freighters, one B747-200 freighter and one B737-300 freighter (see Appendix 4b on Fleet Development).

The airline is the youngest of all international carriers with an average aircraft age of five years two months compared with an industry average of around ten years. SIA was the first airline to recognize the demand for more non-stop services that offer travelers, especially businessmen, uninterrupted travel to long-haul destinations, ensuring they arrive earlier and in better shape.

SIA believes that, other things being equal, most travelers would prefer to be flown in new and modern aircraft, which are usually more reliable, quieter and roomier. It would also serve to enhance inflight service. These are the operational and commercial advantages that have sharpened SIA's competitive edge (Christopher, 1992).

Strategy II: Automated Airport Facilities

As emphasized by SIA's managing director, the expected increase in the world air traffic could lead to congestion at airports. For customer confidence to be maintained, the hassles on the ground so prevalent in other parts of the world will have to be overcome.

The airline industry faces a formidable challenge as it is not easy to expand airport capacity overnight to match surges in air traffic. In 1975, the Singapore government decided to build a new international airport at Changi. At that time, SIA viewed the move of its operations to the new airport as an opportunity for the company to renew itself and to upgrade its services and capabilities. With the government's investment of US$760 million in the airport and SIA's investment of US$118 million, the airport was equipped with the most up-to-date automated systems to facilitate airline operation and customer services.

With the second air terminal now complete, Changi Airport's passenger-handling capacity has been expanded to twenty-two million a year, and there is already provision for the building of a third terminal and a third runway by the turn of the century.

Strategy III: Ground Service with the Human Touch

With the surges in air traffic, the battle that has for so long been waged between airlines in the air has shifted to the ground. As a service industry the human touch, the day-to-day personal contact with passengers, is still the most important consideration. In addition to providing excellent inflight services, SIA has launched the 'Outstanding Service on the Ground' program to motivate the airline's frontline staff on the ground to provide genuine innovative service. Frontline staff are encouraged to show genuine interest in their customers, and through a series of motivating and booster seminars, they are taught to gain self-confidence and become more resourceful in their dealings with passengers. Through this, SIA has earned a reputation second to none for its customer services.

Strategy IV: Profit-Driven Free Aviation Trade

While airlines from the Association of Southeast Asian Nations (ASEAN) member countries have prospered due to government subsidies, SIA's existence is based on its profit making. In 1972, shortly after the airline was formed, then Prime Minister Lee Kuan Yew made it clear that SIA had been set up to provide services and economic benefits — not prestige. If the airline failed to operate profitably, it would be closed down (SIA, 1988).

Hence, SIA has always been an organization driven by the profit motive. It maintains the firm strategy that only routes that are profitable in themselves or make a valuable contribution to the network will be accepted. It is also very ready to take out a destination with no regard for sentimentality. In all, SIA remains a lean organization with no excesses or extravagant ways.

Strategy V: Deregulation, Privatization and the 'Trigger' Mechanism

SIA has always been a staunch advocate for freer airways. Protectionism is SIA's traditional aversion. It appears in different forms: denial of access to a destination, restricted capacity or special fares that can be sold only by the national airline. There are other disguises but these are the most common.

As deregulation is gaining momentum, the highly protected, subsidized national carriers may find survival in the new, more highly competitive international environment difficult. Thus, there will be an trend towards privatization and commercialization of national flag carriers. Travelers will then experience an increasing seat-shortage problem due to the artificial capacity restrictions in several sky markets.

SIA believes that the solution lies in adopting what has been described as a 'trigger' mechanism whereby, when an agreed load factor is achieved over a defined period, each airline would then be automatically allowed to put on additional capacity, without lengthy bilateral negotiation.

Strategy VI: Strategic Alliance

SIA has entered into a trilateral alliance with Delta Air Lines and Swissair to form a global network spanning three hundred cities in more than eighty countries. The alliance provides passengers with coordinated flight schedules, reservation linkages and shared check-in facilities. The airlines benefit from cooperation in engineering and cargo warehousing, and joint marketing and advertising. Of the fifty projects in the trilateral agreement, one is the offer of 'a commonality in ticketing'. The idea is this: a passenger walks up to Swissair counter holding an SIA ticket and gets service as good as when he walks into an SIA ticketing office. Another project is the interfacing of computers. A passenger may check in at Changi on an SIA flight and join a Swissair flight in Zurich without having to check in again (*Singapore Business*, 1992). It is a long-term competitive alliance. When customers realize the benefits of this type of alliance, they will come back and use the airlines more often.

Apart from its Swissair-Delta alliance, SIA has entered a partnership with Scandinavian Airlines, which allows joint marketing of an all-cargo service between Copenhagen and Singapore. SIA has also formed an alliance with Aerolineas Argentinas to offer one of the cheapest round-the-world economy fares for a trip via the South Pacific.

SIA's strategic plans involve investments in other airlines and the computerized reservation system Abacus, as well as plans to expand capacity and increase revenue. Besides the formalized alliances, SIA also fosters understanding and friendly ties with other airlines like Garuda on a more informal note through golf games and other activities.

5.6 Quality Objective and Performance Measures

Management guru Peter Drucker has been quoted as saying, 'a company has but one objective, to create a customer.' This is an oversimplification of a company's objective but it is very relevant because it is a concept that directs us towards the objective of quality. Once quality has been chosen as the pivotal part of the company's mission, other objectives, such as cycle time reduction, cost reduction, competitive standing, return to shareholders and so on, fall into place. Motorola and Digital Equipment Corporation (DEC) are among those companies that have 'quantified' an objective by adopting six sigma as a basis for consistent company vision and language. Six sigma is a statistical measure that indicates one reject in a million parts.

An objective is a quantitative statement of the desired result to be achieved within a specified time. It is an aimed-at target. Thus, it can be seen that objectives form the basis of detailed planning of activities.

5.6.1 Critical Quality Factors

Quality objectives may be established through the identification of critical quality factors (CQFs) which are those measurable characteristics, conditions, or variables that when properly sustained, maintained or managed, will have a direct impact on customer's satisfaction, and hence, the company's success. A critical quality factor may be a specific outcome, result, service level or performance target (Motorola, 1993).

5.6.2 Quantitative Performance Measures

Performance measures are metrics identified by the management team to monitor the achievement of its objectives. Performance measures are stated in terms of units of measurement for the critical quality factors. Characteristics of good performance measures are:

- Use customer focused measures as often as possible.
- Use a measurement that can be checked periodically and frequently.
- Use normalized measures whenever possible, expressing them as per person, per unit, per dollar, for example.
- Use dimensionless measures, expressing them in the form of ratios or percentages, which can be graphically displayed.
- Judgmental measures may be appropriate for some factors, such as customer, peer or expert opinions.

5.6.3 Benchmarking and Objectives Setting

A prevalent approach for setting quality objectives is benchmarking, in which the performance of the best organization is used as the standard. A 'benchmark' is simply a reference point which is used as a standard of comparison for actual performance. Benchmarking is one of the distinguishing features of modern strategic quality management and it is the key to companies achieving greater levels of excellence.

Quantitative measures of critical quality factors would allow a company to compare its performance with the industry standards or with excellent models through an annual objective-setting process designed to identify the gaps. Hence the expected results are established to close the gap. These expected results are set as quality objectives for the critical success factors.

5.6.4 SIA's Corporate Quality Objectives and Performance Monitoring

On examination of SIA's corporate mission and goals, one could categorize its three performance areas as:

- Customer Service
- Safety and Reliability
- Profitability: prices, return on shareholders' funds and contribution to the economy

Quality of *customer service* is usually measured by international bodies such as *INTRAMAR*, where critical quality factors are identified and the world's top airlines are assessed according to how they fare in each factor. The top twelve quality factors influencing passenger choice and satisfaction as identified by *INTRAMAR* (1991) are:

Punctual flights	76%
Excellent inflight service	59%
Superior aircraft	52%
Comfortable seats	48%
Efficient reservations	44%
Discounts	43%
Good check-in service	43%
Clean cabin	38%
Good food and beverages	36%
Frequent flying programs	28%
Superior business class	26%
Superior first class	17%

Bearing these considerations in mind, SIA has established a performance monitoring system whereby a service performance index (SPI) is computed each quarter in order to assess service quality standards. Multilingual inflight surveys were used to itemize customers' impressions on key issues. This information is then compiled along with data on punctuality, baggage mishandled/recovered per one thousand passengers and the ratio of complaints to compliments addressed to management.

For *safety* and *reliability*, the regulatory authority for Singapore registered planes is the Civil Aviation Authority of Singapore (CAAS). SIA's top level quality control document states the airline's adherence to the Singapore Air Navigation Order, Singapore Airworthiness Requirements and also to the US Federal Aviation Regulation 145.

A reliability control board (RCB) headed by a Quality Control senior manager and comprising representatives from line, base, workshop, technical supplies, planning and CAAS has been established. Board members meet monthly to review airworthiness and reliability concerns such as, aircraft and component performance, integrity and maintenance quality, and dispatch reliability, etc. Details will be provided in subsequent related chapters.

Financial statistics and operating statistics are compiled and audited once a year, with contributions to the economy analyzed and comparisons made with the previous year. An example of critical operating quality factors and performance measures are shown in Figure 5.3.

Figure 5.3: Critical Operating Quality Factors and Performance Measures

Operating Quality Factors	Performance Measures (% Change)	Reasons for Change
Capacity utilization: Aircraft payload in tonnes X Million km flown	+ 17.8	Increased frequencies of flights.
Overall load factor (%) = Traffic/Capacity	– 2.1%	Traffic growth was lower than capacity growth.
Yield (cents) = Operating revenue/ Traffic (tonnes-km)	– 10.5	Intense competition and strengthening of Singapore dollar.
Unit Cost (cents) = Operating expenditure/ Capacity (tonnes-km)	– 7.8	Capacity growth was higher than increase in operating expenditure.
Breakeven load factor (%) = Unit cost/Yield	+ 1.7%	Yield fell at a higher rate than unit cost.

Monthly data is also compiled for the above and released in the airline's monthly journal, *Outlook*, under the subheading 'How we performed this month' to provide timely feedback for all staff members.

In addition to the above, staff productivity indicators are computed once a year by obtaining the average of changes in capacity produced, load carried, revenue earned, and value added per employee.

5.7 Organization for Quality

Various experts have emphasized the importance of organizational structure to quality's effectiveness. An analysis of these experts' opinions has revealed that there are many different approaches towards organizational hierarchy that can be adopted to achieve a company's desired quality objectives. Case studies of similar organizations have proven to be a source of useful information but it must be remembered that operating conditions, environments and other factors are rarely exactly comparable, and as a result, the case studies must not be thought of as universally applicable. A full appreciation of the differing factors involved is necessary when these case studies are used for purposes of comparison.

In general, the organizational structure pertaining to the quality system should be clearly established within the overall management of a company, with lines of authority and communication clearly defined.

In addition to the formal organizational aspects indicated above, there are supplementary organizations that can be used for achieving quality objectives such as a quality council. A quality council is a group of upper managers who assist in the development and implementation of quality strategies. This is of particular importance for strategic quality improvement and the council can be developed at different levels. The council addresses complex quality issues that require a single-minded focus; as a result, although the regular top management team usually has the same membership as the council, it cannot be combined until a later stage. This ensures that quality issues are dealt with properly.

5.7.1 The Organizational Characteristics of SIA

SIA's organization chart is included in Appendix 5. In line with its corporate goals, several of its organizational characteristics are observed in the following:

- Despite the airline's expansion, staff increases have been kept to a minimum unless additional crew is needed to fly extra flights. Emphasis is placed on productivity improvements through automation and better work methods. Technological improvements are harnessed and made use of in the air, on the ground, in the hangar and work shops and in the office.
- SIA has attempted to maintain minimum-sized units to carry out its tasks.
- The airline has maintained its adaptability and flexibility because it realizes the need to make quick decisions and respond promptly to changing conditions in a volatile environment. There has been no proliferation of formalized systems or unnecessary increases in hierarchical tiers and bureaucracy. Responsibility and authority are delegated to the lowest possible levels and the chief executive has easy access to his senior managers.
- The tightly integrated nature of SIA's operations ensures that there is no question of one department being more important than another. There are frontline and back-room activities and although the back-room activities may not face the same types of pressure as frontline operations, any failure is bound to have serious long-term consequences. It is thus evident that it is utility and relevance, not relative importance, that plays an important part in the organizational structure of SIA.

5.7.2 Quality Control Division of SIA

A quality control division has been established in the SIA Engineering Company with a quality control manager assigned for standards and another for services as will be presented in Chapter 7. Authority, responsibilities and activities for each quality management staff member are stipulated in the company's exposition document and will be discussed in the later parts of this book.

The concept of TQM involves everyone in an organization being devoted to satisfying customer needs and continuously improving their part of the process. Therefore, individual department managers need to take the lead and become responsible for the execution of matters pertaining to quality improvement in their particular chain of command. However, a quality assurance manager should advise on and assist with all quality tasks, and monitor and coordinate them through-out an organization wherever possible.

5.8 Quality Policies

Policies act as guides to actions and indicators of how resources can be allocated and assigned efficiently to the organization.

A firm's policy choices help to motivate quality differentiation and determine which activities are to be performed. Policies should be broadly defined, yet they should be specific enough to provide useful guidance.

5.8.1 SIA's Policies for Ground Services

Quality policies, as related to safety and reliability, are stipulated by CAAS and present less difficulty for an airline company such as SIA. Problems arise when frontline people, providing quality ground serv-ices, have to face dynamic problems that possess no clear-cut solu-tions. SIA keeps a record of all the incidents that occur at different line stations such as excess baggage, fare differences, payment for mishandling of baggage, etc. Functional operations managers read and analyze all these cases and generate policies like: 'How can we help? What is our policy here? In which way are we right?' for pro-viding better ground services and they have these policies published in the monthly journal, *The Higher Ground*, as guidelines for frontline staff. It is this kind of dedicated quality effort that makes SIA a success.

5.9 Planning for Quality

The plan for quality achievement should be made in conjunction with other functions such as research and development, marketing and production engineering. Manufacturing companies such as Ford Motor, make it a point that quality planning is the cornerstone of de-fect prevention and continuous improvement (Dale *et al.*, 1991).

Written quality plans (or control plans) consistent with all other requirements of a company's quality system should be prepared for projects relating to new products, services or processes. They are considered a pre-production requirement and are used to summarize the quality planning for on-going quality assurance for a specific service, part or group of parts. The plan should provide key elements in the products or service that are necessary to achieve fitness for purpose, and the means by which they are to be measured.

5.9.1 Dexterous Planning in SIA

The word planning suggests a formalized, centrally directed process in a large corporation. SIA's planning is also shaped by preparation and anticipation because of the volatile nature of the industry. The objective of SIA's planning process is to keep the airline vigilant, prepared, and ready to act.

Flexibility is the key to SIA's success. The company does not adhere strictly to immutable five-year plans but instead responds sensitively and quickly to changing conditions. Bureaucracy is not allowed to interfere with the company's decision-making process.

Although SIA shuns rigorously strict planning, the basic elements of a corporate planning process are still present. Every operational detail is planned carefully before it is executed. No plans are considered inviolable in the company because SIA realizes the importance of flexibility and dexterity in planning. The following examples help to illustrate this.

5.9.2 Fleet Planning

The periodic oil price increases that occurred in the years following the first oil crisis affected SIA's operational viability. After the first oil crisis, the search for an aircraft with better operating economics than those of the Boeing 707, but not an aircraft as large as the 747, was needed for the airline's long- and medium-range routes. This led to an order for eight DC10s in 1977 with delivery scheduled from 1978 to 1980. This was all according to a five-year operating plan to match the need. However, it was realized that 747s could be employed profitably on the routes to Perth and Auckland, which were targeted to be serviced by the DC10s. This was contrary to the earlier belief that these routes would not be able to support the 747s and SIA's leadership moved quickly to modify the plan. What ultimately evolved was an order for eight Airbus A300s for the shorter regional routes and the purchase of 747s for the long-haul services, to replace the DC10s which SIA quickly sold off. If SIA had procrastinated, unnecessary wastage and cost would have been incurred.

5.9.3 Route Planning

The need for flexibility is most evident in route planning. Bilateral air service agreements between countries that dictate the capacity and frequency of air transportation act as an artificial barrier to natural growth. SIA's five-year operating plan is based on the availability of traffic rights to operate new routes or to increase frequencies on existing ones. This, in turn, depends upon the outcome of negotiations between airlines and governments. Sometimes, negotiations do not turn out as expected and this results in changes in operation patterns and modifications in delivery schedules. Thus, flexibility is needed. In Southeast Asia, airlines enjoy flexibility in exercising traffic rights on international sectors and this has led to the airlines flourishing and air traffic surging, making the region one of the fastest growing in the world.

5.9.4 Relocation to Changi Airport

In 1975, the Singapore government announced its intention to build a new international airport at Changi. Despite losing all the infrastructure that it had developed at considerable cost in the old airport, SIA adapted itself positively to the government's decision. Plans were quickly drawn up to develop modern facilities in the new airport that would be equipped with the most up-to-date systems. The corporate offices and hangar were built at a cost of US$118 million. This was considered money well-spent, taking into account that the SIA hangar, the world's largest column-free hangar, has helped to make SIA fully self-sufficient in airframe and engine maintenance, and capable of selling engineering services at all levels to other airlines. The air freight terminal, which services thirty airline clients, the Inflight Catering Center, the world's largest flight kitchen under one roof which provides meals for thirty-one scheduled airlines operating in Singapore and an ultra-modern computer center have enabled the airline industry to grow steadily. In 1983, according to *Air Transport World*, SIA ranked fourteenth among international airlines in terms of passenger-kilometers carried, ahead of well-known names like KLM and Swissair. This has been another example where flexibility and adaptability have played an important role in SIA's planning process.

5.10 The SQM Cycle and Strategic Alignment

Implementing strategic management for quality can be addressed in five phases: decide, prepare, start, expand, and integrate (Juran and Gryna, 1993). The decide phase requires management to form a quality council, appoint quality executives and staff, and train selected managers. The preparation phase involves explanation of needs, setting up visions, goals, objectives, policies, long-range plans and implementing plans. The start phase includes the development of quality management processes, revision of current management systems, such as, reward, recognition, training, merit rating, and the conducting of pilot quality projects. The expansion phase develops and communicates lessons learnt from pilot projects to entire organizations. It also updates implementation plans and long-range plans. Integrating is the ultimate phase, where quality becomes a way of life. Goals and strategies are finalized and plans deployed to various levels; people are trained to participate in teams as well as to carry out individual quality roles; key business processes are identified and analyzed; assessments, reviews and audits are in place. In summary, quality is no longer a program, it is a part of the business planning. In most organizations, after initial development of a quality culture, a normal SQM cycle of decide-prepare-start-expand-integrate would require about six years.

With quantitative quality objectives and performance measures, strategies can be checked after each SQM cycle to examine their consistency and appropriateness for accomplishing the goals. This would involve the assessment of the impact of execution of each of the strategies on the achievement of quality objectives. As an example, strategic alignment among strategies, objectives and goals can be expressed as:

$$\underset{\text{Strategy I + Strategy IV}}{\text{Execution of}} = \underset{\text{Objective 2 + Objective 4}}{\text{Achievement of}}$$

$$\underset{\text{Objective 2 + Objective 4}}{\text{Achievement of}} = \underset{\text{Goal 2 + Goal 3}}{\text{Fulfillment of}}$$

Execution of strategies helps to achieve corporate objectives, and achievement of objectives will lead to fulfillment of goals. Thus there is a direct alignment between strategies and goals as:

$$\underset{\text{Strategy I + Strategy IV}}{\text{Execution of}} = \underset{\text{Goal 2 + Goal 3}}{\text{Fulfillment of}}$$

The purpose of establishing this kind of strategic alignment is to assess whether the execution of all strategies would ensure the achievement of goals. The benefits are:

1. If an alignment can not be established between goals and strategies, revise the strategies and improve the plan until an alignment is achieved.
2. Establishing linkages between strategies and objectives, objectives and goals, and strategies and goals will increase the probability of success of SQM.
3. If goals are not met, an organization can trace the objective performance through the performance of strategies.
4. Strategic alignment can improve the planning process used to set the strategies by determining why the process produced ineffective strategies. The same type of errors in data analysis and decision making can then be avoided in the future.

References

1. Airline Business (1991). *World Airline Monitor: INTRAMAR.* December.
2. Allen R.L. and Bailes C.V. (1988). '*Managing the Startup of a Corporate Quality Improvement Effort - Translating Corporate Strategies into Field Operations.*' *Impro Conference Proceedings.* Connecticut: Juran Institute, Inc. Pp.6A-13 to 6A-18.
3. Christopher M. (1992). *The Customer Service Planner.* Oxford: Butterworth-Heinemann.
4. Dale B.G. and Oakland J.S. (1991). *Quality Improvement Through Standards.* Cheltenham England: Stanley Thornes (Publishers) Ltd.
5. Delaplane G.W. (1987). '*Integrating Quality Into Strategic Planning,*' *Impro Conference Proceedings.* Connecticut: Juran Institute, Inc. Pp. 4B-21 to 4B-29.
6. Drucker P. (1989). *The Practice of Management.* Boston: Butterworth-Heinemann.
7. Glueck W.F. and Jauch L.R. (1984). *Business Policy and Strategic Management.* Ackland: McGraw-Hill. Fourth Edition. P.5.
8. Juran J.M. and Gryna F.M. (1993). *Quality Planning and Analysis: From Product Development Through Use.* New York: McGraw-Hill Inc.

9. Motorola (1993). *Benchmarking BMK220.* Singapore: Motorola Inc. ISSUE No. 1. Dated 2/93 PG-1-6.

10. Paine F.T. and Naumes W. (1982). *Organizational Strategy and Policy: Text and Cases.* Chicago: The Dryden Press, Holt-Saunders.

11. SIA (1985). *OUTLOOK,* May. Singapore: SIA.

12. SIA (1988). *Perspective.* Singapore: SIA.

13. Singapore Business (1992). *Singapore Airlines Sticking by Its Strength.* Singapore: Singapore Business. August.

14. Utzig L. (1980). 'Quality Reputation - A Precious Asset,' *ASQC Technical Conference Transactions.* Milwaukee: ASQC. Pp.145-154.

CHAPTER SIX

Management of Market Quality

6.1 Elements of Market Quality Management

A closer look at Figure 4.1 in Chapter 4 would reveal that the evolution of quality management is actually centered around the development of market survivability, market presence and market leadership. The simple reason for this is that any quality philosophy has got to be market-oriented; that is the basic concept of market quality management. It is pointless to have a product or service whose key quality characteristics or parameters are uniform around a nominal value, but for which there is no demand. Marketing concepts are the fundamentals of total quality management.

Elements of management of market quality are:

1. Concepts of market quality
2. Marketing function in quality management
3. Design of market quality
4. Research in market quality

6.2 Concepts of Market Quality

6.2.1 Definition of Market Quality

In a market-driven economy, the interplay among suppliers and customers gives rise to an equilibrium for the various elements of purchase considerations: product or service quality, price, delivery, customer services, warranty, etc. The resulting *competitive strength* based on all these elements gives rise to the definition of market quality. SIA's market quality lies in its competitive strength as a result of customers' combined assessment of its service quality, aircraft safety, flight reliability, and ticket prices.

6.2.2 Market Quality is Customer Focused

First of all, there is the recognition of what quality is. Peter Drucker (1989) stated that:

> 'What the business thinks it produces is not of first importance — especially not to the future of the business and to its success. What the customer thinks he is buying and considers 'value' is decisive — it determines what a business is, what it produces and whether it will prosper.'

6.2.3 Quality is Market-Policies Related

Stated in Section 3.3.3, the level of quality is evaluated by the difference between what a customer expected to, and what he actually does obtain or experience. The customer's perceived level of quality is therefore related to the marketing policies of how a company presents its product through various sales-promotion programs that arouse the customer's expectation for a purchase.

6.2.4 A Change of Customer Expectation

Customers, through experience and through the ability to make choices, have far greater expectations than the minimum acceptable level of product and service quality. Today's customers do not buy products. They buy benefits or values. So, it is not so much what a product or service is that matters, but rather what it does. In other words, what impact on customers in terms of delivered values does the product achieve?

6.2.5 The Decline of Branded Products

As technology advances, the differences in product features and product functions between competing brands become less visible. Brand names or corporate trademarks are no longer sufficient to differentiate a company from its competitors. As stated by Christopher (1992), there is a tendency for the branded markets to slide down to the commodity markets as shown in Figure 6.1 (Christopher, 1992). The ability of a brand name to command a premium price is reduced because alternative brands may embody much the same technology. This holds true particularly for the airline industry, where companies offer similar terms and services, such as the same type of aircraft, airfares and frequency of flights.

6.2.6 Market Quality Shifts the Demand Curve

A recent survey based upon a sample of over one thousand managers across fourteen European countries indicated that when it comes to choice of suppliers, quality and service issues came way ahead of price as a priority index (Humble, 1989).

This is not to suggest that price is not important but rather that a higher market quality, which is the perception of a combination of better product quality, better delivery and other services, would enable a higher price to be charged. Economists' classic demand curve suggests that as price increases, the quantity demanded falls. By

Figure 6.1: The Decline of Branded Products

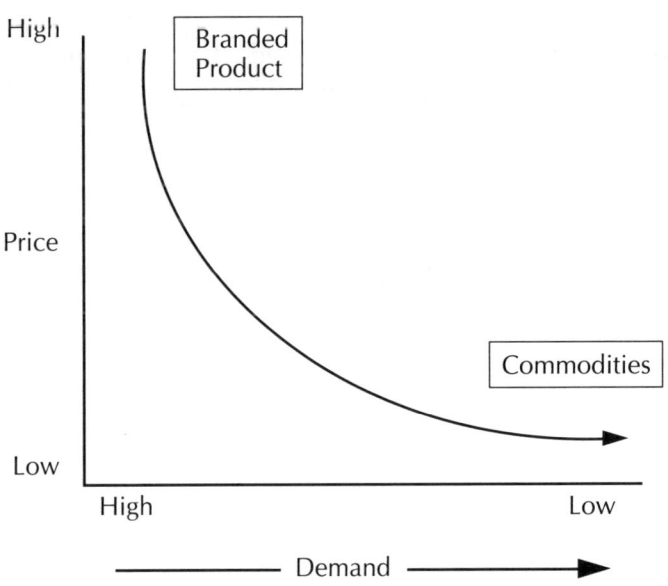

Source: Christopher (1992)

increasing the perception of market quality, the organization is able to shift the demand curve to the right as shown in Figure 6.2, thus implying that a higher price will not necessarily result in a fall in demand.

6.3 Marketing Functions in Quality Management

Dale and Okland (1991) identified some of the key marketing functions in quality management as follows:

1. To accurately define the market sector and demand through market research. This is important in the development of product grades, quantities, prices, and the timing estimate for the launch of a new product. Market research activities also provide intelligence on what industry competitors are doing.
    With reference to the ability of the production systems to satisfy the suggested quantity and quality requirements for the product, the marketing team should ensure that the people at production or operations are consulted and their commitment obtained.
2. To accurately determine customer requirements by a review of contract or market needs. Actions include an assessment of any unstated expectations or biases held by customers. Where necessary, customers should be consulted when developing the product specification in terms of the desired requirements and product characteristics.

Figure 6.2: The Impact of Superior Market Quality

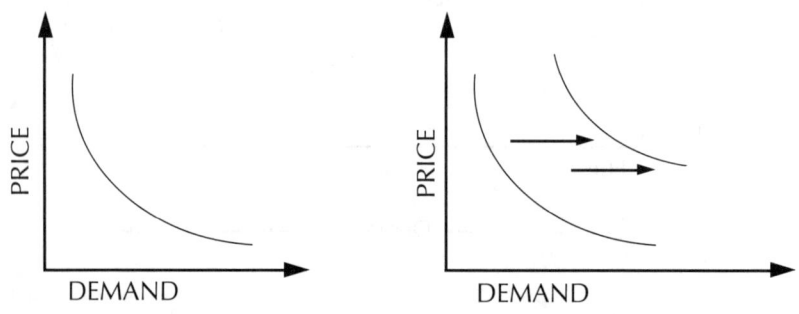

3. To adhere to national and international standards in tandem with customers' requirements while taking into account the financial implications of such adherence.
4. To develop a customer profile database.

6.4 Design of Market Quality

6.4.1 The Concept of Total Product

Collins (1989) using the personal computer as an example, summarized the changing customer's expectations as 'the total product' concept. A total product is the sum of both tangibles and intangibles which continues to deliver benefits in the eyes of the customers. The four components of a total product as shown in Figure 6.3 are:

- The innermost circle — core product: generic and fundamental requirements as stipulated by customers; usually representing customers' requirements related to product functionability/service needs.
- The second circle — expected product: mainly customers' expectations on sales and after-sales services.
- The third circle — augmented product: customers' expectations of seller's offers that are customary, such as discounts, gifts, or bonuses, etc.
- The outermost circle — potential product: customers' expectations on a long-term relationship with the supplier, such as supplier's R&D potential for providing new products and the trade-in conditions, etc.

6.4.2 The Coordination of Three Parties

The concept of 'total product' coincides with 'market quality'. For a product that commands a premium price, marketing personnel would have to infuse the sort of market quality befitting the price of the product. Design of market quality would require the cooperation of three parties; namely, the market research team, the technical and engineering team, and finally the market-promoter team.

The market research people would have to determine customers' requirements in terms of core product, expected product, augmented product, and potential product. Subsequently, it is the responsibility

Figure 6.3: The Total Product Concept

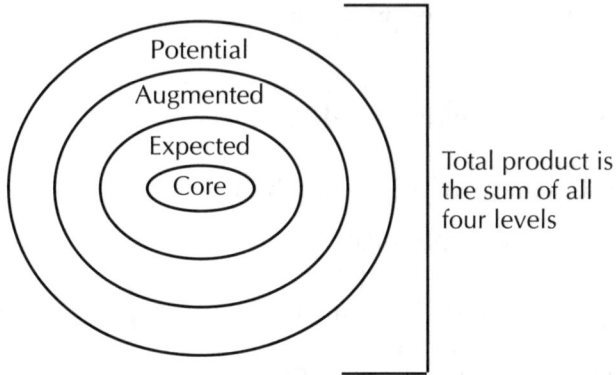

Source: Collins (1989)

of the manufacturing and engineering people to convert customers' requirements of different aspects of a product into technical specifications. Market promoters interpret the technical specifications and product characteristics and translate the information into marketing-friendly activities such as advertisements, and the selection of distribution modes.

A matrix for the design of market quality of any kind of product is presented in Figure 6.4.

Figure 6.4: Design of Market Quality

Product Level	Customers' View	Technician/ Engineers' View	Marketers' View
Core Product			
Expected Product			
Augmented Product			
Potential Product			

As the scope is broad, the following sections will focus on the key issues of design of market quality for an airline company, SIA in particular.

6.5 SIA's Design of Total Product

As observed by SIA's staff in charge of ticket reservations and general administration (SIA, 1993b), there has been a shift in passenger expectations. They want cheaper tickets but expect high service standards. While people in Japan were seeking the three Cs — car, cooler (refrigerator) and color television — the status symbols at one time, today's SIA staff try to live by another set of Cs — don't criticize, condemn or complain. This is the philosophy to win customers.

SIA offers total product to its customers and keeps constantly changing and refining its total product to ensure the airline's performance.

6.5.1 SIA's Design of Core Products

The core product of an airline company is the aircraft and the airport. SIA's bold decision in the design of its core product is to invest heavily and regularly in new aircraft. Customers prefer flying in new and modern aircraft which incorporate the latest in passenger comfort, safety features and facilities that enhance inflight service. New technology also means better on-time performance and more cost efficiency, particularly in fuel consumption, which helps to keep the cost of air travel down.

Design of SilkAir's A310 Product

Based on the type of aircraft used, an airline provides its core product — a seat on board a plane — to its customer. Ensuring the success of a core product requires much careful design and hard work. An example is SIA's launching of its first A310-200 for its inaugural flight to Kunming in China. Before the launch of the new product, the aircraft was given a thorough overhaul and modification for improved system and component performance.

- The aircraft. The aircraft was completely reconfigured from a three-class to a two-class business/economy seating arrangement. It was then repainted in the deep midnight-blue and sea green livery of SilkAir's corporate colors.

- The flight operations. The aircraft was flown by SIA pilots with SilkAir cabin crew. SilkAir's Flight Operations Department checked that the A310 conformed to all safety requirements. The safety equipment procedure was prepared by an external consultant, and the aircraft was operated under SIA's aircraft operator's certificate.

- The ground service. The Traffic Services Department produced an A310 manual as well as a modified handbook which covers all aspects of passenger, baggage and cargo handling for A310s. Procedures were drawn up on how staff should handle flight delays, aircraft changes and emergency situations.

- The inflight service. Service procedures are different for A310s compared with B737s. A new service manual was prepared. Cabin crews with at least one year's experience were rostered to attend intensive two-day training sessions to familiarize them with the new equipment loading plan and galley layout.

It is only with such detailed planning and design that a core product that is comfortable, safe and worth the money is provided.

Changi Airport helps Shaping Out SIA's Core Products

The Singapore government's commitment to aviation also helps to shape SIA's core product design. The continuous development of Changi airport provides SIA with an excellent operational base. Changi helps to enhance SIA's image. The availability of extensive facilities at Changi to serve both passengers and airlines has turned Singapore into a major hub which few airlines operating in the Asia-Pacific region can choose to ignore. The modern facilities at the airport also enable passengers arriving and departing Singapore to go through the formalities quickly and with little hassle.

6.5.2 SIA's Design of Expected Service Products

SIA's design of total product is based on meeting customers' service expectations. In addition to the design for the core aspects of the product mainly based on technology, system design is required to integrate the service components in order to fulfill customers' expectations. The two elements in the design of expected product are:

- The design of customer service system, and
- The design of customer communication system.

Design of SIA's Customer Service System

SIA's three customer service systems are:

- The sales service — phone operations, reservations, ticketing and payments;
- The ground service — check-in, seat assignment, baggage handling, traffic, security and flight delays;
- The inflight service — boarding, safety equipment procedure, meals, announcements and entertainment.

Details of the system operations will be presented in subsequent chapters.

SIA's principle of service design is focused on the use of high-tech facilities. SIA's product line is divided into three classes of travel — First, Raffles (business), and Economy. Those at the top believe that the business passenger market holds the future for the airline both in numbers and yield. SIA uses 'technology in the sky' as a competitive tool for improving service in this market segment. High-tech service design of First and Business Class seats includes the installation of small TV screens, satellite-linked air-to-ground telephone service, and the offering of video entertainment.

Design of SIA's Customer Communication System

A crucial part of the design of expected service product is the meeting of customer expectation. Therefore, customer communication plays a major role in the establishment of service expectation in the first place. It is important that a customer communication system is designed on a proactive basis of reshaping customer's expectations rather than on a reactive basis of responding to stimuli from customers in the form of complaints or their turning to other companies. There are a number of ways that a proactive customer communication system can be established. These are:

- advertising to arouse expectations and promote understanding of the product,
- periodic mailings to regular customers,

- issuing customer service manuals both internally and externally,
- holding workshops with customers to promote word-of-mouth communications, and
- using telephone 'hot lines' or electronic data interchange to communicate.

SIA's customer communication system consists of the following subsystems.

The Strategic Advertising Campaign

The Singapore girl and modern fleet advertisements convey SIA's twin strengths to customers at large and are SIA's centralized strategic advertising decision. The Singapore girl accompanied by the 'A Great Way to Fly' tune has remained the basic theme in SIA's advertising campaign for quite a long period of time. As long as it can meet the inflight promise, the campaign style should be retained. While other airlines have constantly changed their theme, SIA has been able to give the customers a very clear image of what it stands for. The fleet modernization campaign gives another strong message to the market: that SIA is a leader in aircraft technology.

The Tactical Advertisement Communications

SIA also communicates with smaller, select market segments of customers through its tactical advertising that focuses on specific routes, schedules or product promotions. Tactical advertising is handled locally with strict central monitoring in Singapore to guarantee consistency. The airline directs precise messages at targeted segments of the passenger market to convey information and sell its unique benefits. Leisure or holiday advertisements dominate while others are aimed at special interest categories such as business, convention and incentive travelers, frequent flyers and even children. Singapore is portrayed as the gateway to Asia, Australia and New Zealand as seen in the advertisement which covers both business travelers and holiday-makers.

SIA's US station has sent out fifteen thousand mailers to small businesses likely to send staff on trips to Asia. The mail communication system has drawn a high response rate of 6.3%.

Promotion of the A310 Airbus product includes advertising in the press, organizing aircraft photography shoots, preparation of various promotional materials such as brochures, posters, note pads and T-shirts, and production of A310 scale-model aircraft.

In short, SIA's customer advertisement communication is built on the basis of acknowledging what product customers want and promoting it in such a way that it appeals to them.

The PPS Database Communication

SIA has established a program of Priority Passenger Service (PPS) for First and Raffles class passengers. In addition to other benefits such as automatic flight reconfirmation and priority wait-listing, passengers' personal information about such things as seat and meal preferences is stored in a computer data base to facilitate the airline's communication with a particular passenger.

The CSS Communication Training

Since service is largely a 'perception' industry, it is important that the frontline staff be able to communicate to customers. SIA considers listening to customers the first step in customer communications. Therefore, the airline organizes communication skills seminars (CSS) for its staff from time to time to offset the fact that the human brain processes works six and a half times faster than speech, and that sometimes it is difficult to concentrate on listening because the mind tends to wander (SIA, 1993a). At the CSS, participants learnt how to listen, show understanding, handle requests, manage dissatisfied customers and do other things which are part of a normal day's work in sales. The course tries to represent actual events as accurately as possible and aims to reinforce the different skills needed by people in the airline industry. Many of SIA's experienced staff members agree with the course's concept and its emphasis on customer relations.

6.5.3 SIA's Design of Augmented Products

As defined by Collins (1989) in Figure 6.4, an augmented product is the seller's offering over and above what the customer expects or is accustomed to.

From time to time, the airline industry, like the banking industry, will develop and augment products in the form of package tours and incentive travels.

Package Tours and Special Bookings

SIA has launched many package tours, such as Asian Affair Holidays, Feast of the East program, Singapore Stopover Holidays and Super Singapore Stopover packages, etc. Against the background of a competitive business environment, special booking classes are established at different periods of time. Examples include a 'Q class' booking system which enhances the station performance and is intended to push special fares for a promotional period, and a separate booking class called 'G class' for group booking.

Travel Bonus or Incentive Schemes

As mentioned in the previous section, the PPS is one of them. Other than this, there are Frequent Flyer Programs, Young Explorer's Club, Senior Citizen Programs, and other incentive travel schemes where trips are awarded to top achievers, who are courted in both independent and joint SIA-Singapore Tourist Promotion Board (STPB) campaigns.

6.5.4 SIA's Design of Potential Products

There should be continuous product development in order to attract and hold customers, in response to changed conditions or new applications of existing products. Products that can be potentially improved in terms of customers' benefits are categorized as potential products.

Pushing the Frontiers of Service Products

Pushing the frontiers of service products has become a constant activity within SIA. From the very beginning, the airline has sought to anticipate the needs of its passengers and to meet those needs through product development and innovation. This philosophy has seen numerous attempts being made to improve SIA's quality service. These attempts range from trying to improve the standards of the Economy class by offering a choice of meals, complimentary drinks and headsets in the mid-1970s, to the launch of Celestel, the world's first global air-to-ground telephone service in September 1991.

SIA's Megatop B747-400

The airline's recent product development includes the project to progressively refit its Megatop aircraft at a cost of over US$31 million. The latest enhancements on board the Megatop are part of a tradition of passenger service which has firmly established SIA as a leading international carrier. The B747-400, after refitting, has a host of enhancements ranging from a personal cinema system in First and Raffles Class to new seats in Economy.

References

1. Christopher M. (1992). *The Customer Service Planner.* Oxford: Butterworth-Heinemann.
2. Collins B. (1989). *Management for Engineers.* Cheshire: Longman. P.372.
3. Dale B.G. and Oakland J.S. (1991). *Quality Improvement Through Standards.* Cheltenham England: Stanley Thornes (Publishers) Ltd.
4. Drucker P. (1989). *The Practice of Management.* Boston: Butterworth-Heinemann.
5. Humble J. (1989). *The Competitive Edge.* Management Center Europe.
6. SIA. (1993). *OUTLOOK.* Singapore: SIA. May.
7. SIA. (1993). *OUTLOOK.* Singapore: SIA. September.

CHAPTER SEVEN

Management of Airworthiness: Safety and Reliability

7.1 Introduction

An airline exists for only one reason: to provide swift, efficient and safe travel for people to reach their destinations. All other aspects of airline business must be subservient to this goal. Altruism dictates that for an airline safety is an issue of ethics. However, for the passenger, safety boils down to the very basics of life and death. It is a fact that safety is an important, though often understated, prerequisite when choosing an airline. Service and all the niceties are bonuses when picking an airline but in the recesses of each passenger's mind, the airline's safety record remains its biggest selling point.

On this note, suffice it to say that SIA is one of the world's safest airlines, with an unbeatable zero fatal air-accident record. In retrospect, this has not come about easily for SIA. It is the result of management's unfaltering commitment to aviation safety, the tireless devotion of its quality control personnel, and the high skill and good judgment of its dedicated pilots.

7.2 SIA's 'Beyond Airworthiness' Aircraft Fleet

Both the Civil Aviation Authority of Singapore (CAAS) and the Federal Aviation Administration (FAA) of the United States require that each civil aircraft be certified as airworthy by the original design and construction, operations, maintenance, repairs, and alteration. As one of its corporate competitive strategies, SIA has kept a technologically advanced aircraft fleet with a line of Boeing 747-200s, -300s and -400s, and Airbus A310-200s and -300s, and an average age of fleet of less than five years.

The decision to constantly modernize its aircraft fleet indicates SIA's unique leadership qualities: commitment to customer service, vision and boldness in risk-taking. Modern aircraft, which incorporate the latest technology, will enhance aviation safety and reduce operation and maintenance costs. Newer aircraft also mean better on-time performance. This is particularly so in the case of long-haul trips. SIA was the first airline to recognize the demand for nonstop service, which offers travelers, especially businessmen, uninterrupted travel to long-haul destinations, ensuring they arrive earlier and in better shape (SIA, 1988).

7.3 Auditing New Aircraft in Production

The regulatory authorities, such as the CAAS and FAA, require all aircraft, aircraft engines and propellers to be certified (Kroes *et al.*, 1988).

7.3.1 Aircraft Certification Requirements

As part of the certification process, specifications covering all components of the aircraft are prepared. These specifications may include reference to parts built under the Air Force and Navy Standard, the Military Standard, or the National Aerospace Standard. Replacement or modification of parts for a certificated aircraft must come from the approved sources.

7.3.2 Auditing Purchased Aircraft Quality

The aircraft manufacturers' objective is to provide a safe, reliable and comfortable aircraft in accordance with the specifications, while the purchasers and operators' interests go beyond these basic quality requirements. Thus, there is a need for a quality audit during production. As a part of normal practice, the manufacturers usually provide procedures and facilities for the purchaser's production inspectors to conduct a quality audit for new aircraft during production. The scheduled production inspections at various production stages are conducted after manufacturer's quality control inspections.

For those who do not have the expertise, the manufacturers nominate their own inspectors to conduct the inspections at the request of the purchasers.

The duty of the purchaser's production inspector is to ensure that all products meet the specified requirements and are not likely to pose any in-service problems. The production inspector, who has operational background knowledge which the manufacturer's inspector may not have, usually examines the aircraft structure and components.

A purchaser's quality audit is far more critical than the manufacturer's. Having on-site quality inspection benefits both the manufacturers and the purchasers in the long run. Experience has shown that many human errors manage to escape the quality control process during fabrication. Inspections by production inspectors are a very useful way of minimizing such errors.

SIA sends its quality control inspectors (QCIs) to the aircraft manufacturing plants to oversee the production of their aircraft from start to delivery in order to ensure that each aircraft is built to the regulatory requirements and those of the company.

For a new aircraft, surveillance inspection is carried out at the manufacturing plant to:

- ensure that the aircraft is built in accordance with manufacturer's specifications/standards and the airline's requirements.
- inspect the significant areas.
- verify the functional test of important systems.
- review the rejection tags (reject items).
- ensure incorporation of customized modifications.

7.4 Organizing for Aircraft Quality

With all the requirements of airworthiness, the commitment to customers' safety and reliability, and the vast sums of money involved, it is essential that adequate resources, such as personnel, information, equipment and materials, be properly organized and applied to the management of aircraft quality.

The overall goal for quality management is to maintain the SIA aircraft fleet in airworthy condition and to fully utilize them. All direct and indirect activities contributing to aircraft quality are identified, with responsibility and authority delegated to each of the activities; these are well-documented in the company's quality exposition documents. Two organizations have been set up for this purpose: the SIA Engineering Division (SIAED) and the SIA Engineering Company (SIAEC). (See organization charts attached in Appendix 6 for details.)

The SIAED's Quality Control Department (SIAED-QCD) and Technical Services Department (SIAED-TSD) are responsible for the performance and reliability of the company's fleet of aircraft, while the Engineering Planning Department (SIAED-EPD) is in charge of scheduling the airplanes for smooth and efficient in-service operations. The SIA-EPD does this through tight control of maintenance work packages and scheduling the timely accomplishment of requirements stipulated in the approved maintenance programs and schedules for aircraft and engines operated by SIA. The SIAEC-QCD performs the major portion of the quality control functions for the airline. The engineering and quality control functions of aircraft and engine maintenance activities are shown in Figure 7.1. (See also Appendix 7.)

7.5 Aircraft Quality

7.5.1 SIA's Aircraft Quality Policy

A corporate quality policy should provide focus and direction for all employees at all levels as they strive to achieve the overall goal. The SIAED and SIAEC quality policies are:

- SIAED: 'The Engineering Division of Singapore Airlines is committed to ensuring that SIA's fleet of aircraft is maintained to the highest standards at reasonable cost to the airline, and to providing the best technical support to the SIA Group in aviation engineering activities.'
- SIAEC: 'The SIA Engineering Company is committed to providing aviation engineering and support services of world class quality which meet recognized world safety standards to fully satisfy customer needs. We achieve this through working closely with the customer and pursuing continuous improvement by quality enhancement measures.'

Figure 7.1: Quality Control Functions at SIA Engineering Company

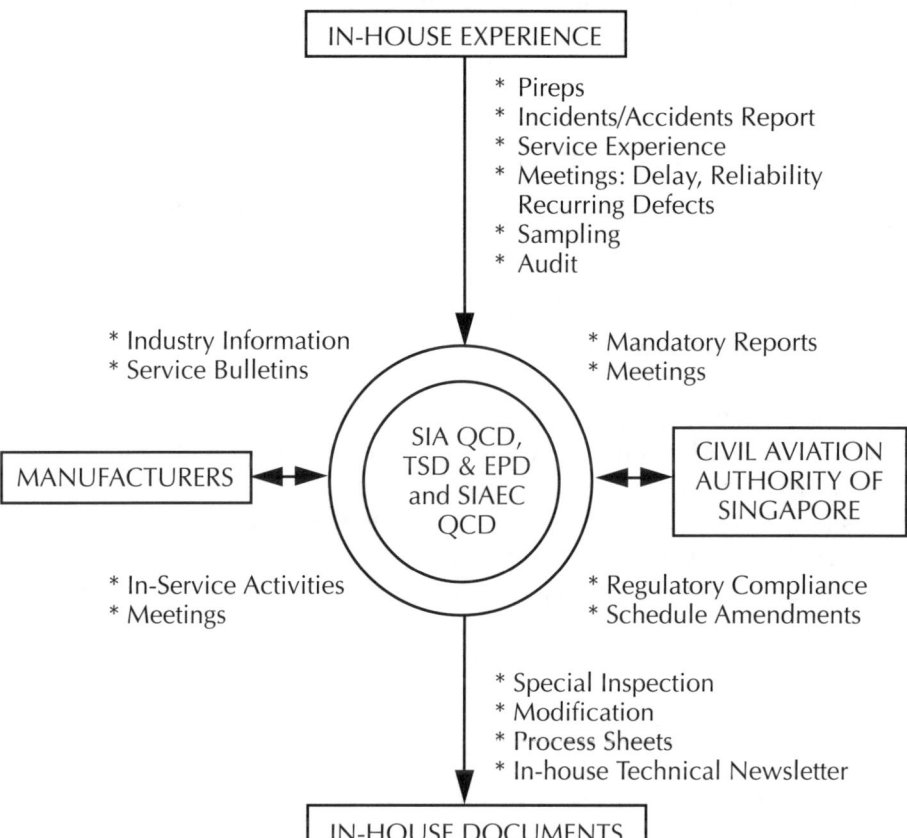

IN-HOUSE EXPERIENCE

* Pireps
* Incidents/Accidents Report
* Service Experience
* Meetings: Delay, Reliability
  Recurring Defects
* Sampling
* Audit

* Industry Information
* Service Bulletins

* Mandatory Reports
* Meetings

MANUFACTURERS

SIA QCD, TSD & EPD and SIAEC QCD

CIVIL AVIATION AUTHORITY OF SINGAPORE

* In-Service Activities
* Meetings

* Regulatory Compliance
* Schedule Amendments

* Special Inspection
* Modification
* Process Sheets
* In-house Technical Newsletter

IN-HOUSE DOCUMENTS

7.5.2 Definitions

For effective aircraft quality management, terms will have to be defined. The terms used in SIAED and SIAEC's quality manuals are in accordance with definitions commonly found in airworthiness requirements of other civil aviation authorities.

- Quality of a product: The degree to which it meets the requirements of the customer. For manufactured products, quality is a combination of quality of design and quality of manufacture.
- Quality control: A management system for programming and coordinating the quality maintenance and improvement efforts of the various groups in a design and/or manufacturing organization, so

as to permit production in compliance with CAAS requirements and any specific customer requirements affecting airworthiness.
- Quality assurance: Overall supervision by the manufacturer of the quality control tasks to ensure that the quality required is obtained.

7.5.3 Regulatory Compliance

SIA's aircraft engineering quality policies are stipulated in the SIAED and SIAEC expositions and quality manual. The documents have been prepared in accordance with the current Singapore Airworthiness Requirements (SARs), and describe policies and procedures which assure compliance with requirements under the Terms of Approval granted by the CAAS and other appropriate authorities.

For any particular airframe, engine, electronic, electrical or radio system, all work should be performed in accordance with current SARs, airworthiness directives (ADs), manufacturer's data, drawings, specifications and bulletins, and other technical data approved by CAAS. SIA does not maintain or alter any articles for which it is not authorized, nor does it provide technical data, equipment, materials, facilities of trained personnel that are not entitled to it.

7.6 Control for Airworthiness

7.6.1 Aircraft Modifications Control

Modifications control is managed by SIAED's Technical Services Department (SIAED-TSD). Modification programs are generated and implemented in accordance with local requirements and in compliance with ADs, service bulletins (SBs) and service letters (SLs).

Modifications are classified in accordance with the degree of urgency as stated below.

- Class A: Covers mandatory modifications or ADs which require incorporation within a specified time limit.
- Class B: Covers modifications which are urgent and require incorporation to alleviate or solve problems affecting aircraft operations.
- Class C: Covers modifications to be accomplished at a convenient opportunity during maintenance/overhaul.
- D1: Spares replacement (interchangeability not affected).
- D2: Spares replacement (interchangeability affected).

7.6.2 Aircraft and Engine Performance Monitoring Programs

During an aircraft's normal operations, data are collected inflight for the purpose of monitoring the performance of an airplane, its engine or system. Data are either recorded manually on the performance log sheet by flight crew during flights or automatically on aircraft models fitted with the Airplane Condition Monitoring System. The programs are also maintained by the SIAED-TSD.

Aircraft Performance Monitoring Program

The purpose of this program is to assist in tracking the long-term cruise performance of airframes and engines to determine the performance trend. The performance parameters are recorded during stabilized cruising of the aircraft. The data are either recorded manually on the performance log sheet by flight crew during flights or automatically on aircraft fitted with the Airplane Condition Monitoring System. A sample copy of a typical aircraft performance data sheet is shown in Appendix 8. The completed performance data sheets are collected by SIAED-TSD for analysis. Abnormal parameter trend are analyzed so that any necessary surveillance or rectification action can be done. A sample copy of an aircraft performance analysis is shown in Appendix 9.

Engine Performance Monitoring Program

Engine parameters are recorded for each sector of the flight in stabilized cruise condition. Engine data are collected the same way as data for aircraft performance monitoring. Recorded parameters are then corrected to those of the standard day conditions, are compared with performance parameters of standard engines and deviations are plotted. Abnormal engine behavior is analyzed to determine the need for any necessary close surveillance or rectification actions. A sample copy of engine performance analysis is shown in Appendix 10.

Compass Performance Monitoring Program

It is a CAAS requirement to carry out periodic compass swing. The objective of this program is to collect compass data in flight and analyze such data to determine whether an annual compass swing is required. Compass data are collected in the same manner as data for aircraft performance monitoring. Collected data are summarized in a report. A sample copy of the compass performance analysis is given in Appendix 11.

Fuel Conservation Program

The program is to identify and rectify problems causing an upward shift in aircraft drag and/or fuel consumption. It includes several maintenance packages to 'clean-up' the aircraft to reduce drag and fuel consumption.

7.6.3 Aircraft Reliability Control

The reliability of an item has been defined as an item that will perform a required function under specified conditions, without failure, for a specified period of time.

Reliability Program

SIA has established a reliability program. The objectives of the program are as follows:

• To provide indications of performance reliability of the fleet
• To provide an approach for monitoring of component performance, aircraft system integrity, and maintenance quality
• To provide maintenance alerts to prompt timely corrective action for major or recurring defects
• To provide an information system for reporting operational experience and corrective actions
• To provide review and adjustment of time limits and maintenance schedules

A reliability board (RCB) has been formed with members including representatives from CAAS, Quality Control, Technical Services, Line Maintenance, Base Maintenance, Workshops and Engineering Planning. RCB members meet every month to review airworthiness and reliability concerns, including the following issues:

• Reviewing and approving time limits

- Adjusting maintenance schedules where necessary
- Reviewing previous month's operations
- Discussing current problems that exceed alert levels and recommending a course of action

Actions recommended will be implemented through the maintenance schedules or a special inspection, the modifications committee, and the operational divisions.

Reliability Alert Levels

To assist in the assessment of reliability, alert levels are established for the items which are to be controlled by the program. A reliability alert level (or equivalent title, such as performance standard, control level, reliability index, upper limit) hereinafter referred to as an 'alert level', is purely an 'indicator' which, when exceeded, indicates that there has been an apparent deterioration in the normal behavior pattern of the item with which it is associated.

When the alert level is exceeded, the appropriate action has to be taken. It is important to realize that alert levels are not minimum acceptable airworthiness levels. Alerts are based on the representative period of safe operation (during which failures may well have occurred) and they may be considered a form of protection against erosion of the design aims of the aircraft in terms of system function availability.

Establishing Alert Levels

The most commonly used data and units of measurement are pireps (pilot reports) per thousand hours, component removals/failures per thousand hours, delays/cancellations per hundred departures, etc. A sample data sheet is attached in Appendix 12.

Pireps are reports of occurrences and malfunctions entered in the aircraft technical log by the flight crew for each flight. Pireps are one of the most significant sources of information, since they are a result of operational monitoring by the crew and are thus a direct indication of aircraft reliability as experienced by the flight crew.

Alert levels can range from 0.00 failure rate per thousand hours both for important components and where failures in service have been extremely rare, to perhaps as many as seventy pireps per thousand hours for equipment/furnishings, or for twenty removals of passenger entertainment units in a like period.

Calculation of Alert Levels

- Based on pilot reports (pireps)
  A minimum of twelve months' operating data has to be available, and the calculations of resultant alert level per thousand hours are shown by Example 1 and Example 2 as included in Appendix 13 and 14.
- Based on component unscheduled removals
  A minimum period of seven quarters' (twenty-one months') operating data has to be available. The resultant alert level rate for the current quarter may be set by calculations of the mean of the individual quarterly component unscheduled removal rate for the period of seven quarters, plus two standard deviations of the mean. The maximum acceptable number of 'expected component unscheduled removals' in a given quarter is determined by using a statistical process in association with the Poisson distribution of cumulative probabilities as illustrated by Example 3 in Appendix 15.
- Based on component confirmed failures
  The period of operating experience has to be the same as the component unscheduled removals and the resultant alert level rate for the current quarter is the 'corrected' mean of the individual quarterly component confirmed failure rates for the period, plus one standard deviation of the mean as illustrated by Example 4 in Appendix 16.

Recalculation of Alert Levels

The method used for establishing an alert level, and the associated qualifying period apply also when the level is recalculated to reflect current operating experience. However, if during the period between recalculation of alert levels, a significant change in the reliability of an item is experienced, which may be related to the introduction of a known action such as modification, changes in maintenance or operating procedures, then the alert level applicable to the item would be reassessed and revised based on the data subsequent to the change. All changes in alert levels are normally required to be approved by the CAA and the procedures, periods and conditions for recalculation are required to be defined in each program.

Alert Values of SIA Aircraft Fleet

Temporary alert values are established on new aircraft and engine systems where there is no previous experience. After three months' actual experience, alert values are re-established using a six-month average rate (i.e. for the long term practices). At the end of twelve months' actual experience, the alert values are established. Alert values are adjusted each year by Air Transport Association (ATA); the limits are set 30% above the mean. Alert values for pireps, unscheduled components removals and inflight engine shutdown, statistical reports and charts indicating fleet reliability and performance at regular intervals are compiled.

7.6.4 Reliability Summary

A fleet reliability summary should be kept for each particular type of aircraft. Information that should be included is:

- Number of aircraft in fleet
- Number of aircraft in service
- Number of operating days (less checks)
- Total number of flying hours
- Average daily utilization per aircraft
- Average flight duration
- Total number of landings
- Total number of delays/cancellations
- Technical incidents

A sample of SIA's aircraft fleet reliability summary is attached in Appendix 17.

7.6.5 Aircraft Maintenance Program

SIA's aircraft maintenance program is developed based on the Maintenance Steering Group's (MSG) 3 concepts of maintenance planning. The MSG is made up of regulatory authorities, manufacturers, prospective operators, systems and structural experts.

The Maintenance Review Board Documents

An initial maintenance program is developed by the MSG at the design/development stage of a new airplane. The group derives results from studies based on predicted/simulated failure modes, failure consequences and impact on safety, operability and economics, and wear/tear of normal functions, hidden functions and critical functions. The MSG develops the broad maintenance concepts and requirements and presents them in the form of the Maintenance Review Board (MRB) document. The MRB document prescribes minimum mandatory requirements.

The Maintenance Planning Documents

The Maintenance Planning Document (MPD) is generated by manufacturers based on the MRB documents. The MPD contains detailed maintenance procedures and requirements used as the basis for new/inexperienced operators to develop their maintenance program. Maintenance programs require the approval of regulatory authorities and may include special provisions to meet unique environmental/operator's circumstances. The program consists of different levels of maintenance checks at scheduled intervals as listed below.

- Monitoring under normal operating conditions
- Periodic function checks
- Health checks (internal leak analysis)
- Condition monitoring using non-destructive testing, trend monitoring and failure analysis
- Hard and soft life control
- Reliability programs for maintenance time escalation and failure prevention

Refinements of the program are based on experience, service evaluation and trade requirements, and in consultation with authorities and manufacturer are conducted with the considerations as stated below.

- Reliability based programs may be used to vary or relax requirements
- Maintenance processes are normally controlled by cycles or hours operated
- Most structural items and some components have fixed life limits

Definitions Applied to Maintenance Programs

- Reliability: Reliability is the ability of an item to perform a required function under specified conditions, without failure, for a specified period of time.

- On condition: It applies to components on which a determination of continued airworthiness may be made by visual inspection, measurements, tests, or other means without a tear-down inspection or overhaul.

- Conditioning monitoring: The data collection and analysis of components and systems which will give information upon which judgment(s) relative to the safe operation of the airplane can be made.

Technical Log

For any discrepancy entered in the aircraft technical log by the flight crew, positive rectification work has to be carried out.

Maintenance Actions Recommended

Actions recommended will be implemented through the Maintenance Schedule or by Special Inspections, the Modifications Committee, and the Production Divisions of SIA.

7.6.6 Quality Control Inspection

Quality control inspectors (QCIs) conduct inspections to ensure that maintenance and engine overhaul are performed in compliance with the requirements of the *airline, manufacturers and regulatory authorities*. QCIs also review records of work performed during Certificate of Maintenance Reviews (CMR). They conduct investigations of major and recurring aircraft incidents and accidents and prepare reports and recommendations on preventive and corrective actions. QCIs are also responsible for reviewing airworthiness directives, preparing service bulletins, raising special inspections as required, liaising with pertinent authorities on company approval, and monitoring the approval systems.

7.6.7 Aircraft Interior Inspection

Aircraft interior, exterior and cargo compartments are inspected regularly to ensure high standards of cleanliness and aesthetics. Regular checks are also conducted on aircraft seats, galleys, toilets and carpets, aircraft paintwork and cargo hold, and the quality of the aircraft potable water system.

7.6.8 Dispatch Reliability

Dispatch reliability is defined as the percentage of scheduled revenue flights which depart without incurring a ground interruption. A ground interruption may include any of the incidents listed below.

- Flight dispatch delay
- Flight cancellation
- Ground turn back
- Aborted take-off
- Aircraft substitution

A flight cancellation is counted when a scheduled revenue flight does not take place due to an inherent aircraft malfunction. Cancellation of a multi-segment flight is counted as a single cancellation.

Substitutions are not counted as interruptions unless a service interruption occurs. When an interruption involves a substitute airplane, the interruption is counted as though it occurred with the originally scheduled airplane.

Only a single interruption is counted for a single schedule departure. However, a single interruption may be attributed to more than one cause. In such cases, each cause is assumed to have contributed an equal amount, and the single interruption is divided accordingly. For example, in a single interruption with three causes, each cause will receive a count of one third.

Dispatch Authorization (DA)

During operations, an aircraft may experience damage or defects that are not covered by the approved documents. When the damage or defect cannot be rectified at the place of occurrence and if it is deemed that the aircraft is safe for flight, a DA may be issued to allow the aircraft to fly to a station where the defect can be rectified.

After the issuance of the DA, quality control personnel should monitor the technical and defect logs to ensure that the damage or defect that necessitated the DA is rectified when the aircraft next returns to home base.

Concession Request

A concession request is normally supported by inspection or in-service performance records of the aircraft or component. A request may be made for a maintenance or overhaul schedule concession for short-term escalation of check permitted by authority. Extension of check period shall not exceed the following:

- AD limit
- Life limit
- Limitations specified by Minimum Equipment List (MEL) or Configuration Deviation List (CDL)
- Structural sampling periods imposed by the Maintenance Reliability Board of the Federal Aviation Association (FAA MRB).
- Special structural inspection program or damage tolerance requirement.

7.6.9 Control of Recurring Defects

All defects that exceed 'alert values' are printed out automatically by the Computerized Aircraft Reliability (CARE) system. Defects are monitored daily by defect analysis engineers and QCIs. Recommended troubleshooting procedures are established for the rectification of defects. A recurring defect is one in which positive rectification work has been carried out and the system tests show it functions properly but the identical defect is reported in the following or a subsequent flight.

Recurring Defects Committee

The Recurring Defects Committee aims to provide long-term solutions and improvements for enhanced aircraft reliability. It meets fortnightly to review the history of defects and to recommend corrective or preventive actions.

Modifications Meeting

The Modifications Meeting is held monthly to table all modifications for approval and allocation of Modification Approval Form (MAF) numbers. No MAF is raised for Class D1 and D2 modifications. The

SIAED-TSD is responsible for the procurement of modification kits and the SIAED-EPD for the planning of the scheduled modification. Modification work is accomplished during maintenance or overhaul checks.

All modifications must receive final technical and financial approval from the assistant director of engineering.

7.6.10 Engineering/Airworthiness Audit

Auditing is defined as any systematic investigation or appraisal of procedures or operations for the purpose of determining compliance with regulatory requirements and conformity with prescribed procedures, specifications and standards. SIA conducts regular internal audits among in-house technical departments, and external audits of vendors and suppliers.

Internal audits cover the verifications of documentation and records, appraisal of work processes, tools, equipment and facilities, housekeeping and personnel in order to identify strengths and weaknesses, and to seek effective remedies for shortcomings.

7.7 Management of Line Stations

7.7.1 Types of Line Stations

SIA has three types of line stations:

- A line station administered by SIA Engineering Company's own technical representatives. In this case, SIA technical representatives are responsible for all the technical handling arrangements. Certifications are to be performed by the technical representatives or other appropriately authorized personnel.
- Line stations which are handled by ground engineers accompanying the aircraft. At these stations, the accompanying engineers are responsible for all technical handling and certifications. SIA Engineering Company Line Maintenance ensures that the appropriate ground support arrangements are made prior to the dispatch of aircraft.
- Line stations handle contracted handling agents. At these stations, ground handling agents are appointed to provide ground support and certifications by appropriately authorized personnel.

A list of SIA's line stations is attached in Appendix 18. Functions of line station management are:

- Evaluation, negotiation and appointment of ground handling agents at line stations.
- Planning and positioning of spares and equipment at line stations.
- Coordination of spare parts pooling arrangements with other carriers at overseas stations.
- Quality surveillance at line stations.

7.7.2 Quality Surveillance at Line Stations

As included in the list attached to Appendix 18, overseas handling agents play a significant role in maintaining the service quality of SIA. Hence, surveillance is conducted to ensure the line engineering quality.

Over a period of three years, the frequency of quality surveillance is planned by CAAS and accomplished by SIA's Quality Control Inspectors (QCIs) or by SIA's QCIs and the CAAS airworthiness surveyors or engineers. Inspections are done at SIA facilities and/or handling agents' facilities at stations.

Areas of surveillance are:

- Storage facilities:
  adequacy of premises
  - proper segregation and storage of spares
  - control system of shelf life
  - tracebility of spares
  - control of poor spares
- Maintenance documents:
  - receipts of documents
  - amendment of documents
  - availability of check sheets and manuals
  - retention and dispatch of check sheets
- Transit procedure:
  - to ascertain that SIA procedures are adhered to through observation of a transit (refueling stop) check.

References

1. CAA (1990). *Civil Aircraft Airworthiness Information and Procedures, Leaflet 1-7. Appendix B.* Civil Aviation Publication. CAP 562. July 1.
2. CAAS (1993). *SIA Engineering Co. Exposition,* Issue 1, Rev 1, February 1. Singapore: CAAS.
3. Kroes M.J. et al. (1988). *Aircraft Basic Science.* 6th ed. New York: McGraw-Hill.
4. SIA (1988). *Perspectives.* Singapore: SIA.
5. SIA (1944). Singapore: SIA. August.

CHAPTER EIGHT

Management of Flight Operations

8.1 Excellence in Technical Operations

Operational excellence in the air and on ground has become the hallmark of Singapore Airlines. Among the many factors in SIA's success are its extensive training programs for pilots and engineering staff and its heavy investment in state-of-the-art aircraft, ground equipment and maintenance facilities (SIA, 1995).

Technical excellence in flight operations and engineering has been a central element in the airline's excellent safety record. Passengers can fly SIA in the knowledge that they are traveling in an aircraft from the youngest fleet of any airline, with the highest standards of equipment maintenance.

8.2 Goals of Flight Operations Management

SIA's Flight Operations Division has set the following goals:

1. To contribute to the overall objectives of the company by ensuring that there is a ready pool of qualified pilots to operate the company's present and future services.
2. To maintain the outstanding safety record of the company through systematic, modern, and cost effective training.
3. To cultivate high morale, team spirit and comaraderie amongst pilots, and between the pilots and other staff in the division as well as employees in other parts of the company.

8.3 The Importance of Competent Pilots

In addition to the preparations and maintenance which ensure airworthiness of aircraft, an other important consideration for an airline is the quality of its pilots.

A pilot must be 'fit for duty' — in physical health, temperament and in his breadth of training. In aviation, many activities require human performance under pressure, in sometimes physically challenging surroundings and in shifts occurring round-the-clock.

This unique mix of human and technical demands in flight operations requires a specialized and customized management approach.

8.4 Pilot Training

8.4.1 Training from Scratch

Cadet pilots go through a three-stage training program. The first is basic flying training at the Singapore Flying College. The second is flight training in Learjets, and the third is advanced transitional training and on an aircraft simulators.

8.4.2 The Singapore Flying College

The establishment of the Singapore Flying College in April 1988 enabled the airlines to train its own pilots in-house rather have them trained externally. The college is a wholly-owned SIA subsidiary for the training of cadet pilots, who undergo an intensive thirteen-month course in Singapore and at the College's branch at Jandakot, near Perth, Western Australia, which was established in 1990.

Training Mode and Duration

In Singapore, cadet pilots receive classroom tuition and instruction in basic flying, and in Australia, they develop their flying skills, Cadets must complete two hundred flying hours and a series of examinations before graduating.

Training Facilities and Infrastructure

The college has:

- six Cessna 152 aircraft in Singapore, while the Jandakot branch has:
- five Beechcraft Bonanzas,
- three Beechcraft Barons, and
- three Cessna 172 aircraft.

In March 1994, the Singapore Flying College opened a A$1.7 million student residence at Jandakot. The building can accommodate eighty-eight students and has an annex housing four staff members. The student residence brought total investment by the college in facilities and infrastructure at Jandakot to A$7.3 million.

8.5 The Flight Crew Training Center

8.5.1 The Use of Flight Simulators

SIA's Flight Crew Training Center has eight flight simulators representing the airline's four main aircraft types:

- the B747-400/the B747-300;
- the A340;
- the A310-300/A310-200; and
- the Learjet 31.

SIA took delivery of its third B747-400 simulator in early 1994. A Learjet flight simulator was also acquired and has been used for training since February 1994. It enables the trainees to experience some of the more exacting exercises, such as failures in a safe and realistic environment. It also helps to speed up crew training, as repetitive exercises can be performed quickly. The airline uses its other flight simulators to train pilots in normal and emergency flight and ground procedures, as well as to test pilots in their bi-annual checks for license renewals.

8.5.2 SIA as the Pioneer of Flight Training

In 1998, SIA was the first airline in the world to install a B747-400 flight simulator. The airline uses the flight simulators to train pilots in normal and emergency flight and ground procedures as well as to test pilots in the bi-annual checks for license renewals. The Airline's state-of-the-art simulators reduce the time required for training and flight checks, thus reducing costs.

The Use of Learjets

When SIA launched its Advanced Training Program in November 1991 using two Learjet 31 aircraft, it was the first major airline to use an all-jet training fleet for such a program. A further two Learjets were delivered in 1993, raising total expenditure on these aircraft to US$33.5 million.

In February 1995, an order was placed for two Learjet 31 and four Learjet 45 aircraft at a value of US$56 million. The new Learjet 31 was delivered in January 1996, while the Learjet 45s will replace the Learjet 31 fleet in the last quarter of 1997.

SIA was the first commercial airline to use Learjet 31s to train its cadet pilots from the ab-initio stage to First Officer rank. There are distinct advantages in using jet aircraft equipped with Electronic Flight Instrument (EFI), Flight Management System (FMS) and up-to-date avionics for transitional trainees. The following sections outline SIA's Learjet program.

Learjet Training

From the outset, SIA wanted to provide a cockpit environment that would bridge the gap between the basic, piston-engined, propeller trainers in which the cadets learn to fly at the Flying College and the actual aircraft in the SIA fleet. All cadet pilots are posted to the Learjet fleet for a period of two to three months before converting to the A310, B743 and B744 aircraft. During this period, they are taught highspeed jet operations on daily line training flights to southern Thailand, East and West Malaysia and occasionally to Western Australia.

Added Benefits

The use of Learjets enables Senior First Officers from the B744 fleet to accumulate experience towards their command qualification. If left to acquire flying experience on the B747-400 alone they could take fifteen to twenty years to meet the qualification requirements. The annual target for the use of Learjets is to provide transitional training to one hundred Cadet Pilots and supplementary flying experience to SIA First Officers. SIA's Advanced Training Program using Learjets has proved to be an excellent investment for the future growth of the company.

8.6 The Human Aspects of Flight Operations Management

The following sections introduce SIA's approach towards the 'human' aspects of flight operations:

8.6.1 Management Approach

Management believes that all employees, both Singapore nationals and expatriates are valuable assets of the company, and that division objectives can be met through extensive training, frequent refresher courses and espirit de corps.

The management team adopts a consensus style, encouraging discussion and debate before making decisions on issues. Overall, relationships between management and union, superior and subordinate, is cordial and professional. Staff service conditions, which may differ slightly between local and expatriate employees, are applied consistently and compassionately. Because of the strong company-staff relationship, it is not unusual to see flight crew go beyond the call of duty, for example, in cases such as the Gulf War when frequent changes to routings and flight schedules occurred.

Periodically, Collective Agreements (CAs) come up for renewal. These are negotiated between the company and the various house unions of SIA. In-between negotiations on CAs, specific issues which may fall outside the collective agreements are reviewed. All issues are discussed frankly and openly and work carries on unabated throughout the period of discussion, negotiation or even, on occasion, arbitration.

8.6.2 Management by Exaction and with Dynamism

For effective flight operations, all employees must conform strictly to procedures laid down in various SIA manuals and meet SIA Proficiency Standards. SIA does, therefore, exercise management by exaction — over pilot training, behavior and discipline. Staff members are required to be mindful at all times of safety and legal requirements.

Recurrence Training

SIA requires all pilots to attend on-the-job training four times a year and to attend an annual in-depth and broad-based safety program. This is mainly a legal requirement.

State of Preparedness

While SIA's financial performance has been better than most airlines' in recent years, its management has never rested on its laurels. Complacency has always been the enemy. Management takes every opportunity to remind staff of the turbulent environment in which the airline operates. One analogy which has been used for this purpose is that of an aircraft encountering bad weather in flight. The corporate message is that SIA staff should not get disoriented by any turbulence which the company may encounter and instead focus their attention on minimizing the effects of that turbulence.

Periodic Review of Organizational Structure

The structure of the Flight Operations Division has been reviewed periodically. On a separate basis, the ratios of technical crew, ground crew, ground support staff and management are monitored to keep the organization lean, dynamic, and cost effective. Crew numbers required for line operations are continuously examined to ensure that they are kept to a minimum.

The Future

As SIA plans to grow steadily at eight to ten percent per year for the rest of the decade, the company will need to increase its pilot recruitment both to cater for expansion and to replace the four hundred pilots who will have retired by the year 2000.

8.7 Strategic Information Systems for Flight Operations

SIA is aware of the significant high-tech information systems other airlines have adopted. It regards information technology as an investment to be deployed in the pursuit of its corporate goals, rather than a means of reducing operating costs via routing automation. Senior executives believe that information technology holds great promise for innovation and corporate leadership, and that is how the term 'strategic information system' was coined.

The Management Services Divisions of SIA provides a full range of information systems as described below.

8.7.1 Flight Planning System: PHOENIX

Optimal flight plans with routes to be flown, and the amount of time and fuel required, are generated by a computer software named 'PHOENIX'. Area avoidance and routing specifications as a political and/or economic restrictions are considered when generating optimal operational flight plans.

8.7.2 Flight Watch System

An artificial intelligence (AI) system has been used to monitor the flight movements of all SIA aircraft. Aircraft movement information is captured on-line in the system and a central database is maintained for ready access by various users. In a situation when a flight has to be disrupted, the system is able to explore all possible courses of action and offer the flight controller the optimal solution. It prompts the users to take a series of actions ensuring proper coordination with other departments affected by the disruption. Among the factors the system considers when recommending a solution are the passenger load factor and flight connections. Its aim is to minimize customer inconvenience. The system's decision support function is able to forewarn the flight controller of the consequences of a pending decision.

8.7.3 Airport Analysis Interface System

For each flight departure, the system calculates and checks the take-off conditions based on airport weather, forecast weather and aircraft structural weight limits. This is to ensure that the planned take-off weight for a departure does not exceed the recommended weight limit for the runways in use. The system interfaces directly to the flight planning system, PHOENIX, to obtain the relevant load and weight details.

8.7.4 Crew Rostering and Flight-Crew Tracking: CRAFT

CRAFT is a system for crew rostering and tracking. It comprises the following modules:

- Flight schedules,
- Crew particulars,
- Crew assignment, and
- Crew tracking and re-scheduling,

Data in the Flight Schedules module forms the basis of crew operating patterns (COPs). COPs and crew particulars, the crew assignment module works out duty lines for each crew. After the rostering function, completeness checks are performed to ensure all flights are covered and the CA (Collective Agreement) legalities of the crew are adhered to. Crew tracking and re-scheduling is an on-line process. Legality checks are provided to ensure re-scheduling due to disruptions does not violate any of the agreements.

8.7.5 Pre-Flight Notice to Airman System

The system caters for the maintenance of the pre-flight notice and information to airman systems (NOTAMS and INTAMS) and generates reports on the active NOTAMS and INTAMS relevant to the various flights. It interfaces with the flight planning system, PHOENIX, to obtain route information for a flight.

References

1. SIA (1994). *Highpoint*. Singapore: SIA, June/July p.5.
2. SIA (1995). *Backgrounder 5*. Singapore: SIA, October.

CHAPTER NINE

Managing Key Airline Business Operations: The Use of Customer Focused Technology

9.1 Introduction

Section 8.7 of the preceding chapter presented the strategic information systems for flight operations. This chapter presents the strategic information systems for key airline business operations. As the airline business comprises many operations, only information systems for the key business operations are included in this chapter.

9.2 Strategic Information Systems

The belief that investment in information technology (IT) should result in leadership via technological innovation, and that it can have a significant impact on a company's strategic direction and long-term position in the industry has culminated in the evolution of a new term, strategic information systems (SISs).

Wiseman (1988) defined SISs as information systems in which the primary function of the system is either to process predefined transactions and produce fixed-format reports on schedule or to provide query and analysis capabilities. He stated that the primary use of SISs is to support or shape the competitive strategy of the enterprise, its plan for gaining or maintaining competitive advantage or reducing the advantage of its rivals. In a nutshell, what all this amounts to is a new business weapon or tool to enable an enterprise to forge ahead of the competition.

Strategic information systems shape the competitive posture and strategy of a company whether the business is administrative or technical in nature. Major types of information systems as defined in IT literature include (Frenzel, 1992):

1. transaction processing systems (TPS),
2. decision support systems (DSS),
3. office automation systems (OAS),
4. management information systems (MIS), and
5. end-user computing systems (EUC).

Some of these systems are operational in nature; they improve a company's operations in the short term. Others help the managers in making intermediate or long-term decisions. Overall, all these systems are designed to upgrade a company's competitive position.

9.2.1 Strategic Information Systems in the Airline Business

SABRE

Developed by American Airlines in the 1960s as its computerized reservation system with an initial investment of $350 million, the Semi-Automated Business Research Environment (SABRE) did not achieve profitability until 1983. Today, SABRE is the world's largest travel agency reservation system, serving fourteen thousand agents. It is one of the most widely known and valuable strategic systems in the world. Many airlines have chosen not to compete with SABRE but to lease the service. Air France, KLM and others are customers of American's reservation system. The system generates 5% of the gross revenue of the AMR Corporation, American's parent company, and accounts for 15% of its profits.

Apollo

Another travel agency system was developed by United Airlines in the early 1970s with an initial investment of $250 million. It gives agents access to listings of all major airlines and hotels, car rentals and other travel related services. In 1988, a market value of $1 billion was placed for the Apollo reservation system, and its clients were USAir, British Airways, Swissair, KLM and Alitalia. It is estimated that SABRE and Apollo have annual returns on investment of 50-100%.

The above information is derived from Frenzel (1992). Clearly, a computerized reservation system is a dynamic and profitable business in itself, and gives an airline a competitive edge as well.

The following sections provide details of SIA's strategic information systems for key business operations, and the measurements and analyzes of quality of its business operations.

9.3 Abacus Computer Reservation Operations

At SIA, reservation and ticketing operations are conducted through Abacus, a leading mega-computer reservation system (CRS). The nine partner carriers of Abacus are Cathay Pacific Airways, China Airlines, Dragonair, Malaysian Airlines, Philippine Airlines, Royal Brunei Airlines, SIA, Tradewinds and Worldspan Global Travel Information Services, a mega-CRS in the United States.

9.3.1 Participation Levels

Abacus has the following number of participating airlines:

- basic participants: one hundred and fifty-one
- direct access: fifty-three
- direct sell: twenty-three

Functions at different levels of participation are stated below.

- Basic participation: Abacus displays seat availability for each flight and in each class of service.
- Direct access: It enables a travel agent to see an airline's up-to-the-minute status on seat availability; and bookings are guaranteed.
- Direct sell: The travel agent is able to receive instant confirmation of a booking as well as positive passenger name record acknowledgment from the respective airlines' reservations systems. Facilities such as advanced seat reservations are also available.
- Direct response: This enables a participating carrier to directly acknowledge receipt of Abacus users' teletype bookings. This function assures subscribers that the sale was received by the airline. If the

carrier fails to return the acknowledgment after a specified time, Abacus will then send a second request.

9.3.2 Other Connected Software Systems

- GlobalServe: GlobalServe is a new product to be released in phases. It is a technical link between Abacus, Amadeus (a European CRS) and Worldspan enabling travel agents to access each other's passenger name records (PNRs), customer profiles and other data and information in order to service their corporate clients.
- Daily ticketing information: This provides the most up-to-date ticketing information which is transmitted electronically to interested participating airlines within twenty-four hours, without having to manually key in ticketing data from flight coupons.
- Abacus Transport Network: The Abacus Transport Network (ATN) is an internationally based major network that connects Abacus directly to hundreds of other airlines, hotels, car rental companies and other travel vendors worldwide. The ATN processes information from travel suppliers and provides the most current and unbiased displays available. Users have access to automatic airfare pricing, client profiles, credit card validation, health and visa information etc.
- Asian Frequent Flyers: The software system for Passages, the Asian Frequent Flyers (AFF) program, which was developed by Abacus, consists of two major portions: the AFF system and host-to-host on-line access for Cathay Pacific, Malaysian Airlines and SIA, the partners in the running of Passages. The three airlines' national systems have on-line access to the AFF customer database for more efficient customer service. With Abacus, the AFF system is able to accept and process related transactions submitted by Passages members.
- Bank Settlement Plan: The Bank Settlement Plan (BSP) enables travel agents in Hong Kong, Singapore and Taiwan to settle their ticketing accounts through Abacus. The BSP allows travel agents to issue tickets on behalf of airlines and settle their ticketing accounts with these airlines automatically through a clearing bank. The Abacus ticket record database is used for information collection and submission to BSP. The BSP Processing Center then prepares reports for both travel agents and airlines.

There are quite a number of other travel-related software systems which can be connected to the Abacus to make services available at the touch of a button.

9.4 Schedule and Computerized Route Planning

Schedule planning is a key player in making SIA profitable. The onus is on the schedulers to prudently utilize the airline's two most important assets; namely, the aircraft and routes, thereby producing the best economic results despite the invariable constraints that exist.

9.4.1 Objectives of Schedule Planning

Schedule planning is an intricate process which involves balancing the following multiple objectives:

- Satisfying customers' varied needs
- Achieving airline economics
- Meeting operational feasibility

9.4.2 Planning Cycle

For the purposes of maintaining continuity and catering to changing market demand and customers' expectations, the annual schedule of each new financial year usually starts in April, and is an improvement over the previous year's schedule. Scheduling work peaks after about six months. The year is divided into several sub-periods and for each sub-period, stations are informed early of schedules so as to be able to formulate their sales policies in advance.

9.4.3 Dynamism of Schedule Planning

As a dynamic airline, it is little wonder that major schedule changes are often made. This is usual when new destinations are launched and when improvements are made to existing flight routings, frequencies and timings. Schedule adjustment is an ongoing process throughout the financial year.

Such adjustments are necessary to maintain the airline's dynamism so that the airline can respond rapidly to pressing situations that arise as a result of unexpected operational problems such as flight diversions and delays due to natural disasters, wars or labour strikes. In addition, the airline also seeks new business opportunities by mounting additional unscheduled charters.

9.4.4 Information Sources for Schedule Planning

Schedulers derive information from inside and outside the airline. Valuable input is gathered from the various SIA divisions and overseas stations.

Information provided by external sources such as airport authorities, travel agencies, cargo agents, passengers, shippers, consignees and trade entities, are also systematically analyzed in the decision-making process.

9.4.5 Schedule Planning Parameters

Good schedules strike a balance between what is desired and what is possible, and between commercial viability and operational feasibility. However, this is by no means a simple task.

Passengers and shippers look for convenience in a flight schedule; ideally, one that offers attractive destinations, sufficient seat and cargo capacity to the destinations with the deployment of the right aircraft types, and convenient arrival and departure times. The main schedule parameters are listed in Figure 9.1, and the following sections provide some of the general considerations a schedule planner will have to make in regard to these planning parameters.

Destinations

When establishing flight destinations the following factors have to be taken into consideration:

- Operating rights: Before any air service can be mounted between two countries, the respective governments must represent their airlines in negotiations for operating rights. The rights have to be documented in air services agreements (ASAs).
- Traffic potential: In determining operations to new destinations, traffic potential is a vital consideration. The destinations should be able to attract passenger and cargo traffic with their natural or

man-made attractions, strong commercial sectors and good infra-structure. SIA will not open up routes to new destinations which are not profitable in themselves or which cannot make contribution to the network.

- Type and size of market: By examining the existing traffic flow between the destinations and other key regions, the type and size of market can be projected. The number of services operated by other carriers also gives an indication of the popularity of the destination.

Figure 9.1: The Main Schedule Planning Parameters

The main schedule planning parameters						
	Considerations	Influence over the airline's operating pattern				
		Destination	Frequency	Linkages	Aircraft deployed	Arr/Dep Time
Commercial	Traffic rights	x	x	x	x	
	Traffic potential	x	x	x	x	
	Cost and potential revenue	x	x	x	x	
	Preferences of passengers and shippers	x	x	x		x
	Other airlines' operations	x	x	x	x	x
Operational	Availability of aircraft		x		x	x
	Availability of cabin and technical crew		x	x		x
	Aircraft maintenance				x	
	Airport restrictions				x	x
	Ground handling agents' equipment constraints				x	x

- Cost and benefit analysis: A cost and revenue analysis is done to determine the economic viability of operating to these destinations.

Frequency

Factors to be considered include: ASA constraints, traffic demand, other airlines' operations, crew and equipment constraints.

The ASAs spell out the number of flights that the airline can operate. Using potential traffic volume as an indication, the airline decides how many services it should operate. Certain destinations may not have high frequency. Furthermore, other carriers may have already provided the required number of operations desired by the community. Matching traffic demand with the right frequency can make the operation a viable venture. Operationally, crew and equipment constraints may not permit multiple services to be mounted.

Linkage

Factors to be considered include nonstop services, costs and benefits of intermediate stops, and agreements with other governments. The airline may operate a nonstop service if there is high traffic flow between two points. On the other hand, intermediate stops may be added to the flight route. Apart from local origin-destination traffic, there may be traffic potential between the intermediate points. However, the right to transport passengers and cargo between third countries must be agreed upon by the governments involved.

Operations with intermediate stops may not yield favorable economic results since extra costs are incurred. Generally, passengers prefer non-stop services as airlines operating them usually have a superior product. SIA offers nonstop services to many of its destinations.

Aircraft Deployment

The types of aircraft deployed and frequencies mounted determine the seat and cargo capacity provided by the airline. Passenger and cargo loads on flights will be poor if there is excess capacity.

SIA is known for its modern fleet of aircraft. Much time is devoted to maintenance work so that the airplanes are in tip-top condition. An aircraft maintenance schedule is drawn up each year. During the planning process, the schedulers have to consider the amount of time set aside for the aircraft to be grounded for maintenance.

Other constraints exist that may restrict the operation of certain aircraft types to some destinations. This is because the ground handling agents may not have suitable equipment for handling the aircraft, or the airports may lack the facilities and long runways to cater to these aircraft.

Arrival and Departure Time

- Customers' preference: The preferred flight timings of passengers and shippers is an important factor the schedulers have to consider. For example, on short-haul regional routes, passengers prefer early morning departures so that they can return the same day. Shippers usually prefer late departures so as to enable the production run of the day to be freighted out in the evening.
- Aircraft and Airline Constraints: A good schedule satisfies the airline's customers as well as the aircraft and airline's technical constraints. The use of the 'spoke and the hub' concept in schedule planning facilitates this. Singapore is used as a hub to carry passengers and cargo on an intra- and inter-regional basis. Traffic from SIA flights arriving in Singapore is given sufficient time to make connections with outbound flights.
- Airport facilities: In the planning process, airport restrictions are taken into account. Most of the airlines prefer to arrive and depart at favorite times. This leads to airport congestion. Aircraft movements are restricted during peak hours as some airports lack sufficient facilities such as customs counters, baggage belts, runways, and aircraft parking bays. Curfew hours may also be imposed for environmental reasons. If flights are scheduled to arrive and depart during peak periods, the service provided by ground handling agents will be closely monitored to ensure that SIA's service standards are not compromised.

9.4.6 Computerized Route Planning

The manual process of planning a route is very time consuming and difficult as the schedule planner has to take into account many factors, such as daylight-saving periods, airport curfew hours, block times and traffic restrictions, when working out the schedule. This task is made more difficult when all the routings have to be combined to form the overall schedule plan because, invariably, alterations have to be made in the process of working out the schedule.

SIA prepares its flight schedules through the use of a computerized route-planning system which assists the schedule planners in planning routes. The system is configured on a personal computer. It is easy to use with its user-friendly menus. It takes care of the lengthy process of juggling and calculating numerical data. Users need not memorize special transaction codes to communicate with the system but are assisted by well-documented screens. Users concentrate on experimenting with various alternative plans while the system performs the less creative task of validating and completing the schedule details.

The six major modules of the system are summarized below.

The Timetable Maintenance Module

This module manages the flight schedules and their supporting files. When building the routes, the system searches the files for the relevant data. The system validates input by checking dates, times and aircraft types, does legality checks, and calculates arrival and departure times per day.

The Schedule Information and Analysis Module

An important part of the system, this module helps the user to analyze the schedule in different ways. Some of the analyzes enable scheduling by cities and by aircraft types. Comparative listings of capacity-tonne-kilometers (CTK) and available-seat-kilometers (ASK) for any one schedule, or between alternative schedules, can also be generated through the system. The system compares the ASK and CTK between two schedules and works out the percentage growth across regions.

The Reporting Module

Analytical reports on possible connections and aircraft utilization hours are made available through the Reporting Module. Other reports include summaries of flights and their frequencies for each region and aircraft type, listings of all possible arrival and departure times for proposed new routes, and listings of all city-pair block times.

The Aircraft Utilization Module

The system generates the weekly aircraft utilization plan for each aircraft type. The system can be instructed to display the utilization plan on the screen of the personal computer. Hard copies of the plans and reports of routing sequences are also generated. Through this module, the user is able to determine whether there are sufficient aircraft to operate routes within a given schedule.

The Broadsheet Printing Module

The dissemination of schedule information to line departments within SIA, and the production of the selected schedules plan is handled by this module. With the help of a set-up screen, the user can choose to print season broadsheets for passenger or freighter services. Additional information such as block times, daylight-saving periods, transit times, elapsed times for each flight, and traffic restrictions, are also printed for reference. These broadsheets may be printed in local or GMT (Greenwich Mean Time) time modes.

The Telex Module

Finally, and just as essential, is the transmission of telexes for the purpose of slot filing. It is an activity in schedule planning in which SIA files a schedule with the flag carrier of the country to which SIA proposes to fly.

This telex module provides SIA's slot coordinator with a convenient and quick way to file slots with other carriers. It extracts flight information from the schedule file, rearranges them in the Standard Clearance/Advice Form telex format, and thereafter transmits the information to the respective slot coordinators.

SIA's Market Planning and Projects Department has expressed confidence in the capabilities of the computerized route planning system. In June 1991, the department used the system to prepare the Winter 1991 selling plans. The Summer 1992 selling plans were also prepared by the system in October 1991.

9.4.7 Publicizing Schedules

The final stage of schedule planning involves the dissemination of schedule data to the public through the SIA Timetable and international schedule publications. SIA also provides its schedule data to the various computerized reservations systems (CRS) so that information is available electronically at the fingertips.

9.5 Departure Control Systems

Departure control includes customer check-in, baggage handling and boarding gate control. It is observed that the glamor of air travel is often tarnished by the hassles on the ground: in the queues, at the check-in counter, and in the holding room prior to boarding.

9.5.1 The Kriscom DCS

SIA has upgraded its Kriscom Departure Control System (DCS) to the level of Swissair-based DCS. The new Kriscom DCS is mainly for more efficient check-in and load control.

The Check-In Operations

- Seat Selection: Seat selection service is offered to First and Raffles Class passengers, and it has to be closed sometimes as early as seventy-two hours before flight departure. The new seat selection facility uses one common reservation-departure control seat map instead of two separate seat maps. It enables the seat selection service to be offered up to flight closing time at airport, thus enhancing its attractiveness to passengers.
- Through Check-In: One of the two new features of the system is the Electronic Data Interchange for Administration, Commerce, and Transportation (EDIFACT) handler for the Inter Airline Through Check-In (IATCI). The EDIFACT is an international coding standard to facilitate the communication of transactions. This handler translates messages and codes connected with the IATCI, such as baggage details and passenger data, into common format which is recognized by any airline's system. The IATCI is achieved through the establishment of links between any two airlines' DCS, for instance between the Kriscom DCS and Swissair's DCS, using the EDIFACT handler. The IATCI facility allows ground staff to through-check passengers to their final destinations.
- Seat Assignment: There are auto seat assignment and passenger service message facilities in the system. In addition, the system is able to handle the down-line seat protection problem by making a

protected seat-assignment to different passenger such as, along the SIN-Tokyo-LA Route, assign seat 35A for SIN-Tokyo flight for passenger A and protect seat 35A for Tokyo-LA flight for passenger B. It thus maximizes seat utilization. The system also ensures that through seats are reserved for booked passengers traveling for the longer leg. When performing check-in for up to ninety passengers at a time, the system is able to recognize any duplicate of a passenger's name during check-in process and an error message is generated.

The Load Control System

The other new feature of the upgraded Kriscom DCS is the Advanced Load Planning System (ALPS). ALPS deals with aircraft loading. The system generates the load plan for a flight, thereby eliminating manual load planning errors. It is done by taking into consideration over seventy safety criteria including aircraft weight limitations. Load planning can be done for aircraft hold areas as well as for unit load device (ULD) positions. The latter provide more accurate deadload and thus maximize aircargo capacity. The system also trims the aircraft into ideal trim lines, which results in fuel saving.

9.5.2 The DCS90

The DCS90 is a software for handling pre-boarding and boarding operations. It was jointly developed by SIA and Unisys and is used by SIA and its handling agents at Changi Airport Terminal 2 in conjunction with the Kriscom DCS..

The system is local-area-network based with master computers linked to intelligent workstation (IWS) terminals. The master computers themselves are linked directly to the Kriscom host computer. This arrangement gives faster access to flight information, and thus reduces queuing time for the passengers, as the check-in agent does not have to wait as long for the host computer to respond.

Additional features are stated below.

Baggage Tag Printing

The system is equipped with an automated facility for printing baggage tags. With the automated baggage tags, handling staff no longer have to sort baggage destined for different flights. The bar-coded baggage tags are interfaced with the CAAS's semi-automated baggage sorting system. The system also has the capability for baggage reconciliation: matching a passenger with the storage location of his baggage in the aircraft hold, for quick retrieval in case he fails to board.

Boarding Pass and Boarding Gate Control

The system uses boarding passes with a magnetic strip containing personal and flight data. At the boarding gate, the passenger slots his pass into a Boarding Control Device or Gate Reader. This device is able to give immediate information on the number and identities of passengers who have checked-in but have yet to board. The boarding pass also comes in useful relaying urgent messages to passengers by alerting the Gate Reader so that handling agent can forward the message.

The system also has the capability of handling inter-airline through check-in, and has a link to the worldwide Timatic system for quick access to visa and travel information.

For the passenger, all these systems mean faster and more pleasant pre-boarding and boarding operations. Recent performance studies have shown a 20% drop in average check-in time with the DCS90 compared to its predecessor. With the 'Global Excellence' Alliance, SIA is able to offer passengers the convenience of one-stop check-in for up to six connecting flights.

9.6 Arrival Control Systems

9.6.1 Immigration: The Blue Lane APIS Facility

It happens very often that at certain airline stations such as those in the United States, passengers would experience delays of up to six hours to go through immigration and customs formalities. In 1991 SIA was the first airline to offer a special facility, commonly referred to as the 'Blue Lane', to passengers on US-bound flights. Other SIA line stations such as HongKong, Taipei, Narita, Frankfurt, and New York were subsequently equipped with the same facility.

The 'Blue Lane' allows passengers to use express lanes to clear through the immigration and custom formalities. To be eligible for this service, a passenger has to provide his full name, date of birth and flight details at check-in, and a special sticker is placed on the passport. This information will be transmitted to an 'Advanced Passenger Information System (APIS)' at the destination. This gives the authorities a chance to conduct a more thorough screening of incoming passengers, to weed out any known 'undesirables'. Passengers benefit from not having to queue and wait endlessly at immigration counters while their personal particulars are checked against a computer data base.

With the success of the blue lane in cutting down US queues, as experienced by SIA, there will be more countries and stations offering this kind of facility. Passengers can look forward to a truly hassle-free arrival at their destinations.

9.6.2 Baggage-Claim: The CBTU Information System

A centralized information system has been established at the Central Baggage Tracing Unit (CBTU) to enable queries on baggage incidents to be made at various stations, and analyzes performed when required. The average number of baggage incidents is two thousand five hundred per month. The computerized sorting, collating and reporting systems have halved the workload at the CBTU. Information can be captured directly on to the data base at the CBTU for online stations, and via diskettes for offline stations. Reports are more accurate and timely enabling more effective management of mishandled baggage.

9.7 Quality Measures of Airline Operations

9.7.1 Quality Measures of Some American Airline Operations

Ratios, percentages, and percentage changes are used in the quality measures of some US airline operations. Five quality measures as derived from data submitted to the United States Department of Transportation for September 1989 are as follows (Rosander, 1989):

	Quality Measures	**Measurement Units**
1.	Baggage complaints	Number per thousand passengers
2.	Overall complaints	Number per hundred thousand passengers
3.	Arrival on time	Percentage arriving within fifteen minutes of scheduled time
4.	Late flights	Percentage late fifteen minutes or more, 70% of the time
5.	Departures on time	Percentage of total departures

9.7.2 The SIA Service and Performance Indexes

SIA conducts a Service and Performance Survey once every quarter. Service and Performance Indexes (SPIs) are compiled for benchmarking and to facilitate and measure continuous improvement. Results of a typical SPI survey are listed in Figure 9.2. The human behavioral aspects of the service systems such as those elements related to service attitude will be deliberated under the topic of customer services.

9.7.3 The SIA Reservation Service Indicators

For all SIA stations, passengers are asked to rate the reservation operations from 'excellent' to 'very poor' on the following three service elements:

- Easy to reach office by phone;
- Fast, efficient reservations; and
- Friendly and helpful attitude.

Telephone Service Quality

For the telephone service, statistics are generated by the Automatic Call Distribution (ACD) system, and the four types of reports which are monitored closely for service performance are summarized in Figure 9.3.

A typical comparison of telephone service factor is listed in Figure 9.4.

Complaints and Compliments Ratios

Letters received from passengers provide a good source of information about the operations service. Recurrent complaints can alert the airline to an area of weakness, and will allow management to take action before it gets worse. The top typical areas of complaints of the reservation service are:

- Booking canceled
- Booking on waiting list
- Seat request not met
- No record of booking

Figure 9.2: The SIA Service and Performance Index (SPI) Survey

All elements for Airport Operations, Phone Operations and Ticket Office Operations received better ratings systemwide.

	Change
Airport Operations	**+0.6**
Fast, Efficient Check-in	+0.4
Friendly, Courteous Check-in	+0.4
Efficient Seat Assignment	+0.5
Efficient Transfer At Changi	+2.0

The target of a 0.3 point improvement in each element was also exceeded for Airport Operations.

	Change
Phone Operations	**+0.7**
Easy To Reach Office By Phone	+1.0
Fast, Efficient Reservations	+0.7
Friendly, Helpful Attitude	+0.6

	Change
Ticket Office Operations	**+0.2**
Fast, Efficient Service	+0.2
Friendly, Helpful Attitude	+0.2

Our passengers were also asked to rank our services for Airport Operations against other airlines which they have travelled on. In First and Business (Raffles) Class, we were still rated second, while we slipped to third place in Economy Class. Telephone and Ticket Office Operations remained in second place.

Among these, 'booking canceled' has, by far, the most complaints. SIA has produced 'Guidelines on Cancellation of Bookings', and the Route Revenue Department has issued a reminder to all stations to follow the guidelines.

9.7.4 Baggage Handling Quality

Quality of baggage handling operations is measured by an indicator of the number of Property Irregularity Reports (PIRs) per thousand

Figure 9.3: Telephone Service Quality

Among the many statistics generated by the ACD system, the four reports that are monitored closely-for service performance, are:

1. Telephone Service Factor (TSF)

This is the percentage of all telephone calls received that are answered within twenty seconds. The TSF target for all stations, on a monthly average, is eighty-five percent. In so doing, we are ensuring that when eighty-five percent of our customers call, they will be attended to within twenty seconds. The higher the TSF achieved, the better the service we are providing to our customers.

2. Grade of Service (GOS)

This is the probability of a random call not being able to get through to our phone sales office on the first attempt. The systemwide standard for GOS is three percent.

3. Abandon Rate

This reflects the percentage of calls received that are abandoned while in queue, but before being attended to by our staff. Our systemwide standard of three percent requires that no more than three out of one hundred calls received are abandoned by our customers.

4. Transaction Time

This is the average time taken to complete a transaction on the telephone. The customer service standard. is two to three minutes, depending on which region a station is in. It is recognized that cultural differences affect the duration of a transaction.

Figure 9.4: Comparison of Telephone Service Quality

Telephone Service Factor

Our TSF for the twenty-six stations with the Automatic Call Distribution (ACD) system also registered a significant improvement.

	Jul-Sep 91	Jul-Sep 90	Change
TSF	73.7	67.9	+5.8

The target of having 60% of our ACD stations achieve a TSF of 70% or more, was also exceeded. Sixty-nine percent of these stations achieved the target in this quarter, compared to 57% in the corresponding quarter last year.

---

passengers over a period of time. It is compared with the previous period and gauged against the company's target.

9.7.5 Traffic or Commercial Punctuality

Punctuality within four minutes of STD (scheduled time of departure) and punctuality with fifteen minutes of STD are the two indicators SIA uses. Virtually any malfunction of the airport facilities, of the aircraft engineering components, and numerous other factors, could lead to the delay of a scheduled flight. Delay analysis is discussed in the next section.

9.8 Station Crisis and Delay

9.8.1 Station Crisis and Delay Simulations

From time to time, SIA line stations conduct crisis simulation exercises. During a typical simulation exercise, the staff is put through the rigors of a four-stage exercise: crisis declaration, casualties list, uninjured list, and the confirmation of uninjured, casualties, missing and deceased list. Staff are deployed to act as next of kin, members of the public and press. Sometimes, participants are invited from other airlines. They are requested to bring along their own local crisis plans for discussions and comparison.

Delay simulations have also been conducted at many SIA line stations. These kind of simulation games are usually carried out with several teams trying to outdo each other in terms of being able to handle every type of delay, including the dreaded 'overnighter'.

9.8.2 Computerized Casualties Information Processing System (CIPS)

To improve the overall response in the event of crisis such as an aircraft crash or a hijack, SIA has developed a computerized Casualties Information Processing System (CIPS) for the Crisis Management Center (CMC). The CIPS is a personal-computer-based, in-house developed, real-time system. It replaces the manual processes and procedures of crisis management. The system can be used to process casualty information for any major emergency involving SIA aircraft anywhere in the world. The operating concepts for the CIPS are shown in Figure 9.5.

9.8.3 The SIA Delay Codes

SIA's delay codes for movement messages are listed below.

Passenger Services

PB — Breakdown of baggage conveyor belt.
PC — Congestion at check-in area.
PD — Breakdown of Departure Control System.
PE — Passenger held up in making excess baggage payments.
PH — Retrieval and charging of excessive hand baggage.
PI — Embarking/disembarking of invalid passengers.

Figure 9.5: The CIPS for Crisis Management

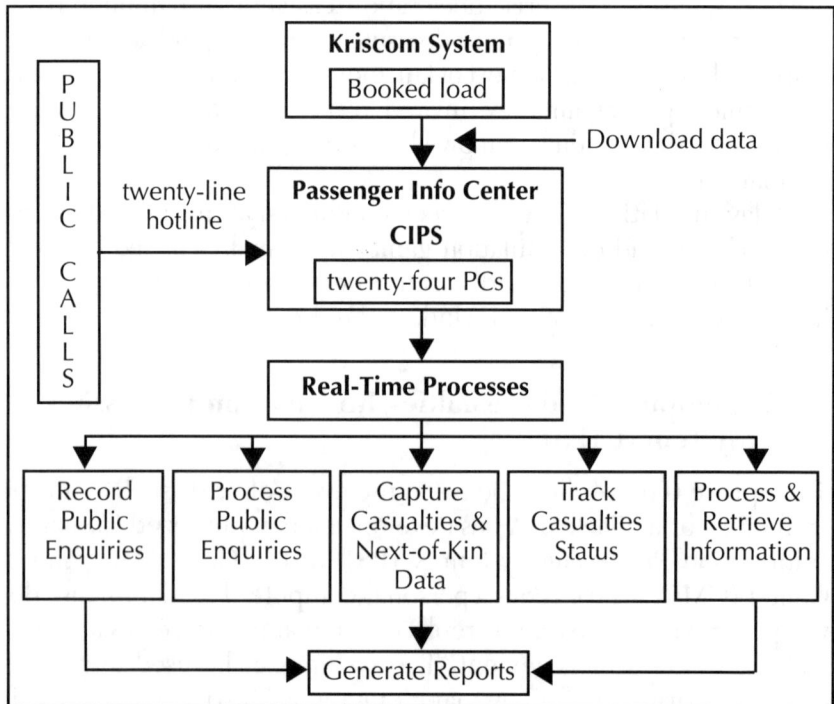

PM — Locating missing passengers/late reporting of passengers for boarding.

PO — Off-loading of passengers bags due to passenger's failure to turn up for boarding.

Traffic/Apron

TA — Breakdown of aerobridge/passenger steps.
TB — Late positioning of baggage/cargo/mail to aircraft.
TC — Difficulty in unloading/loading heavy/bulky cargo.
TD — Late completion of documents/documentation error.
TE — Shortage of loading equipment.
TF — Heavy discharge/uplift of cargo.
TH — Wrong headcount at departure gate/verifying headcount by traffic staff.
TL — Breakdown of loading equipment.
TH — Shortage of loaders.
TO — Error on incoming operational messages.
TT — Reconciliation of transit score.
TR — Retrimming of aircraft.
TS — Sorting out seating confusion.
TT — Shifting of transit load due to over stowage.
TU — Difficulty in unloading/loading due to defective unit load devices (ULDs).
TV — Off-loading of cargo due to volumetric constraint/safety requirements.

Cargo Services

FB — Late built-up of cargo/mail at warehouse.
FC — Late completion of cargo statement.

Catering/Cabin Services

HC — Late completion of cabin cleaning.
HU — Short/late catering uplift by caterer.

Customs Immigration Quarantine (CIQ)/Security

QB — Baggage identification at aircraft side.

QC — CIQ congestion.
QD — Awaiting uplift of departing passenger.
QP — Late clearance of passengers/crew by CIQ.
QQ — Off-loading of passengers by CIQ.
QS — Stringent security checks.
QT — Security checks due to bomb/hijack threat.
QX — Security x-ray machines unserviceable.

Commercial

CC — Late delivery of cargo/mail to warehouse by shipper.
CH — Awaiting passengers retrieving their left behind hand baggage.
CI — Awaiting interline passengers from SQ or other carriers.
CL — Late reporting of passengers for check-in.
CH — Receiving medical attention.
CO — Sorting out overbooking/acceptance of go-show passengers in place of no-shows.
CP — Acceptance of passengers transferred from SQ or other carriers.
CV — Awaiting VIP passengers.

Flight Operations

OA — Aircraft change due operational.
OB — Late boarding clearance by cabin crew.
OC — Awaiting computerized flight plan.
OF — Additional fuel uplift required by technical crew.
OP — Change of flight plan.
OS — Technical/cabin crew reported sick.
OT — Late reporting of technical/cabin crew.
OU — Technical/cabin crew requests for non-standard catering uplift.
OV — Verification of headcount requested by crew.

Engineering

EA — Aircraft defects.
EC — Aircraft change due to technical reason.
EE — Awaiting engineering ground support equipment.
EF — Error/late completion of refueling.
EG — Aircraft on ground (AOG) and awaiting spares.

EM — Late completion of maintenance checks.
EU — Auxiliary power unit (APU) unserviceable.

Consequential

NA — Aircraft damage due to ground accident.
NC — Awaiting technical/cabin crew from incoming aircraft.
ND — Aircraft damaged in flight, e.g. by bird or lightning strikes.
NF — Awaiting aircraft.
NI — Industrial disputes.
NL — Late arrival of aircraft.
NP — Passenger convenience.
NR — Crew rest.
NS — De-icing/removal of snow from aircraft/airport.
NW— Adverse weather restricting aircraft take-off/landing
NG — Adverse weather affecting ground operations.

Air Traffic Control (ATC/Weather)

AC — Runway closure.
AF — Awaiting flight level.
AJ — Jet curfew.
AR — Apron restriction.
AT — Air Traffic Control (ATC)
AV — VIP movement.

Miscellaneous

9.8.4 The Removal of Delay Factors

As observed, there are many factors that may lead to a delay of a scheduled flight. Some flight operations and engineering factors can be removed through the airworthiness regulatory control. Many factors such as Departure Control System (DCS) breakdown, baggage mishandling, airport traffic problems, security check-ups or X-ray machine breakdowns, can be minimized through better ground support facilities.

9.8.5 SATS Facilitates the Removal of Delay Factors

As one of SIA's corporate strategies, SATS, a fully-owned subsidiary of

SIA, has never failed to keep abreast with the latest airport technology development in order to provide SIA with the best that technology can offer. SATS ground support facilities help to minimize many of the delay factors.

Airfield Traffic

After extensive research and investigation, the airfield-bus type of COBUS-300 was selected and two were purchased to joined the SATS fleet at a cost of S\$1.1 million in 1992. The COBUS-300 has a passenger capacity of one hundred, and facilitates faster embarkation and disembarkation because there are more doors. It also provides greater passenger comfort due to air suspension. This type of airbus is also in operation at airports in Zurich, Athens, Dusseldorf, Teheran, and Oporto and Faro in Portugal.

Departure Security

New X-ray machines used for screening passengers' baggage, courier bags and express cargo were installed along with other new equipment purchased in 1992. With a team of sixty police constables trained to detect forged passports, SATS has saved the airlines from the hefty fines imposed by various airports for such infringements.

Ground Transport

In addition to its nine skyloaders, another four Nordco skyloaders and nine transporters amounting to \$1.5 million were added to Apron's fleet and deployed for operations in May 1993 at Changi Airport. The new skyloaders are capable of transferring bulk loads from most types of aircraft and enhance the ground service operations especially during peak hours. New fully covered passenger steps which can be docked on aircraft ranging from the B737 to the B747, are also used for the convenience of passengers.

References

1. Frenzel, C. W. (1992). *Management of Information Technology.* Boston: Boyd & Fraser
2. Rosander, A.C. (1989). *The Quest for Quality in Services.* Milwaukee: ASQC Quality Press.
3. Wiseman, C. (1988). *Strategic Information Systems.* Homewood: Irwin

CHAPTER TEN

Management of Customer Services

10.1 Customer Service and the Spiral of Quality Progress

The attainment of quality requires a sterling performance in every stage of the product life cycle, which can be traced:

1. from market research to product development;
2. from product development to manufacturing, inspection, testing and packaging;
3. from customers' feedback to further market research, thus entering another new product life cycle.

It is important that every stage in a product's life cycle is managed in such a way that it is based upon a 'supplier' providing a 'customer' with total quality. In other words, quality has to be managed in every area that connects suppliers to the business and the business to its customers. This has been particularly true for SIA, where station handling agents are considered as its suppliers for quality services.

10.2 Definition of Customer Service

In a product's life cycle, customer service is the last link in a chain of activities for the current total quality management system. It is also the first link in the chain of activity for the forthcoming, higher level total quality management system. A senior staff member of American Express stated that exemplary customer service, in the form of focusing extraordinary attention to the customer, is the key factor that creates a predictable difference to set a product above the rest.

Christopher (1992) defined customer service as:

> 'Management systems are organized to provide a continuing service link between the time a purchase order is placed and the time goods or services are received and consumed, are with the objective of satisfying customer needs on a long-term basis.'

10.3 Strategic Issues of Customer Service Management

In the context of customer services, there are certain strategic issues that need to be addressed before any functional plans can sensibly be made. These issues are listed below.

1. How important is customer service? This would involve the assessment of the importance of customer service as compared to other elements in the marketing mix such as product performance, price, other promotional variables, etc.
2. What are the dimensions of customer service? This would include the identification of the types of customer service and the operations involved through business transaction analysis.
3. What are the priority components of customer service? These are the components that are seen as priorities by customers when they make their choice of suppliers. Identification of priority service components would help the benchmarking of performance of critical quality factors against the best in class performer.
4. What is the intended service level for each of the customer service components? This includes the analysis of market sensitivity in the context of the level of service offered to each of the service components. For example, in a competitive retail market, offering to double stock availability from 5 % to 10 % would clearly be ineffective. A cost and benefit trade-off analysis helps when making service level decisions.
5. What are the service policies in dealing with customers at the extremes? Different customers will buy a different mix of products. Each individual product has its specific gross margin level; it then follows that the mix of products purchased by a specific customer will have its impact upon profitability. Moreover, it must be recognized that there are substantial differences in the costs of serving different customers. A customer data base should be established for

cost-profits analysis in order to help formulate service policies for different types of customers, in particular customers at the extremes.

6. How to achieve alignment between the customer's and server's view of service? Service performance is very much linked to the motivation and attitudes of people who serve. Unless there is an alignment between how the customers view their priority services and how the staff members view them, there will be occasional problems. It is important that the internal understanding of what customer service should be matches the customers' definitions and requirements.

10.4 Importance of Customer Service

10.4.1 Market Advantage of Beyond-Expectations Customer Services

When purchasing products, customers seek benefits. In so doing, they evaluate competing offers in terms of the totality of product and service as well as the 'relationship' that currently exists, or potentially could exist, between themselves and the supplier. Customer service is an important element of the total quality of a product that influences the purchasing decision. It can be used to help gain a marketing advantage. An organization can differentiate itself from its competitors by providing more than the customer's expected quality of the core product, and by how it manages the 'service surround' to upgrade the total quality of its product as shown in Figure 6.3 of Chapter 6. It should be recognized that every interaction with the customer provides an opportunity to be 'unique' and to go beyond simply meeting expectations.

10.4.2 Shifting to Relationship Marketing for Customer Retention

When customers are satisfied with the totality of a product, that is, the core product and the service package surrounding it, they are unlikely to seek alternative suppliers. This enables the development of a long-term relationship between the supplier and customers. Hence the shifting from transaction-focus marketing to relationships marketing. The logic of relationship marketing is well grounded. The simple idea is that it takes much more effort in terms of time and money to gain a new customer than it does to keep an existing customer.

10.5 SIA's Three Levels of Customer Satisfaction

SIA has set a target of achieving three levels of customer satisfaction. The first level meets the basic needs of the customer while the second level satisfies the customer's expectations in such a way that they are likely to come back. The airline has always been prepared to go beyond the customer's expectations and provide more than they would expect to achieve the third and highest level of customer satisfaction.

10.5.1 Service Above and Beyond The Call of Duty

Almost every day, the frontline staff face problems or requests which have no clear-cut solutions or answers. They could simply ignore the problems or turn down the requests. Instead of doing so, the SIA staff very often provide services that are above and beyond the call of duty. There was an incident when a sensitive and caring staff member helped take care of a young passenger who was ill in a foreign country and acted as an interpreter for the family and medical staff at the hospital. There was also an incident when an off-duty staff member helped colleagues provide well-handled delay services to customers. All these laudable deeds are part of SIA's common practice.

10.5.2 Value-Added Services at Stations

Many SIA stations give unique touches to their customer services by doing something a little different, or by giving that extra bit that personalizes their services without sacrificing overall consistency. These may include practices such as offering a flower voucher to passengers who have been mishandled, adding a nice finishing touch to ground service by having ground staff make a departure announcement on board, and wishing all passengers who have boarded a pleasant flight, etc.

10.5.3 Customer Retention through Service Recovery

SIA realizes the importance of prompt service recovery actions to keep customers. Recovering from a mishandling is important because the passenger has been inconvenienced through no fault of his own, and therefore holds the carrier responsible. Recovery action is made swiftly to ensure that the passenger suffers minimal inconvenience. SIA sees every customer's problem as an opportunity to prove the airline's commitment to outstanding service.

10.6 Types of Customer Service

Business is accomplished through the process of negotiation and settlement, that is, a transaction between the suppliers and the customers. In this process, a supplier can generally provide three types of customer service:

1. the pre-transaction services;
2. the transaction services; and
3. the post-transaction services

Pre-transaction services refer to the systems, structures and operational environment an organization established before the sale takes place. Transaction services are those which the customer experiences during the sales process and the post-transaction refers to the after-sales services (LaLonde and Zinszer, 1976; Rakowski, 1982). Thus, for the airline business, customer services can be classified as pre-flight, inflight and postflight customer services; these will be presented in Chapter 11.

10.7 Critical Quality Factors of Customer Services

The business environment of the airline industry has become so competitive that no airline can afford to confine its operations to an insular, local domain. To remain competitive, an international airline must keep abreast of what other airlines offer in order to achieve total customer satisfaction. To systematically and continuously compare an organization's performance of priority service components with the best performer in the industry is defined as a benchmarking process. Benchmarking involves the following steps (Motorola Inc., 1993).

1. Defining what needs to be done to be competitive in offering quality customer services, that is defining the critical quality factors

(CQFs) of priority service components that lead to business success.

2. Comparing how well the company performs on the CQFs to the toughest competitor or Best in Class (BIC) performer.
3. Using comparison results to develop functional plans that are aimed at making the very best in class.

To go into detail about the identification of priority service components and the benchmarking process is beyond our scope. However, lists of CQFs of each of the three types of customer services in the typical manufacturing organizations are provided in the following sections.

10.7.1 Critical Quality Facilities for Pre-Transaction Customer Services

Management Commitment to Service Pledge

Every SATS Airport Services frontline staff member is required to take the following commitment to service pledge.

THE PLEDGE
We, the Staff of Terminal Two
Pledge by these Qualities towards Service Excellence
To greet each Passenger at the beginning and at the end
of their journey
To address them by Name, Rank or Title
To give Personalised Service with a friendly Smile
To maintain eye contact during our transaction
Customer Service is what we are out to give

The pledge shows SIA's devotion to providing outstanding customer service. The emphasis on 'soft standards', such as greeting passengers and addressing them by name, shows the company's perceptiveness in handling customers. Employees are trained in the handling of difficult passengers and the staff's quality of service is evident in the abilities and dedication that they show.

Organizational Structure

Customer Affairs Department of SIA: The department is organized with a set-up of a Service Audit Unit within it. The department responds to customer complaints and inquiries while the Service Audit Unit monitors service standards and compiles data.

Passenger Services Division of SATS

The division is established to manage the ground customer services at Changi Airport.

Written Customer Service Policy

SIA's Service Procedures

Services provided by SIA are guided by procedures to ensure that services are consistent throughout the entire network, and that services are provided efficiently.

SIA's Service Policies

Customer services in the airline industry encompass many eventualities which can not be covered by the procedure manuals. Even if they could be covered, the manuals would run into volumes, and would be too cumbersome to be used in real situations. Underlying the procedures is a rationale or a set of policies which guide staff members in the handling of unfamiliar customer situations.

Personal Guide for SIA Staff

SIA provides a personal guide to its frontline staff in a form of updated information handbook which is a useful reference to help them to serve their customers better.

Service Accessibility

Telephone SPI of SIA

Telephone operations are assessed by customers on whether:

- it is easy to reach office by phone,
- it is fast and efficient for making reservations, and
- the service attitude is friendly or helpful. Service performance indices (SPI) are computed monthly and quarterly to monitor the accessibility of customer services.

The CRS of SIA

The use of Abacus Computerized Reservation System (CRS) has also helped making the customer services more accessible.

Service Flexibility

The Pro-Active Mindset

With a proactive mindset, SIA staff would not just give up in awful or unexpected circumstances. If situations warrant, they would provide flexible services such as open the Silver Kris lounge before check-in time to accommodate exhausted long distance transit passengers, help locate passengers with seriously ill daughter at home, issue new a ticket for a misplaced ticket in emergency case. They should remain calm, helpful, efficient and flexible.

10.7.2 Critical Quality Factors of Transaction Customer Services

- Seat Availability or Aircraft Capacity.
- Service Delivery Rate: Preflight service time, flight punctuality, flight hours, and postflight service time.
- Information Dissemination and Response Rates: Telephone response rate, ticket reservation efficiency, and timely dissemination of delay information.

10.7.3 Critical Quality Factors of Post-Transaction Customer Services

On-the-spot After Care Services

Availability and Promptness of Involuntary upgrading and downgrading of seats, meet and assist services (MAAS), etc.

Product Tracing and Warranty

Interim relief and follow-up actions: in cases such as baggage being lost, the passenger should receive an overnight kit bag and interim payment for baggage lost. Other kinds of service recovery facilities are provided.

Baggage Repair and Replacement

All SIA stations have their baggage repair services contracted, so that suppliers can collect, repair and deliver the damaged bag to passenger at the airline's cost. If the bag is damaged beyond repair, the airline should replace it with a similar bag, or reimburse the passenger for the cost.

Post-Transaction Complaints

Complaints have been viewed positively as opportunities for service improvement.

Promptness in Dealing with Claims

An example of this type of quality service can be seen in SIA's offer of a goodwill sum of money paid at check-in for involuntary downgrading of ticket holders due to flight operational requirements. This is offered with the intention of neutralizing any negative perceptions arising from the downgrading and so as to maintain good customer relations.

10.8 SIA's Principles on Extreme Customer Service

10.8.1 Definition of Outstanding Service

Overservice, in particular for passengers with extreme and demanding requests is discouraged by SIA. Frontline staff members are reminded that outstanding services do not mean pleasing passengers regardless of costs and consequences. Staff members must learn how to say 'no' when necessary.

This is made clear in SIA's internal news bulletin *Higher Ground,* which has columns such as Service Tips, "Fragile — Handle With Care" and Learning Points. These columns cite examples of difficult service situations encountered by frontline service staff and the solutions to these often trying situations. Some examples are given below.

Special Meal Request

First and Raffles Class passengers are already given choices of various set menus but some passengers insist on meals which are not catered for in any of the menus. In such situations, the cabin crew are instructed to firmly deny such requests.

Compensation for Loss in Income

Under no circumstances should SIA's staff members promise that the company will compensate a passenger for any loss in income, business or missed opportunities resulting from a flight disruption. SIA sticks to the terms and conditions of carriage covering international airlines; loss in income is not the liability of the uplifting carrier.

10.8.2 Stick to Principles of Customer Service

In addition to strict adherence to the international terms and conditions of carriage as in the case of liability for loss of income, the airline has kept its customer services in conformance to a set of principles. An example is cited below.

Seat Request

SIA's Reservations Office is given specific guidelines with regard to the allocation of Emergency Exit row seats (EMEX) and it is to firmly deny requests by passengers for such seats who do not fall within the criterion for these seats. Some priority passengers are denied these seats because priority passengers, which include the handicapped, sick or infirm, the pregnant and so forth, may obstruct the emergency exits and thus hinder speedy evacuation. SIA sticks to the principle that the safety of all is the most important consideration.

10.8.3 Avoid Negligence Through Preponderance

In addition to the scenarios cited above, frontline staff are also reminded not to occupy themselves with serving 'nit-picking' passengers and by so doing, neglect other passengers. Among the many common causes of delays, such as long queues, late transfers, aircraft defects, etc., there are delays that are caused by overservicing one passenger. There have been numerous instances of this, such as the time a passenger caused his flight a thirty-minute delay because he completely lost track of time when shopping at the airport's shops, and the time when a flight was delayed because efforts had to be made to find a passenger who had been detained in one of the lock-up rooms because of visa problems.

Whilst emphasizing the need to exercise discretion in preponderance, the airline also cautions against the other extreme where First and Raffles Class passengers' privileges are neglected.

References

1. Christopher, M. (1992). *The Customer Service Planner.* Oxford: Butterworth-Heinemann
2. LaLonde, B.J. and Zinszer, P.H. (1976). *Customer Service Meaning and Measurement.* Chicago: NCPDM
3. Rakowski, J.P. (1982). *The Customer Service Concepts.* In Review of Business and Economic Research, vol 17, No. 2
4. Motorola Inc. (1993). *Benchmarking,* BMK 220. Singapore: Motorola Inc.

CHAPTER ELEVEN

Towards a Total Customer Service System

11.1 SIA's Principle on Customer Services

It is SIA's principle that every passenger receives outstanding service from the time he makes his booking until he reaches his destination. To stick to this principle, every effort has to be made by the ground staff and the cabin crew to uphold and to further upgrade the service quality in every stage of its total business transactions.

11.2 SIA's Total Transactional Customer Services

As stated in Chapter 10, the pre-transaction customer services are more or less in the form of a service system design in which an organization indicates its commitment to providing quality customer services by setting up a service pledge, service organization structure, and proper service systems with high levels of accessibility and flexibility, etc. The following sections will deal with the transactional customer services provided by SIA. Transactional customer services take place where business transactions are conducted with customers interacting with staff or service equipment to obtain their services. These include the two types of transaction and post-transaction customer services as categorized in Chapter 10.

Preflight services, airport services, and inflight services are all transactional customer services. The postflight services belong to the post-transaction customer services. Hence, the total transactional customer service system consists of subsystems as follows.

1. Preflight customer services:
   - Telephone service

- Reservations
- Reconfirmations and cancellations
- Ticketing and flight information
2. Airport ground customer services
   - Check-in service
   - Baggage handling
   - Delay handling
   - Boarding
3. Inflight customer services
   - Seat auditing
   - Safety demonstration and other mandatory announcements
   - Inflight amenities
   - Food and beverages
   - Shopping
   - Prelanding services
4. Postflight customer services
   - Arrival handling
   - Services for transfer passengers
   - Meet and assist services
   - Airtropolis services

11.3 SIA's Approach Towards Quality Customer Services

11.3.1 Policies and Procedures

SIA provides customer services that are guided by procedures. These procedures are there for good reasons as firstly, they ensure that SIA's customer services are consistent throughout the entire network and secondly, they enable services to be provided efficiently, thus avoiding unnecessary waiting. Underlying the procedures is a rationale or a set of policies that SIA staff members must understand in order to enable them to handle different customer situations. SIA's policies and procedures for customer services will be presented subsequently.

11.3.2 Case Studies on Eventualities and Casualties

In a service industry such as the airline industry, there are many eventualities and casualties. When confronting these situations, the airline staff will have to exercise their discretion because policies and procedures cannot be written to cover all eventualities and casualties or they would run into volumes. In the case of an unpredictable event, unfamiliar customer situation or a casualty, it is SIA's practice to study and to analyze the case in terms of: what has been done incorrectly? What has been done correctly? What is the company's policy? And what are the learning points? The analysis will generate guidelines and service tips for each individual case. These guidelines and service tips will also be presented in subsequent relevant sections.

11.3.3 Service Information

SIA provides a wealth of service information to its staff through the publication of Service Info in its news bulletin *Higher Ground*. Listed in the Service Info section are many instances that can serve to update and refresh the staff's customer service knowledge. The following are some examples.

- The IATA three-letter codes generally use the same designators for both airport and the city. As a reminder, the list of stations in SIA network is as follows.
- Transit visa required for Netherlands.
- Minimum connecting time at Cengkareng Airport is:
  - From international to international: 1 hour
  - From international to domestic (non-Garuda): two hours
- The Advance Passenger Information System (APIS) is also known as the Blue Lane. Promote the Blue Lane to your agents and passengers.
- Wheelchair on SIA B747-400 aircraft.
- Extension of non-smoking flights.
- European Community baggage tag.
- Customer control at Heathrow.

11.3.4 Key Stations Practices

SIA's ultimate goal is to offer a level of customer services that is clearly superior to all other airlines in each and every station, systemwide. But there are times when some new service policies are implemented for the first time and the company does not have the resources to fulfill this ultimate goal in the initial implementation stage. In this situation, it is SIA's practice to concentrate on a few key stations rather than scatter resources evenly over the whole system. The other reason for the practice of beginning in key stations is that in the process of raising customer service levels there, the company will learn valuable lessons that will have useful applications to other stations under similar circumstances.

Key stations meetings are held from time to time to unlock the secrets of providing outstanding customer service. During the meetings of station managers and reservations managers, and the staff from Head Office's Ground Services, Route Revenue and Outstanding Service on The Ground (OSG) departments, targets for customer services will be set and agreed upon. These targets usually cover the measurable aspects of each station's airport and reservations functions. Taking these targets back to their respective stations, they then set about formulating action plans in order to attain them. Action plans presented by each station are evaluated, and items added, dropped or amended as required. The final plans agreed upon are then recommended to SIA senior management for approval, with requests of additional resources such as manpower, equipment, etc. An example of some of the action plans are shown in Figure 11.1.

Subsequently, over a two-month period, audit teams from the Head Office are dispatched to each of the key stations. These are not usual accounting audits as conducted by the Finance Department, but rather customer service audits of the existing infrastructure of station's airport and town office operations.

Figure 11.1: Action Plans

Airport	Town Office
• Queue combing • Pre check-In • Ramp and baggage monitoring • Foreign language PROs • Silver Kris upgrade • Improve interim and outfitting payment procedures	• Re-deployment of staff during peak hours • Increase preflight checks • Educate agents to use fax machines more • Replace old Kriscom sets • Town office support teams

Experience derived from key stations' practices has been that not all the customer service enhancements require a lot of additional resources. For example, queue-combers at the checking counters have proved to be highly effective to expedite the check-in process, town office support teams (TOST) can be invaluable in handling a serious flight disruption, etc.

11.3.5 Service Recovery

Being a service industry, things can occasionally go wrong despite the airline's best efforts. Occasional mistakes or circumstances beyond the airline's control can cause a mishandling. However, mishandlings are not entirely negative. What the airline has done for the mishandled passengers after the incidents, or what sort of recovery actions have been taken are most important in turning the mishandlings into opportunities to regain the customers' confidence in the company's excellent services.

It is SIA's management philosophy that recovery from a mishandling is important because the passengers have been inconvenienced through no fault of their own, and therefore, hold the carrier responsible. While the airline usually cannot undo the mishandling, it shows its true concern for the well-being of passengers by extending its outstanding recovery services. This helps to win back goodwill. SIAs' recovery services range from simple to elaborate and can be undertaken by staff members from almost all areas. SIA has received many compliments from its customers for 'putting things right'. Customers consider those service recovery cases as SIA's 'triumph after failure'.

Service recovery guidelines

SIA has laid down guidelines of service recovery for its staff as below.

- Staff members should put their best effort into doing a splendid job by showing the positive attitude of taking a complaint as a golden opportunity to retain a passenger for life.
- Frontline staff members are best for service recovery. Frontliners will have to make service recovery part of their operational duties. They should be encouraged to make decisions and be bold enough to help passengers who are in need.

- Service recovery should not be restricted to the areas written down in the manuals. It should be extended to passengers whenever they come with a problem. Every customer's problem is an opportunity for the airline to prove its commitment to outstanding service.

11.4 SIA's Preflight Customer Services

The preflight customer services begin with responding to customer's telephone enquiries and end with delivery of air tickets and flight information.

11.4.1 Organizing for Preflight Services: SIA's SIN Sales Reservations and Route Revenue Departments

These are the two departments involved in providing the above-mentioned customer services. Services offered by Singapore (SIN) Sales Reservations (SINSR) cover bookings that are made in Singapore and also travels which exit Singapore (ex-SIN). Other functions of SINSR are:

- reconfirmation for flights ex-SIN
- control of all flights within seventy-two hours of flight departure ex-SIN
- preflight for all flights ex-SIN
- reinstatement of bookings canceled during pre-flight ex-SIN
- re-booking of flights during flight delays
- stopover passengers' (STPCs) requests
- special services: medical cases, stretchers, supplementary therapeutic oxygen, medical equipment, handicapped passengers
- all other reservations matters pertaining to Singapore as a station.

The main functions of Route Revenue Departments are as follows:

- control of SIA's systemwide flights
- reinstatement of canceled bookings beyond seventy-two hours of flight departure
- changing of seat inventory during aircraft changes viz. upgrading and downgrading of aircraft
- approval of MEDA (medical) uplift for stations without SQ (SIA flights) approved doctors

- approval of UM (unaccompanied passengers)
- seat selection (guaranteed seats for priority passengers, etc.)

Telephone Service

Telephone communication is the first point of contact with customers. Telephone behavior can impress or annoy the callers and thus generate positive or negative publicity. From time to time, SIA's Reservations and Ticketing Supervisors provide guidelines and tips for effective telephone operations. Some of them are listed below.

- To project a cheerful, attentive and helpful image
- Be attentive
- Take notes
- Respond appropriately
- Be helpful
- Handling the irate caller
  - it's nothing personal
  - hold your tongue
  - act on the requests
  - end positively
- Handling telephone complaints
  - be without fear, listen and be sympathetic
  - direct the complaints to the correct department
  - do not doubt the passenger as if he is making things up
- Handling miscommunication
  - be aware that miscommunication does sometimes occur
  - when in doubt, always say, "I will check, I will get back to you, as soon as I have the information."

11.4.2 Reservations

Reservations Process

The reservations process mainly involves entering customer's information into the Passenger Name Record (PNR) in the SIA computerized Kriscom DCS as below.

- Name and contact reference (hotel or home telephone number and address)
- Itinerary (flight number/date/timing/sector/seat number)

- Booking status (waitlist, confirmed, etc.)
- Medical record (e.g. the passenger is suffering from an illness)
- PIN reference (if the passenger is a priority passenger, PP)
- Personal preference (e.g. meals and seats)
- Traveling companions

Reservations Policies

- Transaction time: Make it short but not abrupt.
- Privacy and safety: Information on a passenger should not be disclosed to a third party, either verbally or in written form. Apart from passenger's information, flight information which should also not be divulged to outsiders includes:
  - Seat inventory of flight (before and after flight departure)
  - Passenger name list (before flight departure)
  - Passenger manifest (after flight departure)
  - Information on passenger's ticket, etc.
- Seat request: Policies governing seat assignment are as follows.
  - The airline does not allow economy class passengers to request specific seat numbers. However, reservations staff should solicit information from passengers on their preference at the time of reservations. This will enable airport staff to pre-seat passengers accordingly. It will also prevent last minute requests at check-in.
  - The Center of Reservations Control (CRC) accepts requests by economy class passengers for emergency exit (EMEX) row seats from two categories, the priority passengers (PPS) and the genuinely tall passengers above forty-eight hours to the standard time of departure (STD). Between forty-eight hours and flight opening, no requests will be accepted, and staff will have to advise passengers to try at check-in and the seat planner will allocate EMEX seats according to Wait-Facilities List on a first-come first-served basis.
  - Requests for EMEX seats from passengers other than the two categories mentioned above will be politely turned down. Eligible requests will be immediately sent for record and further actions.
  - Seats that cannot be sold at reservations stage: These are the Raffles Class seats 26AK on SIA's B747 Megatop aircraft. These seats have limited recline. They are not even reflected on the seat map. However, these seats can be allocated under certain circumstances provided passengers have been told of the nature of the seats.

- Medical request: Medical cases require clearance for uplift from an SIA approved doctor, and all relevant medical information should be included in the passenger's PNR for easy reference. The PNRs with special medical requests should be sent directly to the Center of Reservations Control, the CRC's printer SIN02 for immediate actions.
- Special meal request: Special meals are provided to passengers for medical or religious reasons. In addition, a number of other types of special meals, such as a birthday cake, may be provided under certain circumstances. Any meal requests other than these will be firmly refused. When accepting a booking, it is better to ask the passenger if he has any dietary restrictions instead of asking if he wants a special meal.
- . Waitlist versus standby: When a passenger's booking status for a flight cannot be confirmed because there are no more seats available during reservation he will be waitlisted. Confirmation of the booking will be made when a seat becomes available through a cancellation of a firm booking by another passenger. Standby refers to passenger's queue position for acceptance at the airport will be based on the time he reports for the flight. Except for priority passengers, standby passengers will be accepted on a first-come, first-served basis when the flight closes and booked passengers fail to turn up. There is no relationship between a passenger's waitlist position and standby acceptance. A passenger may be the first on the waitlist, but if other waitlisted passengers report at the airport ahead of him, they will be accepted first on standby. Reservations staff should avoid telling passengers their position on the waitlist and advise them to report early for a better chance of being uplifted on a flight.

11.4.3 Reconfirmation and Cancellation

Reconfirmation Policies

- A passenger is required to reconfirm his intention in using the reservation he made earlier. It is the practice of all airlines (not just SIA) to protect themselves against losses from unutilized seats, and to provide a better service to genuine passengers who will ultimately board the flight. To allow for those who do not show up for travel on the day fixed during reservation, airlines deliberately accept more reservations than there are seats for a flight. After reconfirmation, if more than expected turn up, the airline may either try to put them on another flight or pay some form of compensation. SIA staff must remind their passengers about the importance of reconfirmation and the consequences of not doing so.

- Reconfirmation needs to be done seventy-two hours before the scheduled time of departure (STD). Passengers who break their journey for more than seventy-two hours also need to reconfirm their onward flights.
- Terminal 2 at Singapore Changi airport offers its passengers the convenience of on-the-spot reconfirmation of their onward flights upon disembarkation in Singapore. At the reconfirmation counters, passengers have the choice of reconfirming through direct-access telephones (hotlines), reconfirmation slips or with the staff manning the counter (on duty from 0700-2200 hours). By using the confirmation slip, a passenger can avoid queuing, as all he needs to do is fill in a simple slip and deposit it at the counter. This can easily be done while waiting for the baggage to appear on the belts. A good service system design.
- For the First and Raffles Class passengers' convenience, reconfirmation slips are distributed onboard the aircraft for reconfirmation of onward connections. Cabin crew collect these slips and pass them to ground staff on arrival for their action. Qualified priority passengers do not need to reconfirm, but their contacts should be requested and noted in their passenger name record (PNR).

Cancellation Policies

Cancellation of a reconfirmed booking should be handled with care.

- If a person calls to cancel his reconfirmed booking, staff should politely inform him that you will call back (at the contact originally indicated in the PNR) to confirm the cancellation.
- If a person comes to the Ticket Office to request a cancellation, for verification purposes the person must first produce his ticket or passport.
- It would be nice if staff could briefly explain that these practices are taken to safeguard his booking and ultimately, his convenience.

Ticketing and Preflight Information

Ticketing and payment are handled by the Abacus Connected Software

Systems, the Daily Ticketing Information and the Bank Settlement Plan. Preflight information for passengers includes:

- Departure and check-in time
- Confirming special requests or arrangements
- Advising flight timing changes or delays.

11.5 SIA's Airport Ground Customer Services

11.5.1 Management of Service Partners: Ground Handling Agents

Working hand in hand with SIA's staff in providing check-in, baggage handling, ramp, aircraft cleaning and load control services at various airports are its ground handling agents. They play a vital role in delivering high quality services at the airports. It is common for passengers to mistake the handling agent's staff for SIA staff, and this perception can be beneficial if managed positively.

SIA considers handling agents its partners in services on ground, and takes measures to equip them with the relevant SIA product information, motivation and to make them more aware of SIA's corporate philosophy in providing outstanding airport ground services. Many handling agents' staff have been invited to Singapore to participate in familiarization programs and seminars that provide briefings such as, 'Show You Care', 'Dare to Care', and 'Be Service Entrepreneurs'.

11.5.2 Check-In Services

Importance of Check-In Services

Check-in handling is a critical test of an airline's quality of service. Frequently, constraints of time, space and equipment culminate to make this area of customer contact a difficult one. Many passengers make their first face-to-face contact with the airline at check-in. The impression an airline makes during check-in will influence the passenger's perception of his entire journey.

Check-In Queues

- Goals of queue management: SIA's goals are to strive towards providing a queue-free check-in, at least for most of the passengers, and if there must be queues, make them pleasant for the passengers.

- Maximum check-in time: SIA's Ground Services Department has set the maximum check-in time as seven minutes for First and Raffles Class and twelve minutes for Economy Class passengers. Staff must try their best to keep check-in times within the limits for their stations.
- Queue management:
  - Ensure sufficient number of counters and staff are available, based on joining passenger load.
  - Ensure accuracy in sign-posting the flight number and departure details.
  - Uphold exclusive use of First and Raffles Class counters. If Economy Class passengers are directed to these counters, there must be arrangements to service the First and Raffles Class passengers when they arrive.
  - Assist passengers such as wheelchair cases, unaccompanied young passengers, the elderly, parents with children or infants, and the non-English speaking.
  - Draw difficult passengers away from the queue.
  - Attend to general enquiries by queue-combing.
  - Keep passengers informed of delays, if known in advance.

Travel Documents Checks

- Seriousness of travel documents checks
  - Airlines are responsible for ensuring that the passengers they carry into a country have the proper documentation required for entry.
  - If a passenger is found not to have documents in order, at best, the person is sent back to the original station, at the carrier's expense.
  - Some countries have very stringent regulations and impose heavy penalties and possible court proceedings on airlines that inadvertently bring in these passengers.
  - The burden then falls on the frontline staff members at check-in to ensure that each and every passenger has valid travel documents i.e. passport, visa. It is a daunting task because of the many countries an airline flies to, each with different entry requirements for citizens of different nationalities. To further increase the burden, illegal asylum seekers wishing to go to another country often attempt to do so with forged travel documents, and those

fake documents are so difficult to identify that it requires special training to detect them.

- Management of travel documents checks
  - Profiling: To identify and also to profile possible illegal asylum seekers on certain routes. Passengers who fit a given profile, and who have tell-tale signs on their documents that indicate possible forgery are referred to the senior manager on duty. The suspected documents may either be verified by immigration officials, photocopied or taken into custody and kept in the aircraft locker until arrival at destination to prevent actual asylum seekers from destroying their documents prior to arrival and claiming refugee status upon disembarkation.
  - Remedy: Profiling has mistakenly inconvenienced genuine passengers who unfortunately fit the profile. SIA must try to regain their goodwill with Service Recovery action.
  - Prevention: To minimize document-check mishandling, training on authenticating passports or visas has been provided for check-in staff at some stations. However, staff should be reminded of the sensitive nature of this issue and attempt to avoid embarrassing the passengers. While the airline does have the right to verify, photocopy, question and even withhold some travel documents, it should always be done with plenty of tact and a good explanation.

Seats Assignment

- The basic principles
  The basic principles which should be observed by seat editing staff and check-in personnel are as follows:

  - Seat passengers who are booked on the same PNR together.
  - Seat non-smokers and smokers in NSST and SMST zone respectively. Pre-seat groups, if there is no special request, in the NSST zone.
  - Seat selection is available for First and Raffles Class passengers, VIPs, invalids or the disabled, qualified Priority Passengers and mothers with infants who require bassinets.
  - Assign bulkhead seats to passengers with infants, and to passengers traveling to the next station or short-haul sectors if they are not otherwise occupied.
  - Do not assign Emergency seat rows to the following passengers.
    - handicapped or invalids

- unaccompanied young passengers
- passengers with children or infants
- wheelchair cases
- obese passengers
- pregnant passengers
- elderly or frail passengers

- Do not assign to joining passengers seats which are protected for transit, through check-in, one shot through check-in or guaranteed seats.
- Do not assign criminals, prisoners or violent passengers under escort to the adjacent seats of any other passenger or in the Emergency Exit rows. They should be seated in the rear of the aircraft cabin.
- Do not assign least preferred seats to VIPs and PPs. Whenever load permits, these seats should not be assigned to passengers.
- Input through check-in passengers' PIN numbers into Kriscom DCS under comment field.
- When the seat requests of passengers who check-in late cannot be met at check-in, liaise with gate staff to find passengers who might be willing to change seats.
- Do exercise discretion when passengers' seat requests are not met and offer the next alternative. Those seat requests that could not be met during check-in, should be allocated prior to boarding, should they become available at flight closure.
- At check-in, inform the passengers what type of seats have been assigned to them, that is NSST or SMST.

Through Check-In (TCI)

Through check-in means that a passenger needs to only check-in once, at his original boarding point, to travel to his final destination, even if he has to board more than one flight to get there. This facility has been well-received by passengers who see it as a vast service improvement from having to re-queue at a transfer counter or a few transfer counters in the case of a multi-sector itinerary. In addition, passengers are assured of the seats of their choice at the early stage of their journey.

- One-shot through check-in (OSTCI): One shot, or single entry TCI is only possible when both flights of a passenger's itinerary are processed in the same departure control system. SIA currently has 17 stations that are on-line to KRISCOM DCS, and OSTCI is available at all these stations. For example, when a passenger traveling SQ222/98 SYD-SIN-NRT checks in at Sydney (SYD), the system automatically detects his on-carriage and checks him for both flights. Two separate boarding passes or a two-stage boarding pass is issued.

- Manual through check-in (Manual TCI): In addition to the seventeen stations that have an on-line OSTCI facility, SIA has twenty-eight other stations that offer manual TCI. SQ flights from these stations are processed in its handling agents' departure control systems, and the connecting flights ex-SIN are processed in KRISCOM. These different systems are not linked. A passenger departing on an SQ flight from Bandar Seri Begawan (BWN) will be checked into the RBS DCS for his flight SQ 181 BWN-SIN. If the passenger is continuing to London Heathrow (LHR) on SQ22, SQ staff in BWN will also check him in for SQ22 on Kriscom and issue him another boarding pass for the SIN-LHR sector.

Gate Check-In for Transfer Passengers

While many other airlines are not in favor of the practice of check-in at the gate for transfer passengers, SIA was the first airline to provide this facility for its intra-European transfer passengers with its Common User Terminal Equipment (CUTE) and the use of the New G. Pier at Schipol. At each gate, there are three CUTE terminals linked to an IER 497 boarding pass printer to enable magnetic coded boarding passes to be printed. SIA has received very positive comments for the improved standard of service to its transfer passengers.

Check-In: Waitlisted or Go-Show Passengers

- Case: A passenger was waitlisted for First Class, and was accepted at flight closure when a booked passenger did not show up. Subsequently, the booked passenger belatedly showed up at check-in.
  Policy: A booked passenger has the right to a confirmed seat only if he shows up before flight closure. The airline reserves the right to assign the seat to another passenger at flight closure.
- Case: An SQ flight was held back in SIN for one-and-a-half hours due to bad weather along the flight path. At the destination station, First and Raffles Class passengers were informed of the revised arrival and subsequent delayed departure time by Reservations.

However, the check-in counter of the station started accepting the First and Raffles Class standby passengers at the original scheduled flight closure time forgetting that the booked passengers would be checking in later than usual.

Policy: Any solution will be an unpleasant experience for some of the passengers. The airline's policy is to honor a passenger's ticket as good for travel if he has already been checked-in. A mistake should not be corrected at the expense of checked-in passengers.

Baggage Handling

Load Control

- Check-in baggage: There are weight and piece systems for the load control of baggage. Excess baggage will be charged at consistent rates. If some excess baggage charges are waived by an SIA station, a passenger with onward connections or transfer to another airline must be informed that the other airline may charge him for excess baggage at the point of transfer. If the charges have been waived by an upline SIA station, the downline transfer SIA stations should never ask the passengers in transit to pay excess baggage charges. However if the delivery carrier is not SIA, transfer station may collect excess baggage charges if the baggage exceeds the limits.
- Cabin baggage: The size and amount of cabin baggage each passenger can carry onboard are also restricted to promote a safe and clutter-free cabin. Failure to implement the restrictions on cabin baggage could result in the passenger being inconvenienced at the downline station. A passenger who transfers from one flight to another with excessive cabin baggage could be stopped at the transfer station, and have his cabin baggage retrieved at the boarding gate.

Baggage Identification

- Baggage identification label: A self-adhesive label is available at check-in counters. It has a pictorial list of dangerous articles that are not to be carried in the baggage on the reverse side. These labels are also to be inserted in the passenger's ticket jacket at ticketing.

- Baggage tag: Check-in staff should ensure that the tag with correct information such as name, tag number, number of pieces of baggage, flight number and destination, etc. is attached to each piece of baggage. The old tags should be removed before attaching the correct tags to prevent short shipment or overcarriage. On some occasions, special baggage tags for baggage not for immediate transfer or baggage for special delivery can be used. Special VIP tags should be used in addition to the priority and destination tags for VIPs.
- Container card: Container cards are used to prevent the mishandling of baggage due to loading of the baggage to the wrong containers. Cards used should have the destination clearly written on them for easy identification by the baggage loaders.
- Baggage container: Different containers should be used for interline baggage and for different types of passengers to decrease chances of mishandling and to ensure quick delivery.
- Baggage messages: Telexes to downline and destination stations must include full baggage details, container numbers, loading positions and a reminder to downline stations not to offload in error in the case of VIP handling.

Interline Baggage

Interline passengers transferred from other flights because of flight delays or other casualties should be accepted, with the correct number of pieces of baggage being transferred by counter checking with the Passenger Transfer Manifest (PTM). In addition, it must be sure that all interline baggage is uplifted for oncarriage.

AOG Baggage

During an Aircraft On Ground (AOG) flight cancellation passengers are frequently transferred to hotels for their comfort. Where possible, passengers are given the option of leaving their baggage with the airline, or taking it with them to the hotel. In such a case, passengers are encouraged to retrieve their baggage. This will facilitate the retagging of baggage later, if passengers are to be transferred to different flights. By physically having their baggage with them when they re-check in, passengers can be assured that their baggage travels with them during a transfer. This advantage should be explained to them when they are given the option of retrieval.

Baggage Mishandling

- Delayed delivery: When the airline fails to deliver the checked baggage on the same flight as the passenger, the goals of the service recovery are to deliver the baggage to him as soon as possible, and to relieve inconvenience of not having the passenger's essential items available.
- Interim relief payment: This payment together with an overnight kit bag are provided for all non-resident passengers in all classes without demand in the baggage collection area immediately upon raising a Property Irregularity Report (PIR).
- Outfitting payment: First or Raffles class and priority passengers who need to be attired for a business appointment that was the reason for the trip, may be assisted and reimbursed for the purchase up to the maximum local cost that is set for the station.
- Information: Two ways to keep the passengers informed are:
  - A written notice to the passenger to apologize and inform him about the tracing and delivery service, and to provide a contact number for enquiries.
  - A call to the passenger informing him of the tracing efforts every twelve hours. Passengers should not be expected to call in to check on the progress of the tracing.
- Delivery: As far as possible the bag should be delivered to the home or hotel of the passenger unless the passenger prefers otherwise. This may mean obtaining the key for the bag from the passenger so that the bag can be opened for Customs inspection. Only when local conditions do not permit this should the passenger be asked to collect the baggage.
- Damaged baggage: All stations should have baggage repairs service contracts, so that damaged baggage can be collected, repaired and delivered at the airline's cost. If the bag is damaged beyond repair, the airline should replace it with a similar bag, or reimburse the passenger for the costs up to US$250 or the equivalent. The goal of this type of service recovery is to ensure that the passenger's bag or replacement is suitable, and he is not further inconvenienced in obtaining it.
- Lost or pilfered baggage: For every kilogram that is checked-in the compensation for lost or pilfered baggage is US$20. The maximum amount of compensation is US$800. Stations should settle all claims within twenty-one days.

Delay Handling

Despatch reliability is of paramount importance not only to passengers but to the airline as well. However, delays are sometimes unavoidable. Air Traffic Control (ACT), weather and crowded airports are beyond the airline's control. It is Singapore Airline's standard practice to strive to minimize the inconvenience for its passengers in a delay. The main areas of delay handling are presented below.

Staff Deployment and Visibility

- Pre-advised Delay Counter: When a pre-advised delay occurs, the Reservations staff will try to contact all passengers and inform them of the delay. However, there will be some passengers who will not be contactable either because SIA does not have their contact number or they are already on their way to the airport. If the airline knows that not all the passengers are contactable, there should be a pre-advised delay counter opened so that passengers who have arrived for the original scheduled time can be informed of the new departure time and can check-in their baggage to enable them to move around without the hassle of carrying along their baggage. The last thing the airline should do is to further inconvenience the passengers.

- Delay Counter: Whenever there is a delay, a delay counter should be set up at the airport and the hotel to allow passengers to make enquiries at their convenience. Staff manning the counter must be equipped to answer passengers' queries, and the counter should be equipped with the delay kit. Visibility of the airline staff during a delay is very important. By mingling frequently with the passengers, the airline can pre-empt problems and to a large extent, relieve their anxiety.

- TOST: A Town Office Support Team (TOST) is very helpful during a prolonged flight delay. TOST comprise of staff from Ground Services and Sales Departments. The team will be activated when passengers have to be accommodated at hotels, and when the airport is short of manpower to attend to the passengers. Handling a delay can be a twenty-four-hour operation. Very often, the Sales Department will have to rely on off-duty staff to handle the re-booking for a delay.

- LM-GS Plan of Action: When an aircraft is still unable to depart after the first Provisional Estimated Time of Departure (PETD) has expired, a delay is considered a creeping delay. A joint Line Maintenance-Ground Services (LM-GS) Plan of Action can be helpful in handling the creeping delay to enable a station to work closely with engineering maintenance personnel. The key objective is to realistically assess the aircraft serviceability status for an early and decisive rearrangement for passengers in addition to giving them more accurate details of the status of the delay.

Delay Information

- Accuracy: Before any information is disseminated, staff and handling agents must be briefed to get the facts right. Giving contradictory messages should be avoided.
- Adequacy: As soon as the briefing ends, an announcement must be made to passengers. It is important that the announcement is clear and informative, and that it contains details as follows.
  - Cause of delay: The real cause should be given. Vague reasons such as 'due to engineering', 'due to operational reasons' should be avoided.
  - Provisional Estimated Time of Departure (PETD).
  - Timing of next announcement: Promises of next announcement must be kept, even if no new developments have taken place.
  - Details on sending delay messages.
  - Apologies to passengers.
- Setting the PETD: In a delay, passengers want to know, above all else, when the flight will depart. Setting an accurate PETD is difficult, as ground service staff have to depend on estimates of aircraft serviceability by engineering staff, Air Traffic Control clearance, crew flight time limitations (FTLs), and a host of other considerations. In the rush to despatch the delayed flight, one aspect that is easily overlooked is the amount of time required to board the aircraft. In setting a PETD, boarding time will have to be included as it can take as much as forty minutes to board a full Big Top or Megatop aircraft depending on the station's facilities.
- Frequency: The hourly announcement is a guideline. If necessary, stations should make more frequent announcements for the benefit of passengers who might have missed the earlier announcement for one reason or another.
- Means: Use all means available to communicate, such as the airport PA system, a portable voice amplifier if the airport PA system

is inadequate, prominent notice boards with delay messages, and Delayed Message Cards distributed at Delay Counter.

Delay Message Facilities

Delayed Message Cards may be distributed to passengers . However, it would be more effective for the airline to offer IDD telephone call facilities if available (usually to a five-minute limit). On some occasions, telexes would be supplied. To switch to telephones would release the ground staff from sending all those messages, giving them more time for other arrangements. At the same time, passengers prefer to make direct contacts, so that they are sure that their messages have gone through.

Alternative Travel Arrangements

- Confirmed bookings: In a delay, the airline must ensure that passengers have confirmed bookings on the next best alternative flight, whether it is on another Singapore Airline's flight or on another airline. When booking for alternative flights, staff must ensure that the passengers are not on a waiting list. If the passengers' bookings cannot be confirmed, it is advisable to meet and assist the passengers.
- Transfer of passengers:
  - Policy: It is SIA's policy to transfer passengers caught in a prolonged delay regardless of the loss in revenue. SIA believes that winning passengers' goodwill makes better business sense than trying to prevent a temporary loss in revenue.
  - Priority: To initiate the transfer of Priority, First and Raffles class passengers followed by those who have important appointments at the destinations, and then other Economy class passengers.
  - Special passengers: Care should be taken when transferring unaccompanied young, elderly and wheel-chaired passengers, and medical cases, etc. and transfer is not recommended if it involves a downline connection on a carrier other than SIA.
  - Baggage: Checked baggage should be transferred to the same flight or the goodwill may be lost again.
  - Escort: Transferred passengers should be escorted all the way to the gates of other flights, as these may be different gates or even different terminals.

- Longhaul transit flights: If a long-haul flight is not expected to depart within two hours of arrival at a station or if at the end of a longhaul sector, the flight is delayed in transit or diverted, arrangements must be made for the passengers to reach their destinations quickly.

Overnight Delay

The handling of a delay can be smooth with quick transfers to the next flight, SIA or otherwise. But often, things aren't quite so easy. The next flight may not be available until the next day, or within a few days in some cases. It is in these difficult times that additional service recovery arrangements would have to be used. SIA provides flexible service recovery in meal, transport, and hotel arrangements. On some occasions, usually for long delays, tour arrangements have also been made by the TOST.

Boarding

The simple act of boarding an aircraft can be a hassle for passengers if proper control of the flow of passengers into the cabin is not exercised. Congestion along the aisles, the rush for overhead compartments and the resultant chaos will reflect badly on an airline's professionalism. As a guide, boarding by rows is recommended. It should start aft of the aircraft cabin, moving progressively towards the front cabin of Economy Class. It is also recommended that the boarding announcement be made in English, and, whenever possible, in local languages as well. Usually, four announcements will be made and the key words to be announced are as follows.

- Pre-boarding announcement: Boarding wiil be by rows, please remain seated until your row number is called, exercise caution when opening and closing the overhead compartments, etc.
- First boarding announcement: To invite First and Raffles Class passengers to board followed by the elderly and those travelling with young children.
- Second and subsequent announcements: To invite passengers to board by rows.
- Last announcement: To announce that this is a final announcement for the flight with flight number announced in particular. To urge all remaining passengers to board.

11.6 SIA's Postflight Customer Services

11.6.1 Arrival Handling

Arrival services are handled by SQ staff together with staff of the SIA's ground handling agent (GHA). Guidelines for arrival handling are stated below.

Disembarkation

Once the aircraft doors are opened, disembarkation services will be provided as follows.

- Mobile steps and telescoping walkways are used for disembarkation.
- Station manager and SIA staff are positioned at mobile steps to welcome arriving passengers.
- GHA tally disembarking passengers at the bottom of the mobile steps to ensure accuracy.
- Local newspapers are provided at some SIA stations for First and Raffles class passengers, and SIA and GHA staff will accompany passengers to the arrival hall and assist them with Customs and Immigration (CIQ) clearance.

Baggage Collection

- Announcements are made in the Arrival Hall to provide information and encourage passengers to contact SIA or GHA staff for assistance.
- First and Raffles class passengers' baggage will be discharged and delivered immediately followed by crew and young passengers' baggage.
- SIA and GHA staff are positioned at the baggage conveyor to assist passengers with their checked baggage, and they will remain in the Arrival Hall until all passengers have cleared CIQ without any problems.
- For passengers whose baggage has been mishandled, SIA and GHA staff offer an apology and assist passengers to complete the Property Irregularity Report (PIR) and to follow SIA's procedure for a baggage claim.

11.6.2 Services for Transfer and Transit Passengers

With the through check-in facilities, transit or transfer passengers should not face any problems on arrival. However, in the case of delays or other casualties, close cooperation between the ground handling agent (GHA) and the Airport Passenger Services (APS) is crucial to providing outstanding ground services for transit passengers as the following two cases show.

To Expedite Passenger Transfer for Tight Connections

SQ9888 departed late from Singapore and was estimated to arrive in Narita at 2020 local time. Two passengers on board had an onward connection to Honolulu on UA826, which was scheduled to depart at 2045 local time. It seemed that the two passengers would have to miss their connection. However the APS and GHA staff were undaunted. They quickly did the following to expedite the transfer of the two passengers.

- Change of gate: Convinced the airport officials to assign SQ9888 to a gate nearer to United Airlines' (UA). A ten to fifteen minute walk was saved by the change of gate.
- Direct-through boarding: Convinced the security guards to allow the two passengers to be escorted directly through the boarding gate to the screening point. By not having to go via the normal route, the passengers saved another five to seven minutes.
- Pre-check-in for connected flight: Informed UA of the tight connection for the airline to pre-check in the passengers.
- Baggage transfer: Positioned three staff at the ramp site to locate and transfer the passengers' baggage to UA.

Due to the close cooperation of the staff involved, the short connection went off without a hitch, and the passengers were very impressed by the quality of SIA's customer services.

Helping Last-Minute-Change (LMC) Passengers

On another occasion, a last-minute-change or LMC couple was assisted by an APS staff member to board their connected flight SQ12 due to the late arrival of their inbound flight. As they were late, they were concerned that they would miss their flight to Los Angeles. The APS staff member confidently assured them that they would not miss their flight. She checked them in and arranged for the baggage to be retagged to Los Angeles. As their no-smoking seats had already been released to other passengers because of their late arrival, they were assigned seats in the smoking zone instead. But the staff did not just leave the situation at that. At the boarding gate, she managed to get two passengers with no-smoking seats to swap places with the couple.

These two cases also illustrate the important role played by handling agents in generating outstanding services for transit passengers.

11.6.3 Meet and Assist Services (MAAS)

SIA provides MAAS to its passengers who are expected to have difficulty in check-in and/or disembarking. Among the categories of passengers to whom the airline extends this type of service are the elderly, unaccompanied minors or young passengers, the non-English speaking, the disabled and medical cases. The service areas in which the passengers need assistance with MAAS at uplift, transit and destination stations areas are as follows.

- Meet and assist at check-in, embarkation and upon arrival.
- Assistance through immigration, baggage collection and customs clearance.
- Assistance in their transfer or interline connections onto other carriers.

Service lapses with MAAS fall under two categories: no proper handover between ground staff and cabin crew; and failure to identify the MAAS passengers. To address these problems, procedures have been developed to ensure that frontline staff will be able to deliver the service as promised.

10.6.4 Postflight Service Facilities at Changi Airport

Changi Airport Terminal 2, officially opened in November 1990, is equipped with the latest technological facilities, particularly those used for postflight customer services.

Airport Capacity

Changi Airport has the capacity to handle twenty-four million passengers a year, making it the largest airport in the Asia-Pacific region. A passenger arriving into Changi can expect to clear customs and immigration and collect his bags all within twenty minutes of landing. If he is in transit, he can transfer flights between the two terminals at Changi Airport in less than an hour.

Airtropolis Facilities

Changi is designed for the comfort of international travelers. It has a gymnasium, a conference hall, an exhibition hall, two business centers, four full-service banks, twenty restaurants, more than one hundred shops, and a host of other services. All these help make a pleasant postflight experience. They also make Changi Airport a destination by itself, or an Airtropolis.

References

1. Speech by Dr Cheong Choong Kong, Managing Director, SIA to Young President's Organization on 8 February 1985. Reported in SIA Company News: *OUTLOOK*, May 1985.
2. SIA Company News: *OUTLOOK*, June 1997.
3. 'Simplified Financial Report 1992-93', by SIA.
4. SIA Company News: *OUTLOOK*, January 1992.
5. Vandermerwe S. and Lovelock C., '*Singapore Airlines*', *The Human Dimension in Services Management*, The International Institute for Management Development (IMD), Lausanne, Switzerland, 1991.
6. *NOTE TO EDITORS* No. 02/94, by Public Affairs Dept., Singapore Airlines, February 21, 1994.
7. *Business Times (shipping Times)*, November 8, 1995.
8. SIA Company News: *OUTLOOK*, November 1992.
9. SIA Company News: *OUTLOOK*, June 1992.
10. *NOTE TO EDITORS* No. 04/94, by Public Affairs Dept., Singapore Airlines, March 10, 1994.
11. Pillay J.Y., SIA Company News: *OUTLOOK*, April 1984.
12. Ross J.E., *Total Quality Management: Text, Cases and Readings*, St. Lucie Press, 1992, P.212.
13. SIA Company News: *OUTLOOK*, September 1988.
14. SIA Document: *TQM as Differentiation Strategy for Service Quality*, S:\DOC\OTHERS\TQM.OTH.

CHAPTER TWELVE

Essence of Outstanding Ground Services

12.1 Paradigm Shift of Competition

Chapter 1 described how quality management emerged as a key issue in the strategic management of a company. The first stage of strategic quality management involves analysis of the environmental changes of a business and the identification of the paradigm shift in competition. SIA has done all of that.

The airline industry is a service industry in which competitors use similar equipment and fly to and from the same places with costs that can be much the same. In an industry whose businesses are similar in so many ways, the distinguishing feature of an airline is therefore the quality of service it provides. For a long time now, SIA's inflight service has been rated ahead of its competitors; however, in the last few years, the gap has narrowed considerably. The competition has thus shifted to ground service. SIA has many line stations all over the world. Ground services are provided by SIA's own staff as well as the service handling agents' staff. Is SIA really ahead of the competition in terms of ground services, and if so, how did SIA achieve its outstanding ground services and what really constitutes the essence of excellent ground services? The following sections will deliberate on these issues.

12.2 Benchmarking Airline Ground Services

From time to time SIA attempts to benchmark its service standards against its competitors' service practices on the ground to assess whether it is ahead of the competition. At one of the presentations of SIA's World Station Managers Conference, a comparison was made with a chosen excellent airline performer, Emirates Airlines (Toh, 1994).

12.2.1 Benchmark Against an Excellent Performer

Emirates started operations on 25 October, 1985 with two leased aircraft. It initially flew to only three destinations. In a little more than eight years, Emirates has grown to a fleet of thirteen Airbuses and two B727s servicing thirty-two international destinations. Along the way, it has built up a reputation as a quality airline, winning awards which include the prestigious *Air Transport World* Passenger Service Award in 1993.

For an airline that has outperformed so many others in the competitive airline industry, Emirates has a surprisingly small number of innovations or enhancements to its name where ground service is concerned. A good example is its home base in Dubai where, despite increasing congestion in the check-in area, the airline has not tried out enhancements like phone or fax check-in. At their home base, practically all ground handling is provided by DNATA Airport Services, the thirty-five-year-old monopolist ground handling company. As part of the Emirates Airlines group, with the same managing director and other shared corporate support services, DNATA gives Emirates an edge over other carriers. Despite this, and the unusual infrastructure advantages enjoyed by home base airlines, Emirates Ground Services in Dubai is ordinary; good, but not spectacular.

A key weakness is the prevailing service culture among the Emirates group's passenger services staff. While generally competent, the staff do not have the same sophistication in customer service and awareness as do the staff in SIA and SATS.

Comparisons of key ground services between the two airlines have been made. The Emirates group has begun to tackle the problems by initiating its first Customer Awareness Program which is similar to SIA's first phase OSG Program — Show You Care (which will be discussed in Chapter 15). SIA's OSG Program bas been used as a benchmark for airline ground service.

12.2.2 Comparative Analysis

At SIA, station managers are eager to compare SIA with, and to learn from, their competitors. They are aware that their competitors are not too far behind them. It is with this mindset that station managers frequently compare their ground services with their competitors. One of SIA's direct competitors in Hong Kong is Cathay Pacific (CX). Over the years, CX's management has placed a lot of emphasis on service enhancements. Its director of customer service has stated that CX's commitment to be totally customer-driven is more than a basic necessity, and if it is to be successful and rated the best airline of the decade, its customers must consider it the best. A comparative analysis of some of the CX ground service characteristics are stated below, provided by SIA station manager C.H. Cheok.

- Check-In Services: CX provides three types of check-in service outside the airport, namely, Citycheck, Telecheck and Faxcheck. CX practices indicate that Citycheck has been quite popular but the other two services are not. SIA has provided fax check-in services since 1992 for certain categories of passengers, but the service is not popular with an average of five users a month.
- On-Time Departure Policy (OTP): CX's punctuality performance for flights departing within fifteen minutes has deteriorated in recent years. After a study conducted in 1993 to determine the causes of delays, CX implemented the On-Time Departure Policy whereby check-in counters close at minus forty minutes and boarding gates close at minus ten minutes to Standard Time of Departure (STD). Regardless of the class of travel, passengers who are late will be denied boarding and their bags offloaded accordingly. A three-month trial in August 1993 yielded a positive result as the punctuality factor improved to 80% or more. Thereafter, the OTP Policy was made permanent by CX. The airline community, under the auspices of AOG (Aircraft On Ground), then asked the Board of Airline Representatives to give its approval for all airlines to implement OTP in Hong Kong effective 1 January, 1994. All airlines in Hong Kong have now implemented OTP and the airlines report that punctuality factors have improved significantly.
- Advance Passenger Information (APIS): SIA takes note that contrary to its current practice of sending APIS through a PC base post-departure, CX has a system that can auto-generate such information, captured at check-in, after the flight is closed. This has led the Management Service Division to carry out a similar project with Ground Services at SIA.

Other comparative analyzes include the CX First Class Lounge and SIA's Silver Kris Lounge in Singapore, the CX Service Quality Plan and SIA's OSG Program, and the management of fraudulent documents.

12.2.3 SIA's Ground Services as the Benchmark

As has been stated in much management literature, benchmarking is becoming an integral part of corporate strategic planning. The results of benchmarking provide input for formulating programs leading to the establishment of standards which then serve as new benchmarks for subsequent management practices.

Using this theory that SIA has continually benchmarked its management practices against others and has eventually become the best-in-class performer of the industry. As mentioned previously, SIA has won the Best Airline Award for the last five consecutive years. In terms of ground services, it has established a significant reputation by getting various ground handling agents to adopt its SIA service standards (Ee, 1994). The IATA Ground Handling Council's Cost Management Working Group has in fact accepted the proposal of making SIA standards a part of the IATA Standard Ground Handling Agreement. Even Japan Airlines has finally agreed to adopt the SIA standards.

When SIA occasionally sends a pre-operations team to certain line stations to discuss the possible handling of SIA's flights, it is not unusual for them to be told by the handling agents that they would very much like to handle SIA because they want to learn from the airline according to station manager W.P. Fong. It is significant that handling agents would like to use SIA standards as the benchmark to serve other airlines.

12.3 Airline's Management of Strategic Partners: The Handling Agents

An airline company has many line stations all over the world. Many of the passenger operational functions such as monitoring baggage presentation, collecting general declarations, immigration, transfer, post flight and delay handling, and other special services are performed by handling agents at the various airports. To finally achieve the ground service goals, an airline, like any other business will have to adopt a consistent long-term approach towards its service suppliers.

12.3.1 The Pro-active Approach

SIA considers its handling agents its strategic business partners who contribute significantly to the improvement of its service performance indices (SPIs). As such, it has been actively managing its handling agents as an important resource, treating them as an extension of SIA rather than a separate entity. SIA has assigned semi-dedicated staff at twenty-seven stations to work jointly with the handling agents. It has also committed resources to help train, motivate and retain the staff of its handling agents (Ee, 1994). SIA has accepted its handling agents as integral components of its various ground service systems. Service standards, procedures and other information is provided; formal meetings conducted; various familiarization programs, seminars and delay simulations have also been conducted together with the introduction of incentive schemes. As a result, SIA has made significant progress in getting agents to adopt SIA service standards as mentioned earlier.

12.3.2 The Cultural Aspects

At line stations in different countries with ground services handled by local handling agents, problems abound. In some countries, it may not be usual business practice to be service oriented. There may be serious language problems and their body-language may be misunderstood by tourists or expatriates. However, as long as they are providing ground services to an airline passenger, they reflect the airline's image. Passengers relate their experiences of having received quality or sub-quality ground services for a certain trip traveled via a certain airline, without making any distinction whether the services are provided by the airline or by the local handling agent.

Hence, it is important to get handling agents on the right track. The airline has to understand and master their cultures. Meetings with handling agents must not be seen as a 'shelling' session but rather as 'brainstorming'. To foster goodwill, airlines must learn to give handling agents moral support and, most importantly, respect. SIA station manager, E. Lim says all mishandling problems must be analyzed and solutions provided to avoid a recurrence, with the understanding that the handling agents possess the manpower and the airline has the expertise in services.

12.3.3 Empowering the Handling Agents

Delegation of operational functions and staff empowerment has been mentioned frequently in TQM. However, in actual practice, when it comes to line stations in some countries, it is not unusual to come up against problems of red-tape, operational inefficiency and a lack of service ideas from the handling agents, says SIA station manager H. Alias. Therefore, there is a tendency for SIA to become self-handling in order to maintain ground service standards. While allocating staff, for the security of being in control of service standards, these staff members are lost from the bigger role of proactive customer servicing, which is the primary element that keeps SIA ahead of the competition. In the long run, there will be a slowing down of customer servicing enhancement. Moreover, in considering the amount of work involved in providing ground services, self-handling would make SIA less cost effective.

Hence, the general direction is to empower the handling agents as much as possible, as is the case in some line stations where handling agents oversee the flight completely without compromising service standards (SIA, 1994).

Upon closer examination, managers of some line stations such as the DAC station in Dhaka, Bangladesh, have found that the main obstacle to empowerment is mindset. SIA has therefore systematically forged a new mindset by educating its staff to accept the new role of customer servicing by, for example, gradually taking them away from the security offered by being behind the check-in counters and introducing them to the more professional and satisfying role of mingling with passengers, according to station manager Alias.

Concurrently, SIA has to ensure that the handling agents are providing good service at check-in counters and not compromising standards. In addition to the provision of superior customer-driven procedures, regular staff meetings are conducted which serve as a forum for discussing the adequacy of handling agent support and for ironing out operational problems. During these meetings, it is impressed upon the staff that while the company pursues operational problems with the management of handling agents, good relationships must always be maintained at the lower levels to facilitate quick problem solving.

12.4 The Handling Company's Management of Ground Services

12.4.1 Belgavia as a True Partner of the Airline Companies

Belgavia is a handling agent at Brussels International Airport. The company performs all the traditional airport handling activities such as passenger, baggage, cargo and ramp handling. Belgavia is also licensed to provide basic line maintenance, inflight catering in Brussels and courier services. Airlines in Brussels have a ground-handling choice between national carrier Sabena and Belgavia. Brussels is one of the most liberal airports in Europe, where a choice and sharp competition is available. The following is an excerpt from the presentation by Luc F. Meurrens, director-general of Belgavia, Brussels, Belgium (SIA, 1994).

12.4.2 Mission and Corporate Values

For every kind of business, management's intention, determination and commitment always play a vital role in the success or failure of the business, and these are usually stated in a company's mission statement. In addition to mission statements, there are often a set of corporate values whereby management lays down what is important to the company, what are their beliefs, what kind of principles the company will adhere to, and what are the major emphases of the company.

Belgavia's mission is to be the top handling agent in Europe. As stated by the company, its corporate values are as follows:

- Customer: He comes first, he is our first responsibility. We are close to our customer, we listen to our customer.
- Quality: Together with our customers we set standards and clear objectives. We do not compromise when it comes to quality. We train, we inspire our employees in the Total Quality Concept.
- Colleagues: Our people make the difference; training is essential. We care for a pleasant working environment. We have few hierarchical levels; we believe in small units with clearly defined responsibilities.
- Creativity: Be critical. Improve your working methods. Provoke an entrepreneurial spirit.
- Continuity We believe in growth. We have a long-term policy/commitment. In order to guarantee our long-term survival, we have to be profitable today.

It is on this set of corporate values and a mission to be the top or best that the following corporate quality strategy and management systems are laid.

12.4.3 Corporate Quality Strategy

In the early 1980s, the management of Belgavia recognized that their competitor, as a national airline handler, had many competitive advantages that they, as a non-airline independent handler, would never be able to acquire. These are:

- an economy of scale through the servicing of their own fleet,
- the marginal cost approach in third-party handling,
- a very political impact on traffic rights, and
- a policy of commercial compensations and *quid pro quo* with other airlines.

However, after years of operations, present-day Belgavia is handling three million passengers annually out of the five million non-national carrier passengers. On average, the company handles some twenty-eight thousand flights per year or an average of eighty aircraft a day. Belgavia is at present active and offering full ground handling services at three airports in France and is expanding its sphere of influence throughout Europe.

All these achievements were the results of its strategic quality management. It has been very clear to the management that if the company wanted to be successful in competition, it would have to keep itself aware of both the competitors' and its own strengths to generate an appropriate strategy for the market. Belgavia has identified its unique competitive advantage as being a neutral and impartial handling agent; not belonging to an airline or an airport authority. Ground-handling is its core business, and it has only one interest — its customers. Belgavia's corporate strategy has therefore been:

- a strategy of differentiation by quality;
- a strategy which is quality oriented and quality driven in every aspect, in everything they do and undertake;
- whereby their service/their product is developed in close contact with the needs and requirements of their customers (a tailor-made product); and
- where their name/their logo is not relevant, not important but where the identity of the customer comes first (dedicated).

12.4.4 Commitment of Resources for Quality

Belgavia's experience has been that:

'writing down and proclaiming a strategy is one thing; the

implementation of a strategy is far more painstaking, and the demands on the organization are tremendous, especially as credibility towards both your employees and your customers must be maintained and not be in contradiction. Credibility is the key word.'

The company's resources commitment for the implementation of its quality strategy includes:

- modern up-to-date handling equipment;
- trained personnel;
- motivated and committed personnel; and
- advanced communication systems.

12.4.5 Quality Management Systems

For success to be forthcoming, daily operations have to be organized and monitored for the provision of a consistent service product. Belgavia's experience in setting up quality management systems are given below.

Measurements, Objectives, Reports, Databank and Performance Monitoring

Quality objectives have to be measurable. Acceptable quality levels (AQLs) have been set in all departments. The company measures everything that is measurable and almost a hundred measurements are available throughout the company.

Some operations, such as baggage handling, are measured on a per flight basis; others are measured at random or at regular intervals. Flight-handling reports must be filed after each flight. This gives the management immediate information on any incident.

All incidents, irregularities and complaints on a per department basis are kept in a databank for statistical purposes. This also helps to detect any structural pattern that might develop in certain areas and to give immediate feedback to the airlines.

A close follow-up and monitoring of quality performance and training process is conducted by the steering committee, basically the executive management of the company. Members of the committee meet every three months to evaluate performance and decide on further quality actions.

Every three months, actual performance and comparison with standards and AQLs are published in a publication called *Quality Mirror*. This is then presented to the management and also issued to all senior staff.

Customer Focus

Careful discussions, running through airline by airline, on any pending difficulty that might endanger the company's long-term relationship with its customers are conducted at the monthly meeting of the marketing committee. The committee also deals with issues such as potential developments in the market and potential new customers.

At regular intervals, the company holds meetings with customers to evaluate its service products. This kind of systematic follow-up is essential to avoid misunderstandings. This is a forum which enables customers to bring up their feelings or misgivings that they were hesitant to bring up earlier.

Every year, the company conducts a customer survey where customers' appreciation on all aspects of the products are assessed. The survey provides valuable input for different quality plans.

Ramp Safety Campaign

Safety has always been one of the most important quality characteristics in airline-related businesses. Ramp safety basically covers the requirements of all related parties: the company's interests, those of the airlines and the well-being of the company's personnel. Belgavia has developed a ramp safety index, which takes into account:

- the result of spot checks;
- aircraft damage;
- material damage; and
- personal injuries.

Rewards for Quality Results

Belgavia gives its managers a financial incentive when their quality objectives at the end of the year are reached.

12.4.6 The Challenges Ahead

To be a service leader, a company requires a clear vision of the future and a fair estimate of its competitive challenges ahead. Belgavia's management has laid down its challenges as:

- the need for better cost and productivity management;
- the struggle for the liberalization of ground handling within the EEC; and
- threat from airline companies wishing to perform third-party handling.

In closing, it can be said that the experiences and the lessons learnt from them are a prelude to outstanding ground services.

References

1. Ee, T. H. (1994) *Beyond Managing Handling Agent*. In Proceedings on World Station Managers Conference, May. Singapore: SIA
2. Meurrens L.F. (1994). *'Beyond Managing the Handling Agent'*. Proceeding on World Station Managers Conference, May. Singapore: SIA.
3. SIA (1994). Proceedings on World Station Managers Conference, May. Singapore: SIA
4. Toh, G.M. (1994). *Are We Ahead of The Competition?* Proceedings on World Station Managers Conference, May. Singapore: SIA

CHAPTER THIRTEEN

Management of Inflight Service Quality

13.1 Introduction

It has been established that the three pillars of SIA's total quality service are: (1) the silk — the Singapore Girl, (2) the steel — the modern aircraft fleet and (3) the ground — the outstanding ground service. For inflight customer service, SIA sets the industry benchmark. Since its inception, the airline's appeal has always been based on the high standards set by its cabin services. Research studies on air travel reveal that when all things are equal in terms of aircraft type, fares, frequencies and reliability, travelers respond warmly to the appeal of high tech and highly accessible personalized quality inflight service (SIA, 1988).

SIA's air attendants, the Singapore Girls, emanate charm and friendliness. Extensive and distinctive advertising programs have been done to promote these attendants dressed in sarong-kebayas, the multicolored, ankle-length dresses designed by Paris couturier Balmain and made from traditional batik fabric (Vandermerwe and Lovelock, 1991). These distinctively uniformed women have become the symbol of the airline's mission to deliver high-quality customer service. They have a very long-lasting impact on passengers.

Yet, the best-looking and most helpful Singapore Girl can evolve only in a modern aircraft with well-equipped avionics facilities and after the management's painstaking training and retraining.

13.2 SIA's Commitment to Inflight Service Quality

Being customer-oriented means introducing innovative service features. It is difficult to imagine airline travel today without a choice of meals, free drinks and free headsets. In fact, many of these have been SIA's innovations (SIA, 1994b).

13.2.1 The Pioneer Inflight Service Features

In 1976, SIA became the first airline to put slumberettes in its B747 lounges. It was also one of the first airlines to introduce fully reclining snoozers on its B747 upper decks. SIA has also been one of the few airlines that provides free drinks, music and other gift items to its passengers on board (SIA, 1988).

In September 1991, SIA became the first airline in the world to offer a truly global inflight telephone service for passengers, allowing calls to be placed to virtually anywhere in the world from any point in the sky. The satellite-based Celestel service opened the way for a whole range of inflight communication services, including facsimile transmission and real time news. In addition, a personal video system has been installed on board Megatop 747s for First and Raffles Class passengers. SIA's personal cinema system offers passengers nonstop entertainment and covers classic and latest release box office hits, sports and current affairs (SIA, 1994b).

In January 1992, SIA became the first airline in the world to globalize its new service: recorded CNN International newscasts are screened on all flights out of Singapore.

SIA's ITN Worldvision News continues to be screened on flights into Singapore. This means that long-haul passengers are kept up to date about the latest world events. On all flights to Japan, a weekly round-up edition of NHK's 'Today Japan' is shown (SIA, 1993).

In May 1993, SIA provided the world's first inflight facsimile facility which allows direct transmission, via satellite, of handwritten, drawn or printed documents. The fax service, together with the recent innovations of high-tech cervices such as the Celestel skyphone, have thus created an 'office in the air' for SIA's passengers (SIA, 1993).

13.2.2 Towards a More Comfortable Inflight Experience: Seat Reconfiguration

Over thirty years, the zeal for inflight service excellence has continued unabated. Recently, SIA spent US$51.5 million for a fleet refit, including cabin reconfiguration, new seats in all classes and the installation of the latest avionics inflight facilities.

In First Class, the improved backrests with better lumbar support offer a more comfortable long-haul journey and the leg rests are designed to ease access to the aisle for window-seat passengers. Backrest recline, leg rest and lumbar support are all electronically controlled at the touch of a button from the armrest.

Seat pitch in Raffles Class was increased to forty-two inches on the main deck, creating more space between seats. Lumbar supports and more comfortable legrests are also features of the new Raffles Class seats. The legrests can now be raised more than sixty degrees, providing greater support. The new Economy Class seating offers increased knee room and space between seats.

13.2.3 The Cabin Management/Interactive Video System

The zeal for innovation has also continued unabated. Keeping abreast of the latest avionics technology, the Cabin Management/Interactive Video (CMIV) system has been added to SIA's long list of pioneer inflight service features. The system was launched in August 1994. It provides movies, digital audio, video games, inflight shopping and destination information to each passenger seat via an arm-rest video screen and a remote control. To run the CMIV in twenty of its B747-400 Megatops, SIA embarked on a US$50 million (S$76 million) investment to install an interactive computer system (*The Sunday Times*, 1994).

In addition to providing inflight pleasure and convenience, the CMIV has a significant impact on the work duties of cabin crew as well as ground staff. The amount of paperwork is reduced and the transfer of data and reports faster and easier with many forms and reports used on board being incorporated into the CMIV system. A few examples of forms replaced by the CMIV are voyage reports, flight records, passenger name list and cabin defect log. With the CMIV, information and data, especially for voyage reports, are channeled more quickly and efficiently to the relevant departments so that any follow-up action that needs to be taken can be done without delay. A better working environment is provided for the crew-in-charge. Apart from the convenience the CMIV provides, the crew's coordination and control are also enhanced.

In short, the CMIV facilitates the crew's duties in maintaining SIA's high standard of inflight service by giving them more time to interact with passengers.

13.2.4 Management of the CMIV System

For any high-tech facility, acquisition and installation does not represent the entire process. Without a proper management system for the use of the new facility, it would result in misuse, malfunctions and the generation of errors. SIA has proper planning for the management of the CMIV system.

Installation of Equipment

The CMIV consists of a video control center (VCC). It is installed beside the staircase in Raffles Class (Main Deck) of the B747-400 Megatops to enable the crew-in-charge to operate the controls while standing up. A work table is provided at the VCC for crew use. Linked to the VCC are three cabin management terminals (CMTs). One master terminal is located in the VCC. The other two 'slave' terminals are scheduled to be installed in Phase 2 in the Raffles Class Upper Deck and Economy Class. The master terminal differs from the slave terminal in that it is capable of previewing all audio and video channels; the slave terminals do not have this capability. Apart from this preview capability, the slave terminals are able to perform all other functions.

Security

For security, staff ID cards are used to access the system. Only leading crew members and above have access to the controls of the CMIV.

Implementation

Currently, crew-in-charge are required to change video tapes for different movie cycles on PCS-equipped aircraft. With the CMIV, the video tapes on these channels will be preloaded so that changing of movie tapes will no longer be necessary.

In Phase 1, an enhanced audio and video system was implemented. Passengers can choose from twenty-one video channels and twelve compact disc channels. Seats in all classes are retrofitted with inseat video monitors. While video monitors in the First and Raffles Class continue to be stored in the armrests, monitors in the Economy Class are located in the seat backs. The exception is the first row of the Economy Class where monitors are stored in the armrests.

Phase 2 is scheduled to be launched with the focus on interactive audio and video functions for passengers. It includes an integrated handset for the inseat phone, games, destination information, broadcast news and probably inseat catalog shopping.

In Phase 3, features such as inflight shopping, gaming and cabin crew applications, for example voyage reports, inflight sales records, cabin defect log etc., will be implemented.

Training

Training is conducted in two phases.

In Phase 1, all inflight supervisors (IFSs) and chief attendants go through a one-day course on handling the CMIV audio and video equipment. This phase takes eight weeks with five classes scheduled each week. Basic procedures of handling the VCC are covered in the course. These include controlling overhead monitors, video players, CD players, airshow, previewing channels and checking the system to ensure that it is operating smoothly. Two mock-up units are installed at the SIA Training Center, and twenty personal computers are required for Phase 1 training. Another twenty PCs are required for Phase 2.

In Phase 2, leading crew together with IFSs and chief attendants have to undergo a one-day hands-on classroom session using touch-screen PCs to familiarize themselves with the passenger facilities. This will provide the crew with the knowledge needed to assist passengers who are unfamiliar with the new retractable passenger control unit (PCU) located in their seats. Flight attendants are to be trained using video aids.

13.2.5 In Touch With Inflight: The Audio Video Unit

With the objective of creating a relaxing inflight atmosphere, SIA has set up an audio video unit to ensure that a high standard of variety of inflight entertainment programs is provided to passengers. To achieve this objective, a lot of details have to be attended to.

Audio Programs

Different inbound and outbound programs are available on all Big Top and most Megatop aircraft and Airbus fleet. The range of audio programs include classical music, pop music, evergreens, comedy, country music and Chinese and Hindi favorites.

The Overall Quality Control of Audio Video Programs

All movie and short feature tapes are checked for picture and sound quality in SIA's fully equipped audio video room. Any movie tape found unacceptable is replaced immediately. This process also ensures that vendors meet SIA specifications. As most movie distributors are situated in Los Angeles, staff members are sent there to gain access to the latest movie releases. Movie editions for inflight viewing follow specific criteria. Care is taken to avoid any display of excessive sex or violence.

The Turner Inflight Programming

It provides all SIA's short feature programs. The programs are reviewed in Singapore after the initial synopses have been provided. Inflight Services keeps in touch with Turner Inflight Programming regularly regarding selection, program content and delivery. Every bi-monthly cycle, eight short features for the main screen and another eight for the personal cinema system are selected. The diverse selections include comedy, lifestyle, sport, documentaries, business and nature programs.

The News

CNN, BBC and NHK are three news providers. BBC reports are packaged in London and couriered to twelve European cities. The same news is also transmitted daily by satellite from Los Angeles to Australia and New Zealand. BBC news reports are screened on inbound flights from Europe, North America and the Pacific Southwest.

CNN International reports are packaged daily in Singapore for showing on all outbound flights from Singapore and on inbound flights from the Orient, Southeast Asia and West Asia.

The weekly round-up edition of NHK's 'Today's Japan' presenting the major developments in Japanese politics, business, society and sports are screened on all flights into Japan. The program is available in English and Japanese on SIA's Boeing aircraft.

The Future Inflight Entertainment

The compact disc and multimedia mini disc do more than music videos. There will be a variety of sources including digital or video tape players that produce hi-definition pictures. Passengers will be able to view a large hi-definition screen or select a program from individual screens at their seats as well as play video games, make phone calls, listen to music, and order duty free items using their personal credit cards.

13.3 Management of Cabin Crew

SIA has for five consecutive years won the title of 'the Region's Best Airline', and made a clean sweep at the Pacific Asia Travel Association award ceremony in 1994 by taking awards for Best Airline (Business Class) and Best Incentive Airline (*The Sunday Times*, 1994). It has been reckoned that the airline's success has its roots deep in its Asian heritage as epitomized by its Singapore Girl (SIA, 1994b). Yet, the Singapore Girl comes into being only after the management's dedicated nurturing.

13.3.1 Cabin Crew Culture: Be Passenger-Focused

It is the people who make the difference between airlines. From time to time, different batches of 'Singapore Girls' and 'Singapore Guys' are taught to learn a new way of life. Their new motto is '**Unless you can make others happy, you can never be happy yourself**'.

This generalizes SIA's culture for cabin crew training. Service tips on product knowledge, attitude, crew-passenger communication and handling incidents in various situations are also provided from time to time.

Crew management puts forward a theme for an annual Service Campaign. In 1993 the theme was 'Lets Prove We're The Best'. There are posters of various interesting personalities in the Control Center and SIA Training Center. These interesting personalities could very well be SIA's passengers — economy, business or first class travelers. The passengers may have difficulties, problems or display uncommon behavior, but they are important to the cabin crew because of the message they put across. The management emphasizes that regardless, they are SIA's passengers and they must be given the best of the airline's hospitality. So, the service campaign motto has been: 'The passengers' habits are up to them but the services are up to the crew'.

Service campaigns usually focus on getting the crew to:

- effectively communicate with passengers
- remember passenger requests
- be more attentive to passengers with difficulties
- give equal treatment to all passengers.

Case materials are collected, and the crew-in-charge will discuss these with crew members during the pre-flight briefings. Service campaign contests are organized to encourage tactful responses to passengers in different, often difficult, situations.

13.3.2 Organization Based on Team Flying Concept

Crew members have also learnt to become true friends as a Team Flying Concept has been applied, organizing them into different wards. There are thirty-one wards of cabin crew: each consists of about one hundred and seventy members under the management of a cabin crew executive as a ward leader. Various teams of eighteen crew members are formed within the ward. For closer rapport and interaction with other crew members, the teams within a ward are reformed once every year and there is a major reshuffling of wards every three years.

13.3.3 Crew Training

Training Doctrine

On the first day of the training program, the crew members are constantly impressed with the correct attitude, rules and regulations of SIA and also the need for them to smile and speak fluent English, even with a fast digestion of distinct phonetic pronunciation so as to prepare themselves for their work. As a matter of fact, throughout the entire training period, crew members are drilled constantly with emphasis on maintaining a correct attitude, a proper knowledge, an empathetic ear and working with a sense of urgency and fitness. They are also taught the importance of teamwork, and that egoism does not have any place in the organization. Crew members are reminded that the junior member has to initiate the greeting whenever staff meet one another, and the need for handing over a name card or an article with both hands.

Cabin crew must attend a four-month basic and conversion training course to certify themselves 'qualified' to take to the sky.

Basic Skills Courses

The schoolroom teaching includes the basics of knowing the galley compartments, the cabin, the aircraft, crew duties, safety procedures, announcements, passenger handling, social etiquette, deportment and grooming. The SIA Training Center is equipped with two B747 cabin mock-ups and one A310 mock-up, an indoor swimming pool with a wave generator, and a cabin evacuation trainer for basic training.

Fleet Training

After the period of basic training, the crew has to go through fleet training. The B747 and Airbus fleet training classes enable the crew to attune themselves to aircraft types and features, seating, service, etc. fire-fighting, security and safety equipment procedure training highlight the crew's other important responsibilities.

In short, to be fully efficient, cabin crew have an immense amount to learn.

Self-Awareness Workshop for Basic Trainees

The inaugural session of SIA's Self-Awareness Workshop began in January 1994 (SIA, 1994a). The one-day workshop is designed for basic trainees. The workshop provides opportunities to:

- Increase the confidence of cabin staff members.
- Gain better understanding of themselves and of interpersonal styles for relating with others in a work environment.
- Acquire skills in assertive management.
- Decrease anxiety at work.
- Increase interaction at work.
- Improve the overall quality of social and professional interactions.
- Enhance individual self-esteem.

Cabin Crew Advanced Resource Enhancement (CARE) Program

The program aims at increasing the overall interpersonal effectiveness

Figure 13.1: The Four Levels of Caring

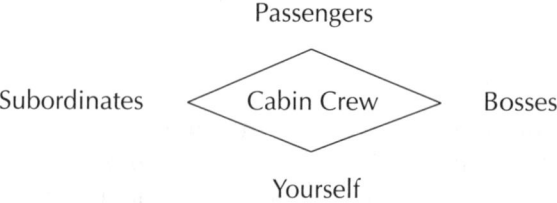

Passengers

Subordinates   Cabin Crew   Bosses

Yourself

of chief attendants and inflight supervisors in relation to their dealings with passengers, subordinates and management. The emphasis is on developing the crew's problem-solving skills to achieve the goal of improving the individual's interaction effectiveness at all levels. The four different levels of caring focused on are: passengers, subordinates, bosses and the crew themselves as illustrated in Figure 13.1.

The net effect of learning and caring about each facet of the diamond is to have one which is neither flawed nor its worth diminished. The training program is thought-provoking as it brings an awareness of the need to sense what the other party wants during an encounter in order to make it a successful one. Merely doing the routine job on board might not necessarily satisfy the passenger if the crew member is not sensitive to the passenger's needs.

Service Excellence Program

This program is designed for inflight supervisors to ensure that interpersonal management skills and concepts continue to be honed and improved. The program explores experiences inflight supervisors have had. Team leadership and coaching skills are also taught providing a structured way of making the crew-in-charge more effective coaches.

13.3.4 New Recruitment Policy for Tapping Human Resource

SIA has a crew size of about five thousand, and it is expected to double by the end of the century. With this increase, the airline needs to ensure that there are sufficient administrative staff — the cabin crew executives (check/training) — to handle the large crew base to maintain its unique management characteristic of not losing the personal touch with individual ward members. Currently, a cabin crew executive (check/training) has to monitor the performance of one hundred and eighty crew members. The situation will deteriorate unless steps are taken to remedy it.

Recently SIA has implemented a new recruitment policy known as the cadet cabin crew executive scheme which enables suitably qualified individuals to join its senior rank cabin crew. Under the new policy, candidates who are graduates, preferably with honors degrees, are invited to SIA as cadet administrative officers. The cadetship covers a period of two and a half years. During their cadetship they will don crew uniforms and function as crew on flights. After a base period of one year as a flight steward or stewardess, excluding the basic and conversion training, they will spend stints of four to five months in various ranks. Upon successful completion of cadetship, the individual will assume the post of cabin crew executive and be assigned wards to manage.

This scheme aims to supplement the cabin human resource leadership pool. Of course SIA will continue to promote suitable qualified crew to administrative positions.

13.3.5 Performance and Discipline

Performance appraisal is conducted for flight attendants, chief attendants, leading attendants and inflight supervisors. Appraisal criteria are as follows:

- Overall appearance: Hair, uniform, make-up, nails, shoes, posture and weight.
- Passenger handling skills:
  - eagerness to serve
  - attentiveness
  - responsiveness
  - visibility/helpfulness
  - professionalism in dealings with passengers, calmness and confidence, etc.
- Duties and procedures:
  - job knowledge: up-to-date procedures, circulars, aircraft and on board facilities, company initiatives, giveaways, etc.
  - performance on: bar service, meal service, food preparation/

heating First Class (PCL) meals, documentation, pre-departure duties, after landing duties.
- tidiness/cleanliness of: cabin/galleys/service equipment.
- monitoring of service standards for example serving special meals, promptness in attending passengers' requests, etc.
- quality of announcements for example diction, pace, clarity, etc.

- Discipline/conduct:
  - response to instructions/guidance.
  - demonstration of respect and courtesy to others.
  - ability to work harmoniously with others such as flight crew ground staff, handling agent, catering staff, Station Managers, etc.

- Man-management skills:
  (for chief and leading attendants, and inflight supervisors)
  - accuracy and clarity of instructions given.
  - follow-up and supervision.
  - acts as a role model.
  - coaching and guidance to subordinates.
  - crew welfare and relationships for example fair allocation of crew rest periods, dealing appropriately with crew sickness on board/ slip stations, investigates and provides information for all crew problems, gives due credit to crew who are helpful and support- ive to each others, etc. effective leadership for example team- work and positive relationships, give feedback and support to crew-in-charge when appropriate.
  - maintains a positive working environment for example offers spe- cific positive feedback, encourage involvement and initiative, han- dles crew complaints and resolves conflict positively, promotes team spirit, etc.

- Safety standards: observation of safety procedures for example.
  - checks/ensures emergency exits/equipment are not obstructed,
  - checks/responds immediately to arming/disarming slides,
  - checks/ensures that passengers are strapped-in for take-off/land- ing and during turbulence when 'Fasten Seat Belt' sign is on, assumes correct crew station for take-off/landing,
  - checks/ensures all compartments security latched,
  - ensures bassinets removed/property stowed for landing,
  - infant seat belts offered to mothers with infants, and
  - exercises/ensures proper care when opening overhead compart- ments/lockers, etc.

An appraisee is allowed to make comments on the performance appraisal and appraisers are advised to be objective and to discuss with the appraisee his/her strengths and weaknesses. Basically, it has been a fairly constructive appraisal system.

In view of the nature of the job, that is, serving passengers, it is reasonable to base crew promotion on the discipline record. This refers to all discipline letters sent to crew for breaching regulations as well as passenger complaints. It is a formal practice to view complaints from the passengers' point of views rather than the crew's so as to better understand exactly what passengers are upset about. Therefore, complaints are not investigated by people with 'line' experience, with knowledge of service procedures and practices. Complaints are investigated by people who have the ability to analyze the situations with an eye for detail to enable them to spot discrepancies and ask the right questions to reveal the truth of the situation and to shed insight on how the situation could have been better handled. However, it is important to note that staff assigned for complaints handling are those who have undergone the relevant sections of crew training and have been on flight observations so as to get a better feel of cabin situations.

13.3.6 Motivation: The WWA Scheme

Though service is every crew member's business, a motivation scheme has been set up to recognize and reward crew members who go the extra mile in serving passengers. The Winning Ways Award (WWA) was started in January 1993 to unveil the crew's specific ways of service to win the passengers' appreciation. The WWA is run for a period of three months to enable every crew member to have the chance of being a WWA winner four times a year. To qualify for the award, a crew member must have at least three compliments from passengers in any three-month period. These compliments must be written by passengers themselves, and the same crew member must not have received any complaints in the same period. To win the award, the number of compliments received must be among the five highest for that period. The best in service deserve the best in awards. The WWA winner with the highest total number of compliments for the year receives a distinctive Omega Constellation timepiece.

The top WWA winner's name will be carved in gold on the Roll of Honour which is on permanent display at the SIA Control Center.

The implementation of the WWA scheme has seen many SIA Cabin Crew's Caring Ways being generated. For example, one chief steward's winning way is:

> 'If a passenger looks at me, I would approach the passenger because he or she most probably would like to request something. Even if it turns out to be otherwise, I can always strike up a conversation with the passenger.'

Another example of good service is reflected in this quotation: 'Passengers are always right, and if you uphold this philosophy to the best of your ability, you are on the right track.' Many of the WWA winners have concluded that crew must be able to provide prompt, efficient and attentive service, must be courteous at all times and be able to anticipate passengers' needs without them having to ask.

Being fairly motivated by the scheme, many winners are apt to sum up their thoughts on walking an extra mile to ensure the safety and comfort of passengers, and almost all of them pledge to be more consistent in their work and continue to put into practice what they learnt during their training days.

13.3.7 Communication and Welfare

While monetary rewards for working as a cabin crew member are attractive with fixed monthly pay, fixed daily allowances, duty travel allowances and some other perks, the communication and staff welfare aspects are also well taken care of at SIA. A communication and welfare section has been set up in the Cabin Crew Division to promote two-way communication between management and crew, and also to provide 'door-step' welfare to crew.

The section is committed to improving communication at all levels within the division. The section has established some vital two-way communication links such as the Crew Communications Task Force and Feedback Column in the crew newsletter (*Highpoint*). There are twenty-three different communication media in the division, notably the cabin crew circulars, upfront bulletin, ward newsletters and overseas briefings.

The Crew Communications Task Force comprises representatives from various cabin crew departments and both senior and junior crew; they meet once a month for brain-storming sessions to examine where it is possible to improve the communication systems within the division. The objective of setting up the Feedback Column is to provide an avenue for the crew to raise any doubts or concerns related to the job itself, service procedures or even matters of a general nature for the respective departments to deal with expeditiously.

The Welfare/Communications Section of the division is also perpetually seeking ways to better address the welfare needs of the crew. The division's welfare activities include; the Crew Performance Hotline to attend to crew queries or problems on work matters, Crew Get-Together Overseas and at Home Base, a 'Buddy System' for new crew members, trainer/trainee one-to-one talks, counseling services and hospitalization visits. Thorough investigations of all accidents on board are conducted to ensure that there was no infringement of safety regulations, and if necessary recommendation is made for corrective/preventive safety measures.

In addition to welfare and communication, a control center has been set up within the division to grant requests for days-off on personal grounds, grant emergency leave on compassionate grounds, to reschedule flights for crew whenever the situation warrants and to assist crew in tracing lost items left on board the aircraft or in crew hotels.

13.4 Seamless Inflight Services

High-tech inflight entertainment and communications, inflight shopping and delicious meals are just some of SIA's service features. SIA's inflight customer service is characteristic in the way that it bridges the service gap between the ground and the air to form a seamless service package for passengers. Seamless service means not drawing a line between SIA's ground staff and cabin crew by seeing all problems arising inside the aircraft as the crew's responsibilities, and those outside as the ground staff's. If such an inflexible attitude is developed, ground staff will 'escape' the problems some times, and the cabin crew at other times, and the passengers will suffer all of the time.

As a seat on-board an airplane is the core product, proper seat management is an especially important area which requires a greater degree of flexibility to achieve higher level of passenger satisfaction. Two examples are given below.

13.4.1 Seat Management as An Example of Seamless Services

Exchange of Seats

An asthmatic passenger was very unhappy with the ground staff at being assigned a seat in the smoking zone. The chief steward put in great effort in persuading someone to exchange seats with the passenger instead of pushing the blame onto ground staff.

Last-Minute Seat Requests

Refusal to handle the last-minute seat request from passengers onboard caused a flight delay of fourteen minutes. A group of eight passengers were unhappy with their seating in the last row of the no-smoking zone. The flight despatcher (FD) gave the inflight supervisor (IFS) the printout of the vacant seats, showing that there were no eight vacant seats together away from the smoking zone. The FD then proceeded to the cockpit to present the loadsheet and informed the IFS that the last passenger had boarded but the IFS insisted the FD handle the eight passengers as they were not satisfied. The FD explained the situation to the passengers, and they finally agreed to try to change seats at the next station. The flight was delayed for fourteen minutes. The delay could have been avoided if the IFS had assisted in handling the last-minute seat request from passengers.

13.4.2 Other Service Examples

The following are some other examples of the seamless services provided by SIA staff.

Loading Urgently Needed Baggage Through Inflight Arrangement

Two Raffles class passengers were rushed to the gate and their urgently needed bags were rushed to the aircraft but due to the late arrival of their inbound flight there were no loaders around to re-open the cargo doors. Through the inflight supervisor's dedicated service effort, their bags were finally loaded in the Business Class (JCL) main deck closet.

Special Inflight Care to UMs

Special care was extended by the cabin crew to two UMs (unaccompanied minors) who were sisters but seated in different zones by ground staff not adhering to the procedure for handling UMs.

Inflight Handling of Excessively Large Hand Luggage

Problems of excessively large hand luggage being addressed on-board to avoid flight delay instead of insisting that the ground staff solve the problem.

IPL at Last-Minute Request

At one of the SIA's airline stations, the aerobridge to the aircraft was unserviceable. Therefore, passengers had to disembark using the passenger steps. An Invalid Passenger Lift (IPL) was provided at the last-minute in response to a request by an elderly lady who had difficulty using the steps.

References

1. SIA (1988). *Perspectives*. Singapore: SIA.
2. SIA (1993). *Higher Point*, Vol. 10. no. 3, April/May. Singapore: SIA.
3. SIA (1994a). *Higher Point*, Vol. 10, no. 12, April. Singapore: SIA.
4. SIA (1994b). *A profile*. Singapore: SIA
5. The Sunday Times (1994). July 10. Singapore: Singapore Press Holding.
6. Vandermerwe S. and Lovelock C.H. (1991). *Singapore Airline.... The Human Dimension in Services Management*. Switzerland: the International Institute for Management Development.

CHAPTER FOURTEEN

Management of Inflight Catering

14.1 Managing Inflight Food and Beverages

Hospitality and excellence are pursued by SIA in various ways: food and drink is one such way. SIA's inflight meals around the world are prepared by SIA-appointed catering centers to ensure that meals have been prepared to SIA's standards no matter which route they are served on. SIA serves around 1.5 million bottles of wine a year. A panel of experts from Britain, Australia and the United States spend several days blind-testing more than one thousand bottles of wine at periodic tasting sessions. The airline ensures the top quality wines it serves are distinctive by placing orders and buying wines years in advance. For example, SIA's consultants in 1992 recommended the purchase of a top red Bordeaux for First Class, to be served in 1998 (SIA, 1994).

14.1.1 Critical Success Factors

To cater to passengers' needs, critical success factors for quality inflight food and beverages are identified based on passengers' views in different classes. Four critical success factors have been identified:

1. quality,
2. variety and selectivity,
3. taste and
4. eye appeal and presentation.

Food quality characteristics include types of food, such as more fish and chicken, less starch, more seasonal and local items, and improved freshness, etc.

Variety and selectivity include different types of cuisine such as Western, Japanese or Chinese, and some special menus providing vegetarian or Muslim meals. Variety and selectivity has been an important factor for quality inflight catering and an item that has been frequently included in passengers' feedback comments.

Taste includes cooking styles; for example, the Japanese and Westerners favor the healthier grilled style while Asians may prefer their food fried. Ninety percent of SIA's passengers want their food with sauce (Lee, 1994).

Passengers eat with their hearts and eyes; therefore the cut of the meat, the colour, the eye appeal of the food, the serviceware and the way food is presented are all important factors contributing to quality inflight catering.

14.1.2 Quality Assessments

Assessments of inflight catering quality have been conducted by passengers who rate, against the critical factors listed above, an overall ranking on food and beverage against other airlines. They also note complaints and compliments, such as a few choices, the unavailability of choice of meals, etc.

14.1.3 Passenger Focus and Menu Plans

Passenger profiles, assessments and interviews, and feedback from staff members on competitors' activities and innovations in inflight service are the ways SIA derives input enabling it to draw a broad picture of how the airline performs according to the passengers' eyes and palate. The picture then becomes a pointer for drawing menu plans. For example, SIA used to cater more local Asian food for Singapore/Denpasar flights until it got feedback that there are more Italians, Swiss and Australians in the months of July, August, December and January, and more Singaporeans in June/December. In response to the feedback, the airline currently provides menu with spaghetti and continental meals for European holiday periods and local Asian dishes in June/December. Similarly for Singapore/Male flights the airline now caters for Japanese, Taiwanese and Chinese from Hong Kong and Australia rather than Europeans because of the change of passenger profile.

Useful input for menu planning can be obtained from passengers' feedback, such as:

- more sauce, less starch,
- use authentic names for dishes,

- more fish, chicken and seafood,
- smaller pieces of meat but same total weight for each portion so as to facilitate eating,
- revamp easy meals: no need for reservation.
- provide in-between snacks,
- avoid locally unpopular raw materials,
- avoid out of season items, etc.

14.1.4 Meal Checks

Meal checks in kitchens and on flights are conducted to enable catering officers to discover whether the caterers have been short-changing the airline by giving compact beef and inferior quality meat. SIA rectifies quality problems straightaway with all the stations. Station managers sometimes conduct reheating checks on food and hold monthly meetings with caterers.

In addition to food checks by catering officers at line stations, SIA head office also conducts the following food checks:

- audit checks on seven to eight stations every year;
- chefs are scheduled to visit each station at least once a year for meal presentations;.
- chefs also conduct reheating checks on board.

14.1.5 Training and Motivation

Currently, SIA is looking into employing a sous chef to train cabin crew on reheating techniques and improve their food knowledge (Lee, 1994). In general, special meals attract about 25% of SIA's food complaints; of this 25%, the majority of complaints, 8%, center on the Indian vegetarian meal. To rectify this situation, SIA has conducted several training workshops for the preparation and presentation of Indian vegetarian meals.

It is SIA's practice for meal presentations attended by chefs to include also special meal presentations at stations where such meals are popularly uplifted so that the airline can improve upon these meals.

SIA's subsidiary company SATS Inflight Catering, has also improved their expertise in Indian vegetarian meals by employing chefs from India.

To motivate SIA's caterers, a working group has been formed to discuss the criteria for the launch of a Caterer's Award at various line stations.

14.1.6 Cost and Wastage Management

SIA cuts costs and reduces wastage for quality improvements. Cheaper but equally good quality suppliers are recommended from various sources for consideration. Staff members are encouraged to help identify items which are not consumed by passengers, but thrown away so as to advise the caterers to serve on board what passengers really want. Some of SIA's wastage trimming program, without affecting the quality of the meals, include:

- preplating the meals,
- change the means of lifting fruits by using smaller baskets to avoid wastage.
- uplifting mineral water by passenger load,
- non-uplift of supplementary store when certain type of load is nil,
- increased sectors for undercatering,
- reduced cocktail garnishes and ice cubes, etc.

14.1.7 Long-Term Approaches Toward Quality Inflight Catering

Based on passenger surveys and feedback, SIA management has set plans to meet passengers' preferences through four approaches:

- Product improvements through design and modern production processes.
- Food quality research, control and assurance.
- Productivity improvement through technology and wastage management.
- Staff training and motivation.

The following sections present the implementations of these approaches.

14.2 Design of Market Quality for Inflight Meal Product

As a passenger-oriented airline, SIA strives to anticipate passengers' needs and meet those needs through product development and innovation. As it has often been said that the way to a man's heart is through his stomach, SIA has a long tradition of innovative design of inflight meal product as in some of the cases given below.

14.2.1 Japanese Cuisine the Japanese Way

- The cuisine: Since October 1993, SIA has offered Japanese cuisine for first class passengers flying to Japan. The passengers who select the Japanese meal are first served a selection of Japanese hors d'oeuvres. Next is the soba, followed by a clear soup. In the Shokado Bento service, the entree is accompanied by a grilled dish, a simmered dish and a vinegared dish, as well as steamed rice with miso soup and pickles. To complete the meal, a delicate Japanese dessert, fruits and green tea is served; alternatively, Japanese brown tea is also be available.
- The serviceware: The inflight Japanese cuisine is served on a full range of Japanese Shokado Bento serviceware to Japanese passengers who place much importance on presentation and form, as well as to other passengers who enjoy Japanese cuisine. The objective of the design of the service product is to ensure that first class passengers on SIA Japanese flights can look forward to a total Japanese meal in true Japanese fashion. Perhaps this is one of SIA's specific ways to gain passengers' favor.
- The market promotion: A food promotion program on Japanese cuisine was conducted to launch the cuisine and serviceware on SQ12/11 Singapore/Tokyo/Los Angeles. The theme of the promotion was 'Autumn' tying in with the beginning of the poetic season in Japan to enhance the saleability of the SQ12/11 product. The highlight of the promotion was the golden sake served with the meal; a specially designed gift, containing very tiny pure gold leaves, usually reserved only for the celebration of special occasions, was given to passengers to commemorate the program.

From the design of the core service product (the meal) to product's serviceware, and finally to the promotion program, the whole process serves as a valid example of the design for market quality of the inflight meal product to enhance its saleability.

14.2.2 The Quick Easy Meal

- Objective of product design: It is designed for First Class passengers who do not wish to sit through an elaborate meal service, but would rather have a quick meal at a time of their choice before getting down to their work. For these passengers, the 'Quick Easy Meal' is ideal. By opting for this meal, a passenger could still have the substantial meal without going through all the courses offered. The unique feature of this product is that it allows the passenger to have his meal served at a time of his choice. In other words, it provides flexi-meal-time convenience for the passengers.

- Design of core product: The meal comprises four courses: hors d'oeuvres, main course, desert and coffee/tea.
- Serviceware: The meal is served on a large melamine tray.
- Product availability: The meal product is available for first class passengers on all flights above six hours when lunch, dinner, or supper is featured. A request for this service can be made at the time of reservation. However, a passenger is still able to request the Easy Meal on board before the meal service even if he has not pre-ordered it at the time of reservation.
- Product promotion: The Easy Meal is featured in the menu in English and other languages depending on the routes. When distributing the menu card, the crew will highlight the availability of the meal to the passengers.

14.2.3 The Singapore Multi-Ethnic Cuisines

Other recent SIA inflight meal product designs include the introduction of a choice of Singapore's multi-ethnic cuisines — Chinese, Malay, Indian, Eurasian and Peranakan as entrees for First and Raffles Class passengers traveling on SQ320 from Singapore to London. Effective 27 March, 1994, passengers can opt for one of the five Singapore dishes available: Hainanese chicken rice, nasi briyani with chicken, Chinese beef noodles, roti jala and mee siam.

The introduction of the Singapore local meals also served as a curtain raiser to the Singapore Food Festival in June 1994. The festival aimed to promote Singapore as a food paradise to international travelers. Passengers on Flight SQ320 can inform reservations staff which Singapore dish they prefer for lunch or dinner when they make their seat booking. Alternatively, they can place their orders at least six hours before flight departure. During the flight, passengers will still be offered a full meal service, including hors d'oeuvres, salad and dessert, as stated in the inflight menu.

Flight SQ320 was selected because it is a daily daytime flight to London, and provides ample opportunity for the serving of Singapore meals. SIA plans to progressively introduce these local favorites on other services if there is sufficient demand for the service.

All these savory goodies are made available only through the hard work of people at the SATS (Singapore Airport Terminal Services) Inflight Catering Center (ICC), which supplies all meals to SIA flights departing from Singapore.

14.3 SATS Inflight Kitchen as a Production Center for Inflight Meals

SATS Catering has become the first flight kitchen in Asia to be awarded the prestigious ISO 9002 certificate for its production of inflight meals. The award is a testimonial to the company's commitment to providing quality inflight meals and services which consistently meet its clients' requirements. It has an unrivalled zero food poisoning record. The company supplies meals to aircraft departing Singapore; it has a clientele of fifty-two airlines; providing 15.1 million meals comprising either lunch, dinner, breakfast or refreshments in 1994. In addition to providing meals, SATS Catering also provides other support services including aircraft interior cleaning to its clients. The company employs more than two thousand full-time staff.

SATS Catering, through a strong sense of mission coupled with sophisticated facilities, has redefined airline catering and cabin services by turning them into a fine art.

14.3.1 Management by Vision: Investment in Inflight Catering Facilities

One of the distinctive characteristics that differentiates a leader from a conformist is vision. Vision involves the ability to foresee a different environment and demand and how to move quickly and meet that demand. Lady Thatcher has it; Kennedy had it; Lee Iacocca of Chrysler and many other successful industrialists and entrepreneurs have it. SIA has become the trend-setter of the industry, especially when it comes to decisions on capacity investment in the facilities development of Changi Airport. The nature of capacity decisions such as the predicaments of overcapacity and undercapacity, the huge investment and the long lead-time involved requires leadership vision. SIA has the vision. In 1975, SIA predicted the demand for an airport with a larger capacity, equipped with sophisticated infrastructure to match the pace and lifestyle of modern passengers, and heavy investment plans were quickly drawn for facilities at Changi Airport. Investment in SATS Inflight Catering Center (ICC) was one of those visionary decisions.

The Building and Plant Layout

The ICC was built at a cost of S\$87 million. It comprises an administration block of 12,500 sq. meters and a kitchen block with a floor area of almost 40,000 sq. meters which is reputed to be the largest single kitchen under one roof in the world. The ICC is within the airport security area and is less than two kilometers away from the Passenger Terminal Buildings. The kitchen has the capacity to produce fifty thousand meals a day.

The layout of the building was planned to ensure minimum crisscrossing of airline equipment, raw and cooked food. The basement of the building is occupied by the Supplies Department, used for the storage of raw materials and airline equipment. The Food Laboratory is also located in the basement. The first storey is occupied by Cabin Handling, the Production Department and the Equipment Department. The offices are located on the mezzanine level and third storey of the building.

The Catering Facilities

Maintenance of Cold Chain and Food Quality

To enable perishable raw materials, ingredients and food to be kept in wholesome conditions, SATS Catering has equipped high bay freezers, walk-in chillers and pass-through refrigerators for separate storage of different types of raw and cooked food. In addition, the outbound loading docks, consisting of twenty-six bays for hilift docking, is enclosed and air-conditioned when the doors of the holding cold rooms are opened for loading of meal carts onto hilifts. The freshness and wholesomeness of food are maintained as the 'cold chain' is not interrupted. The outbound docks air-conditioning project was completed in May 1993 at a cost of S\$700,000. The air-conditioning of the docks has also enhanced the working environment for staff and airline clients.

The Automated Tray Preset Line to Improve Staff Productivity and Maintain Food Quality

Short or late catering uplift by caterer has been one of the reasons for flight delays. SATS Catering was the first airline caterer outside Sydney to use a technologically-advanced automated tray preset line to facilitate the preparation of inflight meals for its airline clients. The line can preset a complete tray of food in four seconds. It therefore takes less than twenty-three minutes to preset three hundred and forty economy class meal trays compared to fifty minutes to preset the trays manually. It is a S$2 million project. The company can reap the following benefits from the investment:

- Increase speed and hence staff productivity
- Improved consistency and hygiene, and thus maintain food quality
- Reduced dependency on labour

Largest Automated Ware Washing System to Maintain Hygiene and to Improve Productivity:

According to Meiko Maschinebau GmbH of Germany, SATS Catering has the largest Meiko completely integrated ware washing system under one roof in the world. This is noteworthy as Meiko GmbH is a sixty-six-year-old company that has installed systems in one hundred and thirty-five airports worldwide. The washing system ensures that equipment and utensils once removed on arrival of aircraft are perfectly clean for subsequent use on departures, and that food produced by SATS Catering is presented on properly and hygienically-cleaned serviceware. One of the features of the system is that the serviceware, which runs along a dishline, moves without intermittent stoppages and does not rely on the speed of the worker to cope with the flow. Productivity is therefore increased. SATS Catering washes about sixty-two thousand trays of items and one thousand eight hundred meal carts a day. With the new machines, capacity has been increased to ninety thousand trays and two thousand carts daily.

The S$170 Million Second Inflight Kitchen

To cope with future demand, SATS Catering is in the process of constructing a second S$170 million four-level kitchen complex with the capacity to produce thirty thousand meals daily. The second kitchen will be equipped with state-of-the-art systems costing over S$37.8 million.

The Built-In Fixtures

At the new inflight catering center, all stores will be kept in a thirty-meter-high storage block adjacent to the kitchen. A three kilometer overhead rail system will link the store to the second and third floors of the inflight kitchen. Chinaware and crockery for first class and business class passengers will be sent to the second floor, the equipment processing area, to be packed into carts. Toothbrushes, headphone sets and items for first-aid boxes will also go to the second floor; so will the bar carts which are replenished with liquor and beer. Carts in which passengers' meals are stored will go to the third floor for meal assembly.

The Automatic Despatch System

In the new kitchen, staff will be able to get canned drinks, biscuits or trays from the store by merely pushing a few buttons on a computer. The automated despatch system will bring them the items they need via an overhead rail system. This state-of-art German system alone will cost S$21 million. Similar systems are in use in London and Copenhagen. The automated despatch system will convey non-perishable items such as trays, side plates, canned drinks, beer, biscuits and duty-free goods. Perishables will still be handled manually but their inventory will be computerized.

The Automated Waste Disposal System

The new kitchen will also have a S$2.5 million Swedish vacuum system for waste disposal. This system will do away food waste lying in litter bins which are full. It means immediate disposal of waste and no odor in the working area. All waste thrown into the 'cat-holes' will be sucked away, compacted and dried out before being discharged into a container trolley.

The Fully Air-Conditioned Kitchen

The entire inflight kitchen will be air-conditioned while in the current kitchen, only the cooking areas and certain parts of the operation area are air-conditioned.

14.4 Culinary Standards of SATS Catering

SATS Catering has a large pool of experienced professional staff comprising chefs and cooks. The group of staff is headed by a master chef and assisting him are the executive chefs, chef de patisserie, Japanese chefs and an Indian chef, a Chinese chef and an Italian chef. The chefs maintain culinary standards by supervising the preparation of dishes in a wide range of cuisines. Not to mention other, improvements recently SATS Catering created twenty-six new varieties of bread rolls, adding to its already wide range of choices available for bread menu. The new creations won rave reviews from well-known food critic Violet Oon, editor of *The Food Paper*. For the introduction of the delicious new breads, airline clients were invited to a sample tasting session. They were so impressed with the array of shapes and textures of the bread displayed that many of them selected the new rolls for their First Class menus.

Special medical and religious requirements are followed scrupulously. Besides normal meals, there are diabetic, low-calorie, low-salt, gluten-free, and Muslim vegetarian meals for passengers who are on special medical diet or whose meals are restricted by their religious practice. SATS has established various kitchens; in addition to the cold kitchen and pastry section where salad and other types of dessert are prepared, there are hot kitchens where Chinese, Japanese, Indian, Muslim, and Western food are prepared. The Muslim kitchen was set up for the needs of Muslim travelers. In the Japanese kitchen, the chef creates traditional Japanese favorites such as soba, sushi, teriyaki and tempura. For lovers of exotic Indian fare, the chef's specialities are a definite boon.

14.5 Maintenance of Food Quality

14.5.1 Quality Control

The Food and Research Department is the quality audit arm of SATS Catering. The department makes regular checks on the quality of raw materials delivered by suppliers and takes daily samples of processed food to monitor their wholesomeness through microbiological tests. Besides testing raw materials and food samples, lab technicians also conduct hand swabs for food handlers working in the kitchen to monitor their personal hygiene. Utensils used for cooking are also bacteriological tested regularly. The department also conducts studies to improve the bacteriological quality or shelf-life of food. This includes the development of new methods in analysis as well as the provision of technical support for troubleshooting in areas related to meal quality.

14.5.2 Food Hygiene Standards: The Bacteria Battle

SATS Catering has maintained a truly remarkable forty-seven-year zero food poisoning record. It has established a total hygiene control system to ensure that meals produced by the SATS' inflight kitchen meet strict hygiene standards.

The Total Hygiene Control System

The total hygiene control system was planned according to the Hazard Analysis Critical Control Point approach. It is implemented as follows:

- Quality control of raw materials: All raw materials are purchased based on strict purchasing specifications which include microbiological quality and are subjected to stringent quality checks by Quality Control Officers upon receipt.
- Personal Hygiene: A high standard of personal hygiene is maintained. Food handling staff are required to attend the certificate course in basic food hygiene conducted by the Society of Public Health Inspectors and in-house hygiene refresher course is regularly conducted by the microbiologist. All staff involved in food preparation need to attend and pass a medical examination which includes stool tests, hand swab tests, etc.
- Food processing and storage: Preparation of raw and cooked food are well separated. Strict time /temperature control of food preparation and strict temperature control of all cold rooms and freezers are implemented. Food cooked in a hot kitchen is blast-chilled to 5°C or below within forty-five minutes and subsequently maintained at a temperature of 5°C or below at all times. Strict maintenance of this cold chain is closely monitored until the food is uplifted to the aircrafts.
- High standard of hygiene and housekeeping: This is achieved by implementing a detailed cleaning/sanitization schedule and pest control program.
- Bacteriological monitoring and hygiene inspection: Intensive

bacteriological analyzes of raw materials, prepared airline food, airline and kitchen equipment and hand swabs of food handlers are conducted by the inhouse laboratory. Frequent hygiene inspections are conducted by qualified microbiological and hygiene supervisors on the whole flight kitchen and raw material suppliers' premises.

Control of Food Poisoning and Other Hygiene Related Complications

Much effort goes into monitoring of bacteriological quality and detecting the presence of harmful bacteria which cause the much dreaded food poisoning and other hygiene related complications. Most of the cases can be avoided by strict control of raw materials, good personal hygiene, adequate refrigeration, proper sanitization of equipment and utensils as well as strict implementation of good food production practice.

For example, Staphylococcus aureus, which is commonly found in nose and throat discharges, on hands, skin, and in infected lesions and boils, is one of the common food poisoning bacteria. However, its presence can be controlled by ensuring adequate refrigeration of foods and good personal hygiene. Vibrio parahaemolyticus has frequently been found in seafood, particularly those harvested from warm coastal waters. Control of this organism includes separation of raw and cooked food to prevent cross-contamination, thorough cooking, or proper storage of food at the right temperature. Salmonella organisms have been implicated in food poisoning outbreaks; the main causes of food poisoning are cross-contamination between raw meat and cooked food, and poor food hygiene practice.

The Food Laboratory

SATS Catering's Food Laboratory, set up in 1976, plays a vital role as part of the total system. The lab conducts a range micro-biological tests including total bacterial count, coliform, E.coli, staphylococcus aureus, salmonella, vibrios, bacillus cereus, clostridium perfringens, yeast and mould counts. The lab has been equipped with high-tech facilities such as an automatic spiral plater, a laser bacterial colony counter, a inverted transmitted light microscope, and an ultraviolet viewing system.

The automatic spiral plater is a machine which takes away the tedious manual chore of ensuring that the inoculations of bacteria samples are uniformly spread on the agar medium. The spread of samples by the machine enables the bacteria colonies to be counted by the laser bacterial colony counter which eliminates manual counting.

The inverted transmitted light microscope enables micro-organisms to be viewed and the image transmitted on a colour monitor. Unlike a conventional microscope, micro-organisms which fluoresce can also be detected on this microscope.

The ultraviolet viewing system enables speedy detection of E.Coli in eighteen to twenty-four hours instead of three to four days. A special culture substrate is split by an enzyme released by the presence of E.Coli; this causes the culture to fluoresce in long wave ultra-violet light and this can be detected by the viewing system.

With the installation of these high-tech facilities, SATS airline clients can be doubly assured that no effort is spared in ensuring that all food uplifted from the SATS Inflight Kitchens is wholesome and has been prepared in hygienic conditions.

14.6 Quality Assurance: The ISO 9002 Certification

SATS Catering management has engaged Novo Quality Services (NQS) as a consultant to upgrade its quality management system to ensure the delivery of highest quality food for its airline clients and passengers. A steering committee involving every area of the organization was formed under the leadership of the manager of the Food Research and Development Department.

Quality policy has been laid down and printed on salary slips and clearly displayed on the electronic signboard at the kitchen's tray assembly area to reinforce the importance of generating quality products. To ensure consistency and traceability, the steering committee formed working groups to develop and document supply and production procedures. The standard operating procedure of each department and the procedures linking departments have been published in the quality procedures manual, and the manual was used to audit how production methods measure against the standards set.

As a result of the dedicated effort from everybody in the organization, SATS Catering has become the first inflight kitchen in Asia to be awarded the prestigious ISO 9002 certificate. The assessment leading to the award includes management and contract reviews, document and process control, purchasing procedures, inspection and testing, corrective actions, handling, storage, packaging and delivery, quality audits and training.

As there is a need to reassess and to update the ISO 9002 certification, it serves as a tool for food quality improvement. Airline clients can rest assure that their inflight meals are catered from a facility that complies with worldwide food standards. SATS Catering has gained greater credibility with the award.

References

1. Lee, G. (1994). *Catering to Passenger Needs*. In World Station Managers Conference. Singapore; SIA
2. SATS (1993). *Excel*, 1993. Singapore; SATS
3. SIA (1994). *Profile*. Singapore; SIA

CHAPTER FIFTEEN

The Human Dimension of SIA's Success

15.1 The Vital Role of Human Behavior in Service Quality

Service involves behavior, attitudes, judgment, decisions and actions. Attainment of quality in service is dependent upon understanding, influencing, directing and improving human factors in service operations. Human errors, mistakes, and blunders are major causes of poor-quality service on the one hand and faulty operations on the other, whether committed by top management, supervisory or non-supervisory personnel.

Total quality management needs to balance the structural dimensions, namely organization hierarchy, strategies, budgets, plans controls and procedures and the behavioral or human dimensions which encompass quality leadership, management commitment, teamwork and total staff participation and the continuous quality improvement programs.

15.2 Characteristics of SIA's Quality Leadership

A review of the management practices established in all the previous chapters against the above description of quality leadership would allow us to summarize SIA's leadership characteristics as follows.

15.2.1 Bold and Prudent Leadership

From the start, SIA's management leaders took a bold step in equipping the airline with a modern aircraft fleet and modern airport facilities that shaped SIA's core products with unique quality characteristics. However, it must be carefully noted that while bold measures were taken by the SIA team, they were not brash, uncalculated ones. The SIA leadership is bold but prudent: a case in point was the astute financial investments made in property and hotel projects that were reliable but also gave SIA extra income.

SIA's success can be largely attributed to its unique leadership. Despite SIA's stake in other, non-aviation related, business interests, its managing director has firmly put down any speculation that SIA might diversify. Instead it will continue to focus its energy on its core business to ensure that it has the best trained staff, a top quality fleet of aircraft and the best product and service standard the industry can offer (SIA, 1992c). It has spurned fashionable ideas about major diversification into hotel chains, travel agencies, car retails and the like (SIA, 1992b). As far as the airline business is concerned, it is known to all that SIA only opens a new route if it is profitable, and it has rejected the lofty ideas of gigantism in establishing the mega-carrier syndrome. In a nutshell, SIA's management leaders believe that there is no point forcing the pace until a critical mass of support is achieved (SIA, 1992b). Being prudent is its mode of operation.

15.2.2 Vested Interest in its Software — The People

The hallmark of SIA has traditionally been the provision of quality services. This distinctive 'human touch' has given SIA a definite edge over other carriers and it is for this very reason that SIA greatly values its software—the people — rather than its hardware, as stated by SIA's group chairman at an annual award dinner held for long-serving staff and retirees. During its Service Excellence Training Course, the senior cabin crew were advised by the managing director that each one of them must be more than a role model capable of setting the benchmark; in other words, the service standard for others to follow. Frontline service staff have been told that they should treat each passenger as an individual and as an exception.

Ability to Attract People of High Caliber

What matters most to SIA is the ability to attract the right kind of people, to train them, to manage them, to provide them with appropriate equipment to do their jobs, and to pay them adequately.

Feedback from SIA's customers has consistently praised the high quality personnel that SIA has managed to attract. Professionalism, pro-activism, enthusiasm, empathy, initiative and perseverance are common words used by customers when complimenting SIA's staff. Some satisfied customers have even derived a conclusion: "SIA staff — they epitomize the quality of service".

The Leadership that Keeps the Followers on the 'Straight and Narrow'

As the chairman of the SIA group shared with his retiring and long-serving staff, he said that the most difficult task for management is to keep to the 'straight and narrow'; that is, to define the objectives with clarity and stick to them (SIA, 1992b). As SIA has confidence in its mission and has remained steadfast to its doctrine of free enterprise and free competition, its leadership has been extremely strict and has been terribly upset by any sub-standard performance. For almost every service sector within SIA, a comprehensive set of operational directives has been drawn up, commonly termed 'Back To Basics', for its operational staff. It is this kind of leadership that has pulled SIA through the trough of a business cycle. In many similar situations, SIA can generally manage better than its competitors and has not been upset too much by the vagaries of the business cycles.

Leadership of Duality

The SIA management practices duality leadership. It is firm and unwavering on safety; the issues of life and death. On the other hand, it is a humane leadership that is concerned with the welfare of its staff.

15.3 Management's Commitment

Management's commitment provides the company with the physical, organizational and cultural environment for business. It is presented in the form of financial investment, values and individual responsibility. SIA's management commitment has been reviewed under the topics of commitment to financial investment, to customer service, and to the motivation of its employees to support and enhance its service quality.

15.3.1 Commitment to Financial Investment

The aviation industry is subject to the rapid changes of technological development. The ability of an aviation business to react quickly to technological change is primarily dependent on its commitment of resources to manage change. Financial investment is required to maintain its fleet renewal program, to update its airline information technology and to upgrade its airport service handling equipment.

SIA's management is fully aware of the importance of skilful and prudent financial management to gather the financial strength to plan for steady and systematic growth, and less bothered than most by the cyclical conditions that prevail in the aviation industry (SIA, 1992c). A key part of its commitment to financial management for long-term competitiveness and efficiency involves identifying those parts of the SIA group that can stand alone, initially as profit centers and ultimately as independent subsidiary companies. A good example is the recently formed SIA Engineering Company. Another example is the formation of its subsidiary company, SIA Properties (SIAP). In Singapore alone, SIAP has developed and managed investment projects in excess of S$660 million on behalf of SIA group. SIAP's acquisition of commercial and residential properties overseas exceeds S$100 million (SIA, 1990b).

15.3.2 Commitment to Customer Service

Customer Service as a Quality Culture

For the SIA staff, providing outstanding customer service is a culture. The institutionalization of such a culture takes the following forms.

The Show You Care, Dare To Care and Be Service Entrepreneurs Programs

Training is conducted and booster seminars organized. Items such as the Outstanding Ground Service (OSG) brochures, OSG badges, posters and T-shirts are provided for these programs.

For the Show You Care program, the attitudinal aspects are included in the service brochure where guidelines for appearance, facial expression, body posture and other aspects of body language are provided. As the airline operational environment is eventful, the frontline staff very often have to face customers who are stressed and tense. Therefore, the major emphasis has been to indicate the need to be friendly, compassionate, attentive, flexible and adaptable. As one quotation says: 'You may not have the power to control every situation but you can control the way you respond.'

The Dare to Care program indicates SIA management's full support of its staff. To achieve a high standard of service quality, it has to be recognized that staff members sometimes will have to go beyond their training, and venture beyond the ordinary matters where there are no guidelines. That is to 'dare'. Not all outstanding service deeds have good endings. Decisions that seem correct at one point of time may turn out to have unexpected and unfavorable consequences in the end. SIA management has emphasized that it will back the decisions of frontline staff, even if they made a mistake. As long as the staff was genuinely trying to help a customer in a reasonable manner, it is acceptable that these efforts may not always turn out successful (SIA, 1990a).

The Be Service Entrepreneurs program is built upon creativity, initiative and perseverance. To enable staff to visualize these abstract concepts, management has tried, after many false starts, using stories of inventions to illustrate each point. It was not quite so simple to do as it sounds because they had to be inventions that were of service to most people, they had to be visually appealing and include the human element, and most of all, they each had to be strongly identifiable with one of the three concepts. Posters were also designed to capture the essence of the Service Entrepreneurs program. Some of them are shown in Figure 15.1.

Figure 15.1: The 'Be Service Entrepreneurs' Program

| **With creativity, a good idea travelled miles.** | **It required initiative to talk when no one was listening.** | **It took perseverence to see in the dark when others lacked vision.** |

The MD's Award in Recognition of Excellence in Customer Service

SIA's staff who have provided excellent customer service are honored as Very Important Employees (VIEs) with the presentation of the prestigious Managing Director's award — a crystal trophy. The common qualities of award winners are:

- Staff who went beyond the call of duty.
- Staff who had the courage to make decisions, and were not afraid of making wrong decisions. They were more interested in helping the passengers.
- Staff who have the milk of human kindness in them.
- Staff who displayed team spirit and good leadership.

The winners are not the only ones on the company with the above listed qualities, but they are the best of the best. They are a special breed, according to SIA's managing director (SIA, 1992d).

The OSG Competition and OSG Award

The Outstanding Ground Service (OSG) competition takes the form of an OSG Feedback, and the form is available to all participants. There are ten multiple choice questions on excellent ground service. There may be more than one answer to each question. But the company is looking for the most appropriate answer. In addition to the ten questions, question eleven is set to invite participants to give ideas and make suggestions on how they think OSG can be further improved. This serves as a tie-breaker for the competition. Twenty prizes of S$1000 gift vouchers are given for each run of competition.

In addition to the competition, outstanding staff and departments are honored by the presentation of OSG or OSG-GM Award at their respective station's annual staff function. The award, together with the OSG training course, has inspired the staff so much that some of them wrote the following rhyme.

Hey! We are SQ
We use our IQ
To give you
Customer Satisfaction

We come forward
Put in our best effort
To show you we care
And Yes! We dare to care

You pay to be with SQ
Our service is of top value
We help as much as we can
You are definitely in safe hands

Fly Singapore Airlines

Continuous Improvement in Customer Service (CICS)

The customer focus: SIA considers its customer — the passenger — as the center around which the bulk of its business revolves. Each complaint received is intensively investigated, and every station, department and staff involved in the case queried. Telexes, reports and documents are dug up and no stone is left unturned.

The SPIs and the numbers: SIA has set up a service audit unit to closely monitor service standards. Regular visits are made to overseas stations to check performance and offer advice. The service performance indices (SPIs) and the numbers of complaints and compliments are compiled monthly and quarterly. They are the numbers that the managing directors and other senior managers watch regularly and closely (SIA, 1992d). Staff are cautioned against complacency and reminded to set targets for making continuous improvements for customer service. An example would be a case where 0.64 compliments were received for every complaint which is a low and unacceptable standard. Staff are urged to set a target of 0.85 for the next period and subsequently to reach a 0.97 target. With a continual resetting of targets eventually the number of compliments will exceed the number of complaints.

15.3.3 Commitment to Staff Motivation and Development

A business organization and its employees depend upon each other for their mutual success. The organization needs the full commitment of its employees' time, knowledge and skills to fulfill its goals and to achieve its objectives of growth of sales and profits. Employees need the success of the business and its commitment to providing employment security, pay and benefits and career opportunities. A business organization must make these commitments and adhere to them over time to create the proper incentives for its employees to help make this joint effort a mutual success.

No organization will be able to render top-level quality service on a sustained basis unless it has the proper personnel policies for employee motivation and staff development.

SIA paid its employees a profit-sharing bonus, including the variable annual wage supplement, of 3.4 months' salary in 1992. The actual amount of bonus for that year for employees whose monthly salary did not exceed $1,500 was up to 3.7 months' salary. Current payment is based on the formula agreed and negotiations concluded between the management and the two unions representing pilots and administrative staff. The profit-sharing bonus is applicable to Head Office staff. The amount of profit-sharing for overseas staff has been worked out mutually on a yearly basis.

15.4 Total Participation

Modern businesses have begun to realize the total potential of all members of an organization. Individuals may be bright and make many contributions that differentiate them from the norm, but a group of individuals working together may generate even more brilliant ideas than individuals. A group's ideas, attitudes and actions are worth more than individuals. Much effort has been focused on the development of participatory management techniques such as, among others, management by objectives and management by walking around. The employee suggestion system has been widely used for the last ten to fifteen years. However, the form of a suggestion system may vary from organization to organization. For SIA, it takes the form of the Staff-Ideas-in-Action (S-I-A) Schemes.

15.4.1 SIA's Staff-Ideas-in-Action (S-I-A) Scheme

The scheme was set up to provide a formal channel by which individuals and groups could contribute their ideas to the airline operations.

Most of the SIA's stations have set up an S-I-A Committee, which usually comprises the senior customer officer, sales representatives, senior reservations officer, staff from accounts agent and administrative and supervisory staff as its members. Annual awards are bestowed on winners of the S-I-A campaign. Themes chosen for the campaigns have included 'Striving for Quality Ideas' and 'Action for Quality'.

Striving for Quality Ideas Exhibition

An S-I-A Exhibition was organized in 1992 whereby ideas for quality improvement were exhibited with pictures of S-I-A divisional and regional facilitators placed on charts to enable new staff to recognize their facilitators, and to increase the awareness of the S-I-A Scheme. Feedback from the exhibition follows.

- It is simple and worth searching.
- It sets me thinking of the ways to improve every aspect of work.
- It is motivating.
- Ideas enable us to make our jobs easier.
- Good suggestions save time and money for the company and we get the satisfaction of knowing that the ideas come from us.
- The ideas improve productivity and service, which make the company more reliable in the eyes of its customers.
- Simple, yet beneficial ideas have somewhat influenced my interest and encouraged me to have a go at it.
- It motivates other staff to participate when they see their colleagues getting rewarded for their ideas.
- With a little thinking, many things can be achieved.

Actions for Quality

Ideas would activate quality actions for operations improvement. An example of this type of achievement is stated below.

Under the S-I-A Scheme, two apron services staff managed to generate new ideas and put them in action to improve the manual emergency operating system of the joint container pallet loaders (JCPLs) used for loading cargo and baggage into the aircraft. They designed a centrally located and electrically-operated control system by grouping the buttons together to overcome the problem caused by the previous system. This helps to avoid aircraft delays caused by the breakdown of a JCPL.

15.5 Teamwork and Networking

15.5.1 Team Concept in Quality Management

As stated by Oakland (1989), the complexity of most of the processes which are operated in industry, commerce and the services places them beyond the control of any one individual. The only way to tackle problems concerning such processes is through the use of some form of teamwork.

The use of the team approach to problem solving has many advantages over allowing individuals to work separately on problems. These advantages as listed by Oakland are below.

- A greater variety of problems may be tackled, which are beyond the capability of any one individual, or even one department.
- The problem is exposed to a greater diversity of knowledge, skill and experience.
- The approach is more satisfying to team members and boosts morale.
- Problems which cross departmental or functional boundaries can be dealt with more easily.
- The recommendations are more likely to be implemented than individual suggestions.

Most of these rely on the premise that people are most willing to support any effort in which they have taken part or helped to develop.

Oakland stated that when properly managed, teamwork improves the process of problem solving, producing results quickly and economically. Teamwork throughout any organization is an essential component of the implementation of TQM for it builds up trust, improves communication and develops interdependence.

15.5.2 Teamwork of SIA for Passenger Handling

Since 1989, after the merging of the SIA-SIN Station and SATS Passenger Services, SIA has made use of the team concept to handle its ground customer servicing operations from check-in until flight departure instead of dedicating check-in duties and terminal functions to separate groups of staff.

Service teams are formed with each consisting of one duty manager, one passenger services supervisor, eight passenger services officers and eighteen passenger services agents. Staff from the 'static' areas — Operations Rooms, Transfer Counter, Nightstop Counter and Special Services Section — are also assigned to the teams, bringing the full team to a total of thirty-five staff. All the flights by different airlines handled by SATS at Changi Airport-Terminal 2 are sub-divided into flight groups and each team is assigned to a flight group. The team is deployed to handle the various stages of the designated flights from the time of check-in until final departure. Other duties include meeting arrival flights and assisting the Special Services Section in the handling of wheelchair passengers and passengers requiring the Meet-and-Assist Services (MAAS).

Each team is a self-contained unit with the duty manager in overall control. The passenger services supervisor is responsible for the deployment of staff, staff discipline and administration matters, and in turn, reports to the team duty manager.

The formation of this type of service team has instilled a sense of belonging among team members which works towards strengthening staff cooperation and morale and thus ensures the quality of flight handling.

15.5.3 Networking at SIA

Networking in SIA's context is the cooperation between two or more people or stations to ensure that a course of action is followed through so that there is no disruption to the service provided to passengers.

By the spontaneous action of a particular station in informing another station or stations of the arrangements made for a passenger, SIA ensures the fulfilment of the passenger's needs. In the course of airline operations, the key factors necessary to fulfil a commitment confidently are established contacts, effective cooperation and subsequent follow-up.

Good Networking

The following are some examples illustrating SIA's good networking effort:

- Networking between SIA and the Alliance partner Swissair in Toronto helped the staff of three stations — New York, Toronto and Brussels — pull through the 'storm of the century' in handling the flight disruptions and delays.
- A tribute to networking in overcoming the big flood in Bombay where all telecommunications and railway services were badly disrupted while an A310 Airbus could not come in to land as visibility was hovering around seven hundred meters and below throughout the day.

- Networking at work to restore stolen tickets, passports, briefcases, money, etc.
- Networking helped a passenger recover one of his cases which contained his collection of five years worth of scientific research materials.
- Other examples include station networking in actions to handle last-minute seat changes, to help stranded passengers, to help a heart attack passenger right from the start of the flight till he reached the hospital.

As a result of good networking, it is not uncommon for SIA to receive compliments from grateful passengers which reflect the warmth they felt when they were assisted. Compliments such as 'things are possible with SIA', are not unusual.

Poor Networking

As many as 15% of the complaints received stem from poor networking. This is especially important in delay handling. Passengers would like to be accurately and regularly informed of the situation. Ambiguities in communication with them can lead to confusion as has happened on a number of occasions as listed below.

- A group of seven paraplegic passengers could not use the Invalid Passenger Lift (IPL) vehicle, neither could they use the wheelchairs because of shortage. A telex was sent by the upline station before the passengers arrived, and the downline station sent back a telex to clear some ambiguities and received no reply. As a result, the connecting flight was delayed for forty-three minutes.
- During a flight delay, a passenger turned to SIA staff at the Hong Kong station (HKG) for a booking on the first available onward connecting flight: Singapore-Jakarta-Bandung. The staff member at Hong Kong station had not received confirmation of the passenger's wait-listed flight but she had not called the passenger. She had neither informed the passenger at HKG Airport before his departure that his connecting flight was not confirmed, nor advised the downline stations.

Greater Networking

Poor communication between stations, and between traffic staff and flight operations/cabin crew, has been a cause of concern pointing to a need for greater networking. SIA records different events that have happened, analyzes passengers' complaints and generates 'lessons from the case'. They are then compiled as a set of 'Back To Basics' guidelines which are published in its news bulletin, the 'Higher Ground'. Some of its lessons from cases showing the need for greater networking can be seen in Figure 15.2.

Figure 15.2: Back To Basics

Case 1: Handling Of Unaccompanied Minor (UM)

Lessons from this case:
• The decision to transfer an UM in transit to an alternative flight because of a flight disruption should be communicated to originating and receiving stations for them to contact parents/guardians.
• Before the day is out, stations should check with one another to ensure all information is received and actions will be taken.
• In keeping with delay handling procedures, get the UM to call his or her parents/guardian. The staff accompanying the UM can keep the parents/guardian informed of the situation. This is a very important

Case 2: The Missing Messages

Lessons from this case:
• Staff should exercise more care. Miri is an off-line station and staff should make sure that telex sent will be actioned by the staff there,
• A telex advice is normally adequate. however, to avoid the onus of proving that the message has been sent, it is better to allow a free phone call for the passenger caught in a flight delay.
• After a telex has been sent, the matter should only be considered closed when the other party has acknowledged receipt of the message. if time permits, a copy can also be given to the passenger.
• Proper networking would have prevented the breakdown in communication.

Case 3: No After-Care Service Done

Lessons from this case:
• Meeting passengers arriving on a delayed flight is a form of aftercare service. We should be present to assist passengers and ensure that they are taken care of right up to the end of their journey.
• At the transit station, it is all the more imperative that passengers are met if they are travelling on another airline.
• You should ensure that the immigration authority has been contacted for the necessary papers or dispensation.
• You should contact all downline parties concerned to ensure that all necessary actions would be taken.
• Proper networking ensures that there is no sudden hitch in our plan made for the passenger.

Case 4: Inconsistent Practices

Lessons from this case:
• Observe the guidelines set by head Office on waiver of excess baggage and the number of cabin bags allowed per passenger. Should an exception be made for a passenger, telex the transit station of the decision to avoid inconvenience to the passenger.
• Inconsistent practices resulting from poor networking not only inconvenience passengers but also make us appear unprofessional.
• Through proper networking. passengers will not be inconvenienced and our need for occasional differing standards of practice will not be seen as inconsistent or unprofessional.

References

1. Oakland, J.S. (1989). *Total Quality Management*. Oxford: Heinemann Professional Publishing
2. SIA (1990a). *Higher Ground*, February. Singapore: SIA
3. SIA (1990b). *Higher Ground*, May. Singapore: SIA
4. SIA (1992a). *Higher Ground*, January. Singapore: SIA
5. SIA (1992b). *OUTLOOK*, April. Singapore: SIA
6. SIA (1992c). *OUTLOOK*, November. Singapore: SIA
7. SIA (1992d). *Higher Ground*, December. Singapore: SIA

CHAPTER SIXTEEN

Training and Development: The MDC Approach

16.1 Introduction

SIA's focus on customer services can only be achieved through an unequivocal commitment to human resource development. Staff training and development is a cornerstone of SIA's human development process. While staff on-the job training has been conducted by each of the line departments, the emphasis on staff management development was demonstrated by the establishment of the Management Development Center (MDC) in 1987.

16.2 Training Philosophy

SIA's training philosophy can be summarized as follows.

1. Training is a necessity, not an option. It is not to be dispensed with when times are bad, nor postponed for operational expediency.
2. Training is for everyone. It covers all aspects of the group's operations, and it embraces everyone from the office assistant to the managing director.
3. SIA does not stint on training. They don't waste, but they don't penny-pinch, and will use the best in training software and hardware that money can buy.
4. Training is systematic and structured. An individual follows a training path that parallels his/her career progress.
5. Training is both specialized and general. Technical training is given to pilots, engineers, and functional training to staff.

SIA's spirit is strong and eager, simply because training is really so much a part of its corporate ethos (SIA, 1993).

16.3 Training Expenses

Training makes up 12 % of SIA's payroll costs. There is, in a practical sense, no other company that spends so much on training even with the understanding that pilot training accounts for a significant proportion of the SIA's training bill. The company believes that the benefits of training will accrue with the passage of time.

16.4 Training Facility: The SIA Training Center

The SIA Training Center (STC) was set up in January 1993. It is a one-stop skills acquisition and training hub for the SIA group. The $80 million training center provides centralized training for SIA group staff as well as programs for external participants. There are five training units at STC: the Flight Operations, Cabin Crew, Commercial Training, Management Development Center, and Computer Training and Development. Training facilities at STC include a cabin evacuation trainer, three cabin mock-ups, seven flight simulators, a lecture theatrette, fifty-two computer training or seminar rooms with one split-level classroom, and break-up/discussion rooms. A total of five hundred and forty-five staff members work at the center. Many of them are directly involved in training an estimated annual throughput of seventeen thousand five hundred participants.

16.5 Management Development: The MDC Approach

SIA does not aim only to develop managers to run its current business, but also prepare them for long-term effectiveness in management. Hence the motto at SIA's Management Development Center (MDC) is 'Training for Tomorrow'.

16.5.1 Concepts and Procedure for Curriculum Development

The MDC aims at developing SIA's managers to meet challenges of the future in the highly competitive global environment. As such, its curriculum is developed based on the concepts and procedure listed below:

- To recognize what the future business world would be like and what kind of challenges an organization would face.
- With this recognition, a vision of the potential future has emerged. SIA believes that the business environment of tomorrow will be:
  - *Increasingly competitive* for gaining market share.
  - A *less predictable environment* with indicators more complex and harder to read.
  - *Faced with faster changes* with the introduction of advanced technology that brings along ever changing and new rules of business competitive games.
  - *Increasingly interconnected,* with the end of the cold war that has broken down political barriers, and with swifter communications that transform the world into a global village, a single market. Thus, the need to be global in outlook is an inescapable fact of life.
- Given the above scenario, SIA realizes that to sustain the business of today and survive in the environment of the future, there are certain corporate values that a manager should imbibe. This is vital in ensuring that the human development strategy is coherent with the demands of the environment.
- The invaluable asset of an organization is its people, whose corporate values can be inculcated and whose knowledge base can be broadened through an enlightened human resource development policy.
- The MDC's curriculum is developed to cater to the above stated requirements of the managers of today and tomorrow.

The characteristics of the successful managers of today and tomorrow, as well as the associated values required to sustain the characteristics are listed in Figure 16.1.

16.5.2 Senior Management's Commitment Towards Management Development

In line with SIA's visionary way of doing business, 'training for tomorrow' is imperative. To ensure that all executives and managers go through the core programs, MDC tracks attendance and manages the nomination of staff for the programs. In a situation where the staff member continually declines the 'offer', a valid reason has to be

Figure 16.1: Characteristics of Successful Managers of
the Present and the Future

CHARACTERISTICS OF THE SUCCESSFUL MANAGER OF THE PRESENT AND FUTURE	VALUES
1. Strategic Orientation	Long term outlook. Preparedness for and anticipation of change. Profit-driven and future-oriented. Competitive. Achievement-oriented. Information management. Networking.
2. Commitment to Service Excellence	Commitment to service excellence. Concern for total quality management. Customer-oriented.
3. Creativity	Innovation. Imagination. Entrepreneurial. Prudent risk-taking. Adaptability and flexibility. Responsiveness to change. Originality. Ingenuity. Resourcefulness. Insight. Versatility.
4. Global Outlook	Internationa awareness. Political and cross-cultural sensitivity. Concern for global environment. Willingness to learn from others.
5. People-Oriented & Professional Approach	Leadership. Professionalism. Drive. Integrity. Teamwork. Openness. Ethical. Good interpersonal skills. Work discipline. Effective communication. Competence. All-round capability. Discretion. A learning and up-to-date professional.

given, and senior management is kept informed. Senior management's commitment to training is evidenced by their strong participation in their core programs. SIA management's approach has never been to stint on training.

The MDC programs are conducted mainly at the SIA Training Center. Various hotels chosen in Singapore and around the region are also used. The venues are selected for their impeccable service facilities.

16.5.3 The MDC Programs

The MDC Programs provide the cutting edge to international competitiveness. The programs aim to develop managers who will succeed in today's business environment and are prepared to face tomorrow's challenges. With this in mind, the programs are pitched progressively at each crucial stage in a manager's career. The programs are categorized into three areas, namely core, complementary, and external/*ad hoc*.

Training follows the structured path of core programs. The core curriculum is derived from a conceptual approach and aims at inculcating values which have been identified. The core programs are spread out to provide training opportunities for a number of years. In between, staff can still attend complementary programs. Participation in the core programs is mandatory.

The Core Programs

The MDC recognizes the changing needs and priorities of managers at different stages in their careers. It therefore offers a series of Management Development Programs tailored to meet each of these broadening needs at various levels of the managerial hierarchy. As the manager moves along the corporate continuum, the programs will provide deep insight into the different challenges of management at each stage of his career. They focus on generic skills, knowledge and principles useful to senior staff and valued by the organization.

Taken together, the Programs form whole, producing a total effect. The Core Programs are mandatory and are completed in a specific sequence.

Complementary Programs

These functional or skill-related courses are meant to meet the specific or operational needs of managers in their day-to-day tasks. Some of these are for self development.

External/Ad hoc Courses

These courses are public programs organized by external organizations or institutes of higher learning, which may be of interest and benefit to some departments.

16.5.4 The Faculty

Management development is a dynamic process to prepare the SIA staff to meet the challenges of a changing environment. Therefore, the programs must be applicable, updated constantly and conducted by a group of people who have an international perspective and the expertise and experience to promote the development of a 'global mindscape', the quality that is highly critical for career development at SIA. The MDC has a faculty of visiting academics and specialists from different parts of the world. There are advantages for establishing this type of faculty. It can be constantly revitalized, either as new specialists bring in fresh knowledge or as an existing pool is rotated as and when the need arises.

16.5.5 The Shared Learning Approach

The MDC aims to enhance the long-term effectiveness of people in management. As such, besides training the twenty thousand staff in the SIA group, the MDC is pleased to share its executive programs with other organizations in the region on a cost-sharing basis. This enables a rich mix of participants bringing about interaction and the exchange of ideas among corporate executives around the region. This shared learning approach has been a notable factor for the continuing popularity of MDC's programs.

16.6 Service Training for Clients: The SQ Center

In addition to the facilities at STC, a Service Quality (SQ) Center has been set up through a venture between the then National Productivity Board (NBP) and SIA.

The establishment of the SQ Center was based on a fundamental philosophy that service quality is not just for the frontline staff; it is an ideology that must permeate the entire client organization for effective results. SIA realized that to strengthen the attractions of its home-base, Singapore, as a worthy destination for international travelers, service standards in the entire tourism industry needed to be improved substantially. Unless supervisory and managerial people recognize the importance of high service standards and take the trouble to analyze the ingredients of good service, the organizations will not be able to introduce the appropriate structural and procedural changes that are essential for success.

The founding of a training organization such as the SQ Center requires a competent team for planning, development of appropriate curriculum, recruitment of qualified trainers, adoption of a sound training doctrine followed by the imaginative marketing of the courses to clients. SIA does not mince matters, and because of the strong foundations it has laid down for the SQ Center, good results were soon achieved. Organizations other than those in the tourism industry have been also attracted to the center. Prominent among them were agencies in the public sector.

16.7 The Training Award

The Training Award was conferred on SIA in the inaugural ASEAN Achievement Awards given by the ASEAN Institute. The award was for consistently providing a high standard of training to staff, which in turn has contributed to the company's excellence.

Reference

1. SIA (1993). *OUTLOOK*, February. Singapore: SIA

CHAPTER SEVENTEEN

Epilogue: Towards the State of 'Beyond TQM' in SIA

17.1 State of TQM Normalcy

The greatest injustice to TQM is to give it a 'special status'. That is the typical approach of business managers. The typical manager would usually set aside a certain number of hours a week when TQM is 'switched on' as a corporate program apart from the normal management processes, rather than a corporate way of life. However, after implementing TQM for a number of years, a business organization reaches a state of normalcy whereby TQM is accepted as the 'proven' way of managing the business. At this state of normalcy, the term 'TQM' is no longer needed. People would just speak of 'management' rather than using a buzzword like Total Quality Management (Bounds *et al*, 1994). It is a state of beyond TQM.

17.2 State of Beyond TQM

The state of beyond TQM is the state of normalcy which can be described as follows:

1. It is the state whereby an organization is able to regard quality as inseparable from whatever is being done, at all levels. It is the era when quality is no longer a conscious effort but more a natural part of every employee's daily process. There would be such thing as being 'meticulous' about work but more a highly unguarded normal standard of doing things. The employee now finds discomfort in sub-quality and slip-shod work.

2. It is also the state whereby an organization's expectations are clear, rules are known, and results are predictable. In this stage, managerial practices unconsciously flow from the principles that firmly reside in the minds of managers, practices taken for granted as the assumed way of doing business.
3. In this state of TQM normalcy, managers would continue to refine and to test new concepts and tools, further perfecting the TQM practices until there is a drastic paradigm shift pushed by big political, environmental or technological waves.

17.3 A Realization of the Normalcy of TQM in SIA

From what has been presented in this book, SIA can truly lay claim to a culture of quality. TQM has evolved from a concept to a normalcy for the people at SIA. The constant education and practice of quality has evolved a culture that makes quality second nature for all at SIA.

Quality has ceased to be separate from SIA's service operations. These two are now synonymous. As long as there is service to be provided, there is quality of a global standard in it. Indeed, quality has been so deeply imbued in the staff of SIA that it requires no conscious effort, it does not need to be forced or coaxed from the staff, but flows naturally. For SIA, the realization of the normalcy of TQM has arrived!

Reference

1. Bounds G. et al (1994). *Total Quality Management: Towards the Emerging Paradigm*. New York: McGraw-Hill

Appendix 1a: Facts and Figures on Singapore Airlines

HIGHLIGHTS OF THE SIA GROUP'S FINANCIAL RESULTS
FOR THE YEAR ENDED 31 MARCH 1995

The SIA Group's financial results for the year ended 31 March 1995 were announced on 22 May 1995. All monetary figures are in Singapore dollars.

HIGHLIGHTS OF GROUP'S PERFORMANCE

- Operating profit rose 13.6% to $931 million.
- Profit before tax was $958 million, up 9.9%.
- Profit after tax and minority interests grew 14.5% to $918 million.
- Earnings per share rose 14.5% to 72 cents.
- Shareholder's funds grew 8.5% to $9.0 billion.
- Net cash decreased 13.4% to $878 million.
- Value added increased 7.3% to $3.3 billion.

FLEET

Aircraft	Engine	In Operation	On Firm Order	On Option	Lease to other Carriers
B747-400 (MEGATOP)	PW4056	32	14	9	1
B747-300 (BIG TOP)	PW JT9D-7R4G2	5	–	–	3
B747-300 Combi	PW JT9D-7R4G2	3	–	–	–
B747-200	PW JT9D-7Q	2	–	–	2
B747-400 (MEGA ARK)	PW4056	4	2	1	–
B747-200 Freighter	PW JT9D-7R4G2	1	–	–	–
B747-200 Freighter	PW JT9D-7Q	–	–	–	1
B777	Rolls Royce Trent 800 Series	–	34*	43**	–
A310-300	PW4152	17	–	–	–
A310-200	PW JT9D-7R4CI	6	–	–	–
A340-300	CFM 56-5C4	–	17	20	–
DC8-73 Freighter	CFM 56-2CI	1	–	–	–
TOTAL		71	67	73	7

Average age of passenger fleet: five years eight months (as at 1 April 1996)

Notes:
*   Includes six aircraft intended for Singapore Aircraft Leasing Enterprise (SALE).
** Includes ten aircraft intended for SALE.

Appendix 1b: Facts and Figures on Singapore Airlines (Cont'd)

SINGAPORE AIRLINES LIMITED

ROUTE NETWORK

Americas	Europe	South West Pacific	North Asia	South East Asia	West Asia & Africa
Los Angeles	Amsterdam	Adelaide	Beijing	Bandar Seri Begawan	Abu Dhabi
New York	Athens	Auckland	Fukuoka	Bangkok	Bombay
San Francisco	Berlin	Brisbane	Guangzhou	Cebu*	Cairo
Vancouver	Brussels	Cairns	Hangzhou	Chiangmai*	Calcutta
	Copenhagen	Christchurch	Hiroshima	Denpasar	Cape Town
	Frankfurt	Darwin	Hong Kong	Hanoi	Colombo
	London	Melbourne	Kaohsiung	Hatyai*	Delhi
	Madrid	Perth	Kunming*	Ho Chi Minh City	Dhahran
	Manchester	Port Moresby	Macau	Jakarta (SQ & MI*)	Dhaka
	Paris	Sydney	Nagoya	Kota Kinabalu	Dubai
	Rome		Osaka	Kuala Lumpur	Durban
	Vienna		Sendai	Kuantan*	Istanbul
	Zurich		Seoul	Kuching	Johannesburg
			Shanghai	Langkawi*	Karachi
			Taipei	Lombok*	Kathmandu
			Tokyo	Manado*	Madras
			Xiamen*	Manila*	Male
				Medan*	Mauritius
				Padang*	
				Pekanbaru*	
				Penang	
				Phnom Penh*	
				Phuket*	
				Singapore	
				Solo*	
				Surabaya	
				Tioman*	
				Vientiane*	
				Ujung Pandang*	
				Yangon*	

SIA's route network covers seventy-three cities in forty-one countries. In addition, SIA operates freighter-only services to Chicago, Bangalore, Basel and Moscow. SilkAir, SIA's subsidiary, serves twenty destinations (marked by*) in eight Asian countries.

1 April 1996

Appendix 2: The SIA Group of Companies

THE SIA GROUP

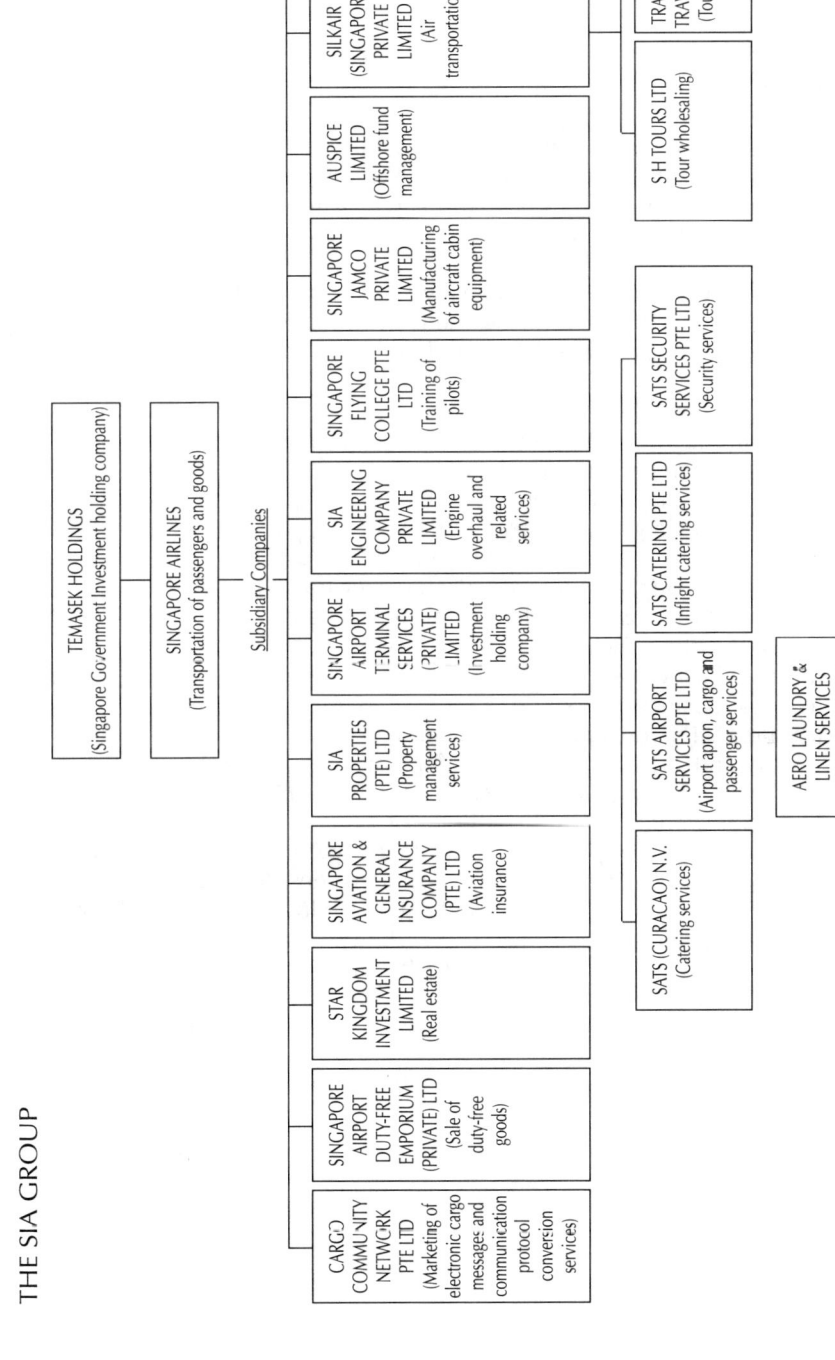

TEMASEK HOLDINGS
(Singapore Government Investment holding company)

SINGAPORE AIRLINES
(Transportation of passengers and goods)

Subsidiary Companies

CARGO COMMUNITY NETWORK PTE LTD
(Marketing of electronic cargo messages and communication protocol conversion services)

SINGAPORE AIRPORT DUTY-FREE EMPORIUM (PRIVATE) LTD
(Sale of duty-free goods)

STAR KINGDOM INVESTMENT LIMITED
(Real estate)

SINGAPORE AVIATION & GENERAL INSURANCE COMPANY (PTE) LTD
(Aviation insurance)

SIA PROPERTIES (PTE) LTD
(Property management services)

SINGAPORE AIRPORT TERMINAL SERVICES (PRIVATE) LIMITED
(Investment holding company)

SIA ENGINEERING COMPANY PRIVATE LIMITED
(Engine overhaul and related services)

SINGAPORE FLYING COLLEGE PTE LTD
(Training of pilots)

SINGAPORE JAMCO PRIVATE LIMITED
(Manufacturing of aircraft cabin equipment)

AUSPICE LIMITED
(Offshore fund management)

SILKAIR (SINGAPORE) PRIVATE LIMITED
(Air transportation)

ABACUS TRAVEL SYSTEMS PTE LTD
(Marketing of Abacus computer reservations systems)

SATS (CURACAO) N.V.
(Catering services)

SATS AIRPORT SERVICES PTE LTD
(Airport apron, cargo and passenger services)

AERO LAUNDRY & LINEN SERVICES PRIVATE LIMITED
(Laundry and linen services)

SATS CATERING PTE LTD
(Inflight catering services)

SATS SECURITY SERVICES PTE LTD
(Security services)

S H TOURS LTD
(Tour wholesaling)

TRADEWINDS TOURS & TRAVEL PRIVATE LIMITED
(Tour wholesaling & tour operations)

Appendix 3a: SIA's Awards for Quality Services

AWARDS 1991-92

- Awards SIA won in 1990 included Airline of the Year by *Air Transport World Magazine*; Best Airline in the Asia/Pacific by *PATA Travel News Magazine*; Best Carrier to the Far East and first runner-up for Airline of the Year in *Executive Travel Magazine*; third in position as best airline overall in *Business Traveller (Europe)*; World's Best Airline and Best International Airline in *Conde Nast* and Best Trans-Pacific Airline by *Business Traveller International.*

- In February 1991, SIA won three awards for financial management, information technology management and general management organized by *World Executive Digest* and the Asian Institute of Management.

Other awards won in 1991 and 1992:
- "Best Airline Program into ASEAN" – ASEAN Tourism Association
- Fifth Asian Freight Industry Awards
- Cargonews Asia, Hong Kong
  - (a) Best Air Cargo Carrier (Asia-Europe)
  - (b) Best Air Cargo Carrier (Regional, Asia) – Cargonews Asia
- Best Airline Magazine Award – Pacific Asia Travel
- 'ARRIVAL' Magazine – Airline of the Year Awards
  - (a) Best Airline Overall
  - (b) Best First Class
  - (c) Best Business Class
  - (d) Best VIP Lounges and Best Catering
  - (e) Second in Best Inflight Entertainment
- "Best of Everything for 1991" and "1991 Asia CEO of the Year Award"
- Financial World
- Top Travel Company in 1992 Travel Industry Awards–TTG Asia and PTN
- "Asia's Most Admired Company"–Asian Business Magazine
- "1st ASEAN Achievement Awards 1992–Training Awards" – ASEAN Institutes (Jakarta)
- "Best Airline in Conde Nast Traveler Readers' Choice Awards"– *Conde Nast Traveler*
- "Best Airline for Business Travel" – *Business Traveller*, Asia Pacific
- "Best Airline Award" in 1993 – *Travel Trade Gazette*
- "Best Business Class Award" – *PATA Travel News*

Appendix 3b: SIA's Awards for Quality Services (Cont'd)

1993

Business Traveller (US-based)
- Best Airline for International Business Travel
- Best Trans–pacific Airline

Business Traveller (UK-based)
- Best Airline for Long Haul Flights

Business Traveller (Asia Pacific)
- Favorite Airline (when travelling on business)

Executive Travel (UK-based)
- Best Carrier to the Far East (third)
- Best Cabin Staff (second)
- Best Lounges (second behind US)
- Best First Class (second)
- Best Business Class (second)

Asian Business (Hong Kong-based)
- Second Most Admired Company
- Top in Quality of Management
- Top in Quality of Products

Asiamoney
- Best Managed Company
- Favorite Airline in Asia (second)
- Best Business Class
- Best First Class
- Best Service
- Best Inflight Catering
- Departure Lounge (second)

Euromoney (UK-based)
- Best Airline (second)

Conde Nast Traveler (US-based)
- Best Airline (sixth consecutive year)

Ministry of Transport (Taiwan) Survey on Passenger Satisfaction
- Top Carrier

Ab-road Airline Image Survey (Japan-based)
- Would like to use again
- Would like to use in future (second to US)
- Inflight Service
- Inflight Meals

Appendix 3c: SIA's Awards for Quality Services (Cont'd)

1994

Air Transport World (US-based)
– Best Airline for twenty years of excellence in internationl service

Business Traveller (HKG-based)
– Favorite Airline (third consecutive year)
– Suitability of destinations served (first)
– Convenience of Schedules (first)
– Cabin Crew (first)
– Awareness of needs of Business Traveller (first)
– Quality of Advertising (first)

Executive Travel (UK-based)
– Best Carrier to the Far East
– Best First Class
– Best Lounges
– Most Efficient Cabin Crew
– Best Ground/Check-in staff

Travel Weekly (UK-based)
– Best Airline to Asia

Nipo Survey of Business Travellers (Netherlands-based)
– Favorite Airline

PATA Travel Awards
– Best Airline
– Best Airline (Business Class)
– Best Incentive Airline

World Travel Awards 1994 (TTG)
– Top Asia/Pacific Airline
– World's Leading Airline (second to BA)

Business Weekly (Taiwan-based)
– Excellent Crew Performance
– Seating Comfort (third behind CI and BR)
– Baggage Handling (second behind CI)
– Punctuality (second behind CI)
– Excellent Overall Performance

Appendix 3c: SIA's Awards for Quality Services (Cont'd)

Flight Performance Review (UK-based)
– Leading carrier for business class seating and cabin crew on
  Southeast Asia routes

Travel Industry Globe Awards
– Best Airline to Asia

ABM Business Travellers Poll (Australian-based)
– Best Service (second to QF)
– Most Punctual Airline (second to QF)
– Best Value (second to QF)
– Best Schedules (second to QF)
– Preferred Airline to Asia (second to QF)

Appendix 4a: SIA's Competitive Scenario

No. 10/95   22 May 1995

FINANCIAL POSITION

The Group's financial position remains strong. As at 31 March 1995, shareholders' funds of the Group stood at $8,986 million, up $707 million (+8.5%) from 31 March 1994.

The Group's net cash fell $136 million (-13.4%) to $878 million at 31 March 1995 mainly because of payments for aircraft purchases, SIA supplies center, the fifth airfreight terminal, second inflight kitchen, and second hangar.

Total assets of the Group amounted to $12,127 million, an increase of $1,173 million (+10.7%) from a year ago. Return on total assets was higher at 8.0% against 7.6% in 1993-94.

ROUTE DEVELOPMENT

In June 1994, the Airline resumed service to Abu Dhabi after a break of eight years, with a twice weekly B747 service routed via Colombo.

Strong growth in intra-Asia travel continued and underpinned capacity expansion for SIA. With the opening of Osaka's new Kansai International Airport in September, SIA introduced five additional weekly services to the Japanese city from Singapore. A further three flights were added in January 1995, bringing the frequencies of B747 services on the route to twice daily. Elsewhere in Asia, additional frequencies were introduced to Denpasar, Dhaka, Hiroshima, Ho Chi Minh City, Hong Kong, Manila, Seoul and Surabaya.

On long-haul routes, the frequency of the airline's trans-Pacific services between Singapore and Los Angeles was increased to twice daily in April 1994, with the launch of an additional weekly service via Taipei.

In October 1994, three additional weekly flights – all departing Singapre in the morning – were introduced on the Singapore-Sydney route, bringing the total mumber of services on the route to ten weekly. Passengers on this 'Flying Start to Sydney' service enjoyed features similar to those introduced earlier on the 'Flying Start to London' service. Additional services to Perth were introduced in October 1994 and March 1995, bringing the frequency of services on the route to eleven weekly.

Appendix 4b: SIA's Competitive Scenario (Cont'd)

FLEET DEVELOPMENT

In June 1994, SIA made headlines around the world by placing a US$10.3 billion order for fifty-two aircraft — twenty-two Boeing 747-400s (Megatop 747s) and thirty Airbus A340-300Es — for delivery between 1996 and 2003. The order was an expression of the Airline's faith in the long-term health of the aviation industry and its own promising future.

The order covers eleven Megatop 747s on firm order and eleven on option from Boeing, and ten A340-300Es on firm order and twenty on option from Airbus Industries. The Megatop 747s will be powered by Pratt & Whitney PW4056 engines, and the A340-300Es by CFM56-5C4 engines. In each case, SIA can convert the optional orders to other aircraft types.

SIA expects to finance the entire purchase from its internally generated cash flow, as in the past, but if appropriate the airline will consider borrowing or lease financing.

SIA maintains one of the largest B747 fleets in the world, and it will be composed entirely of B747-400s by 1997 or earlier. SIA will be the largest operator in the world of B747-400s by the end of 1995.

During the year, SIA took delivery of eight B747-400 aircraft-five Megatop 747 passenger aircraft and three Boeing 747-400 freighters (named Mega Arks). The airline also took delivery of two Airbus A310-300 aircraft in the year.

Although the market for used aircraft continued to be weak, the Airline found several clients for leases. As at 31 March 1995, three B747-200, two B743-300, one B747-400 and one B747-200 freighter aircraft were on lease to other airlines.

In early 1995, two B747-200 freighters were sold, and two B743-300 aircraft leased by the airline were returned to the lessors at the expiry of the leases.

As at 31 March 1995, SIA's fleet comprised sixty-six aircraft: twenty-eight Megatop 747s, seven Boeing B747-300s (Big Top 747s), three B747-300 Combis, two B747-200s, seventeen Airbus A310-300s, four A310-200s, three Mega Ark freighters, one B747-200 freighter and one B737-300 freighter. The average age of the SIA fleet was five years, keeping it the youngest of any major airline in the world.

Appendix 5: The SIA Organizational Chart

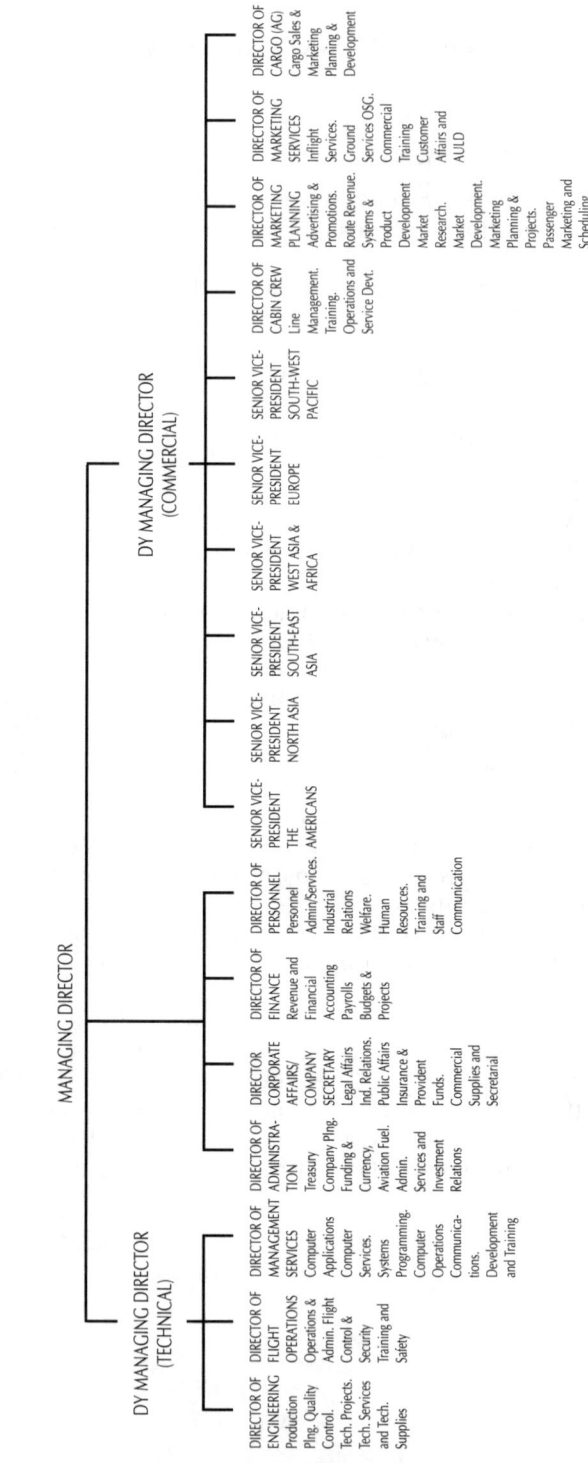

CHAIRMAN

DEPUTY CHAIRMAN

MANAGING DIRECTOR

DY MANAGING DIRECTOR (TECHNICAL)

DY MANAGING DIRECTOR (COMMERCIAL)

DIRECTOR OF ENGINEERING
Production Png. Quality Control. Tech. Projects. Tech. Services and Tech. Supplies

DIRECTOR OF FLIGHT OPERATIONS
Operations & Admin. Flight Control & Security Training and Safety

DIRECTOR OF MANAGEMENT SERVICES
Computer Applications Computer Services. Systems Programming. Computer Operations Communications. Development and Training

DIRECTOR OF ADMINISTRATION
Treasury Company Png. Funding & Currency. Aviation Fuel. Admin. Services and Investment Relations

DIRECTOR CORPORATE AFFAIRS/ COMPANY SECRETARY
Legal Affairs Ind. Relations. Public Affairs Insurance & Provident Funds. Commercial Supplies and Secretarial

DIRECTOR OF FINANCE
Revenue and Financial Accounting Payrolls Budgets & Projects

DIRECTOR OF PERSONNEL
Personnel Admin.Services. Industrial Relations Welfare. Human Resources. Training and Staff Communication

SENIOR VICE-PRESIDENT THE AMERICANS

SENIOR VICE-PRESIDENT NORTH ASIA

SENIOR VICE-PRESIDENT SOUTH-EAST ASIA

SENIOR VICE-PRESIDENT WEST ASIA & AFRICA

SENIOR VICE-PRESIDENT EUROPE

SENIOR VICE-PRESIDENT SOUTH-WEST PACIFIC

DIRECTOR OF CABIN CREW
Line Management. Training. Operations and Service Devt.

DIRECTOR OF MARKETING PLANNING
Advertising & Promotions. Route Revenue. Systems & Product Development Market Research. Market Development. Marketing Planning & Projects. Passenger Marketing and Scheduling

DIRECTOR OF MARKETING SERVICES
Inflight Services. Ground Services OSC. Commercial Training Customer Affairs and AULD

DIRECTOR OF CARGO (AC)
Cargo Sales & Marketing Planning & Development

Appendix 6: Organizations for Quality Control at SIA

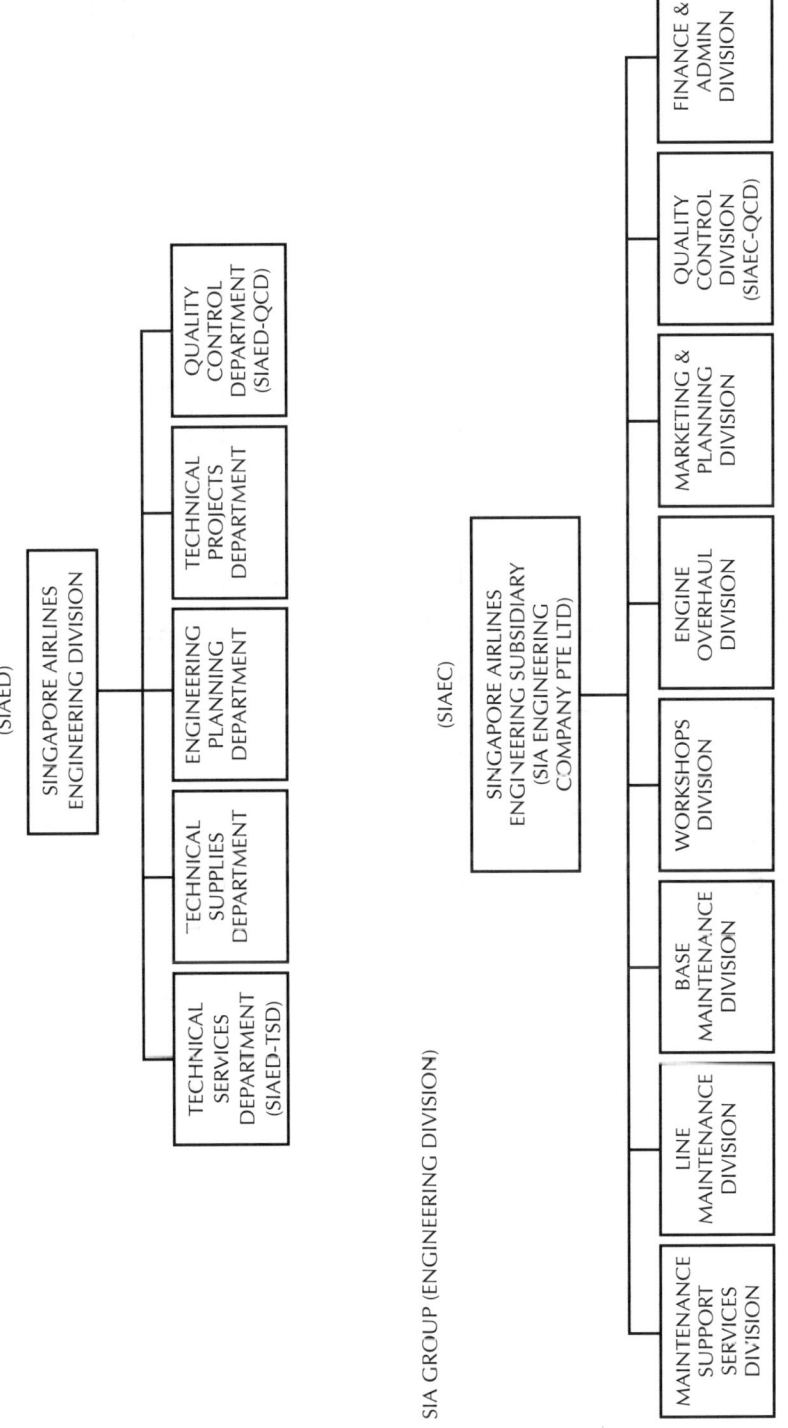

(SIAED)

SINGAPORE AIRLINES ENGINEERING DIVISION

| TECHNICAL SERVICES DEPARTMENT (SIAED-TSD) | TECHNICAL SUPPLIES DEPARTMENT | ENGINEERING PLANNING DEPARTMENT | TECHNICAL PROJECTS DEPARTMENT | QUALITY CONTROL DEPARTMENT (SIAED-QCD) |

(SIAEC)

SINGAPORE AIRLINES ENGINEERING SUBSIDIARY (SIA ENGINEERING COMPANY PTE LTD)

SIA GROUP (ENGINEERING DIVISION)

| MAINTENANCE SUPPORT SERVICES DIVISION | LINE MAINTENANCE DIVISION | BASE MAINTENANCE DIVISION | WORKSHOPS DIVISION | ENGINE OVERHAUL DIVISION | MARKETING & PLANNING DIVISION | QUALITY CONTROL DIVISION (SIAEC-QCD) | FINANCE & ADMIN DIVISION |

Appendix 7: Quality Control Division

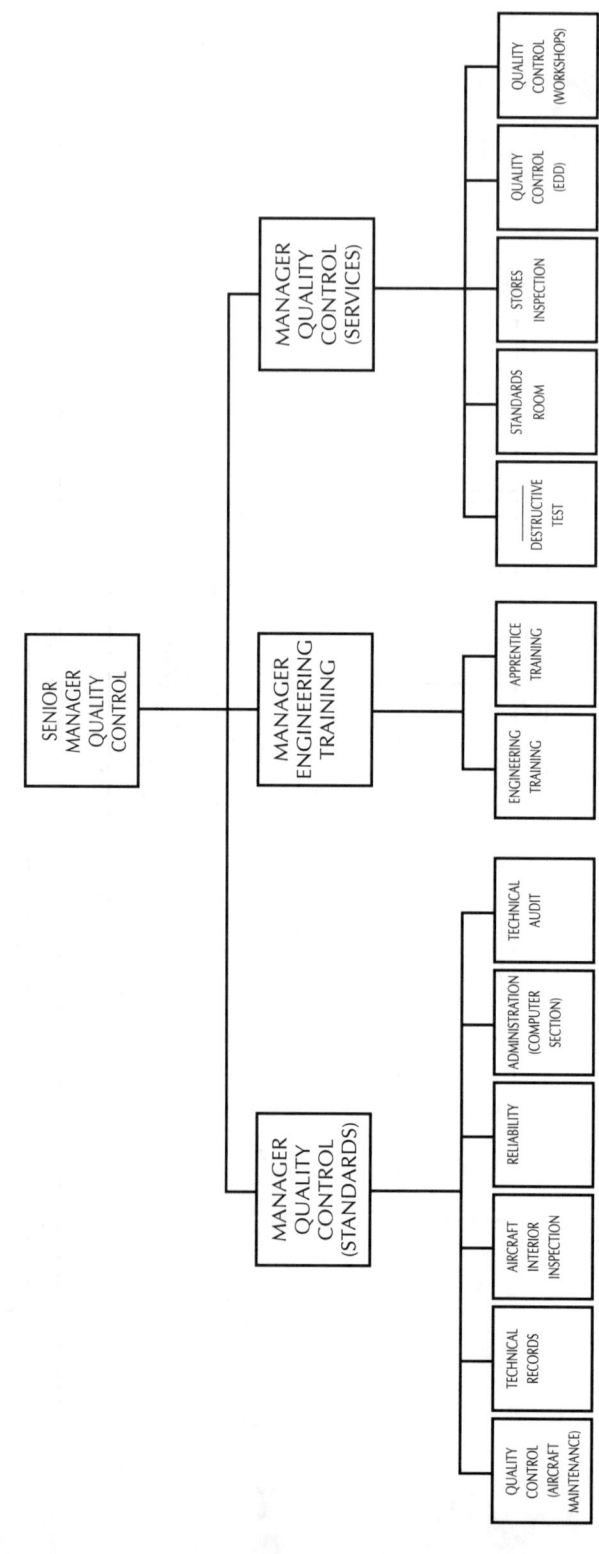

Appendix 8: SIA Aircraft Performance Data Sheet

SINGAPORE AIRLINES

No. 430500

9V —		N ←		TAKEOFF	MAX	ACTUAL	QNH	OAT°C	CLIMB DERATION
SECT. S E L - S I N	SQ 0 1 7	EPR/N1	1 1 · 5 4	1 · 4 0	1 0 0 2	+ 2 5	0 · 00 0 00

	DA	MO	YR	A P U	START (SEC)	E G T	PEAK	NO LOAD		TANK	1	2	3	4
DATE(Z)	2 2	0 6	9 5		5 0		8 1 0 4 4 0		FLUID UPLIFT	OIL	0 0	0 0	0 C	0 0
CAPT MARAIS J.S	E/O WONG CK				OAT°C + 2 5				°QTS/LITRES	HYD	0 0	0 0	0 0	0 0

TIME(Z)	TAT	ALT		MACH	IAS			MACH	IAS	A/C GROSS WT
1 0 4 0	- 9 6 7	3 1 0	CAPT	8 4 7 3 1 1		F/O	8 4 9 3 1 8	9 2 5 0 0

ENGINE	1	2	3	4		SYSTEM	1	2	3	4
EPR	1 · 2 7 5	1 · 2 8 0	1 2 7 5	1 · 2 7 5	O QTY	6 · 8	6 · 8	7 · 8	3 · 8
N1	0 9 0 5	0 9 0 7	0 9 0 7	0 9 0 7	I TEMP	0 9 0	0 8 5	0 7 5	0 8 5
EGT	4 7 2	4 8 2	4 8 0	4 7 5	L PRESS	5 0	5 3	5 2	5 1
F/F	3 0 9 0	3 2 4 0	3 1 8 0	3 2 4 0	HYD TEMP	6 5	6 5	6 5	6 5
N2	0 9 2 0	0 9 2 0	0 9 1 7	0 9 2 4	HYD QTY	0 8 5	0 6 3	0 5 0	0 6 8
AVM	0 · 3	0 · 5	0 · 6	0 · 5	COMP DISCHARGE	0 8 5	0 9 0	0 9 0	No. X
BLEED	3 · 0 PACKS	3 · 0 PACKS	3 · 0 PACKS	3 · 0 PACKS	PACK AIRFLOW	2 5	2 7	2 7	PACK OFF
					OXYGEN: CREW	1 8 5 0	OXYGEN: PAX	1 6 0 0

MAG HDG	RMI	HSI	1 2 1 6 · 5 STBY COMPASS 2 2 0		TRIM UNITS		
CAPT	2 2 0 2 2 1	TRUE HDG INS	2 2 1 6 · 2 LAT 2 6 ° 3 4 4 N	AILERON	LEFT WING DOWN	RIGHT WING DOWN
F/O	2 2 0 2 2 0		3 2 1 5 · 9 LONG 1 2 2 ° 3 6 · E	RUDDER	NOSE LEFT	NOSE RIGHT

	TOC	APU	GUTAN	BVOG				TOD	CHOCKS
TIME (Z)	START 09:30	10:51	12:23	13:06				14:10	
ALT/INTERVAL	310 40	30 81	310 92	310 43				310 64	
FUEL USED 1	2440	26580	11090	13230				16240	16950
2	2470	6750	11470	13700				16720	17550
3	2420	6630	11310	13500				16540	17250
4	2460	6750	11590	13840				16960	17280
FUEL AT START	82300 82300	82300	82300	82300				82300	82300
FUEL USED	9790	26180	45460	54270				66510	69020
FUEL REMAINS	72510	55570	36840	28030				15790	13280
ZERO FUEL WT	235600 235600	235600	235600	235600				235600	235600
AUW	317900 308110	291170	272440	263630				251390	248880
EST LDG WT	249800	25100	250400	251000				250000	
2/3 ENG ALT	28000	29500	31300	32200					
ISA DEV MCT	+18 53	+13 58	+15 64	+14 54					
2R									
1R	1·60	1·60	1·60	1·60	1·60			0·80	
1	13·40	12·90	12·50	7·50	5·40			3·20	3·20
2	26·20	21·80	14·00	9·40	6·90			4·10	3·40
CTR									
3	26·2	22·00	13·90	9·30	6·80			4·00	3·30
4	13·30	12·90	12·50	7·40	5·10			2·70	2·60
4R	1·60	1·60	1·60	1·60	1·60			6·80	
3R									
TOTAL	82·30	72·80	56·10	36·80	0			15·60	12·50

REASON FOR FULL POWER TAKEOFF: N/A

INFO FOR NEXT EO-ENGINEERING: NIL

WEIGHT & BALANCE CHECK		
	WT (KG)	MAC (%)
WT & BAL SYS	NIL	
LOADSHEET		

CHOCKS OFF 0 8 5 9 Z

TAKEOFF 0 9 0 6 Z

LANDING 1 1 6 3 5 Z

CHOCKS ON 1 6 4 5 Z

OM 25.6.86

19

Form ENG 197 J

251

Appendix 9: SIA Aircraft Performance Analysis

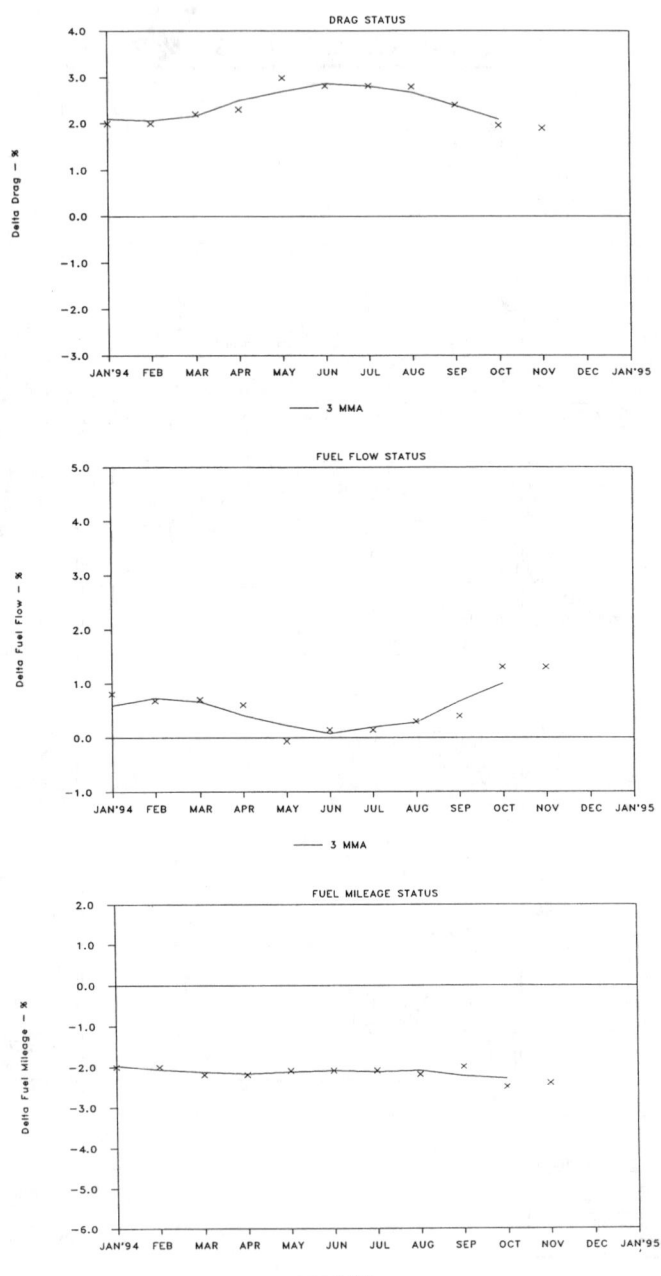

Appendix 10: SIA Engine Performance Analysis

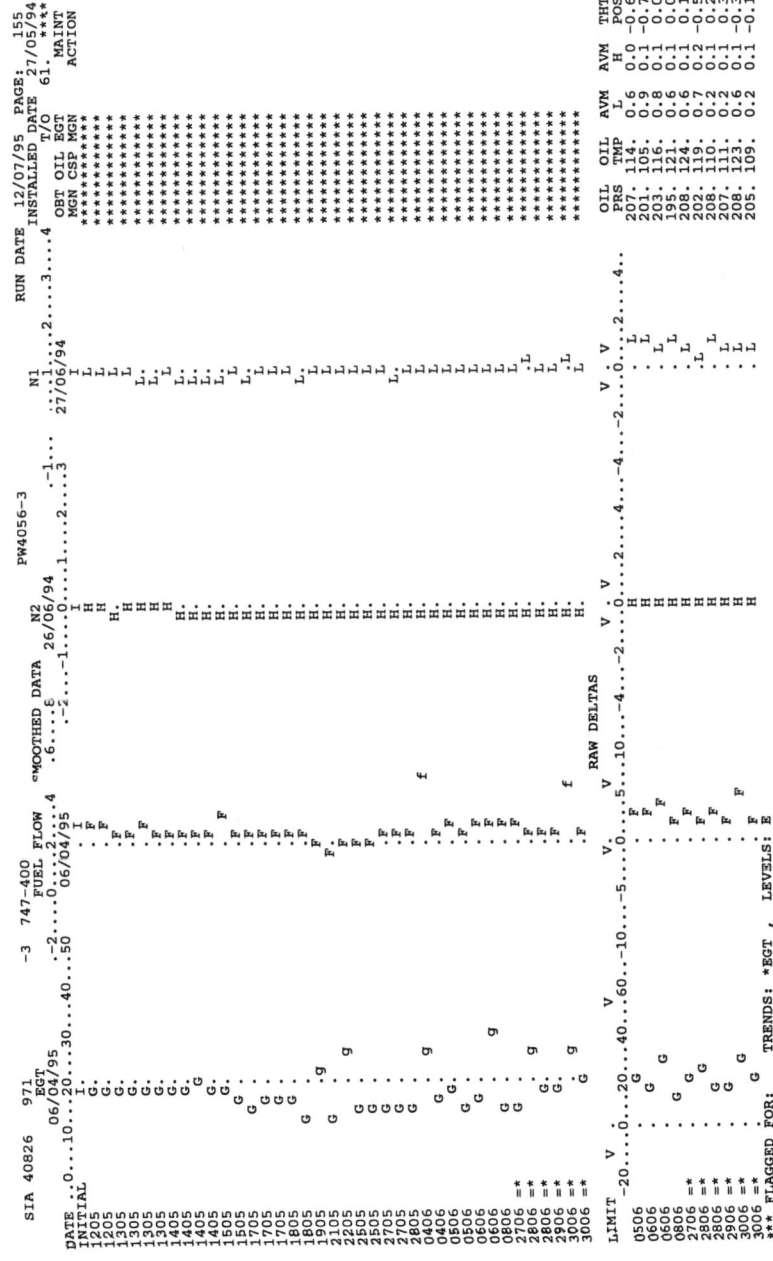

Appendix 11: SIA Compass Performance Analysis

B747 IRU MHDG PERFORMANCE REPORT   < 34 >

ACID	FLT	FM	FLCT	DATE	UTC	FROM	TO	GWT	CODE
	0011	ER	0182	13JUL95	110618	RJAA	WSSS	2885	3401

PALT	CAS	MACH	TAT	LAT	LON	THDG	VER
034960	293.6	.856	−08.75	N33031	E137003	−113.1	S503A513D0000

CHDG (COMPASS MHDG)
0250

IRU	MHDG	LAT	LON
L	−106.9	N33031	E137003
R	−106.9	N33026	E137004
C	−106.9	N33030	E137006

Appendix 12: A Sample of SIA's Pireps

			PIREPS PER 1000 DEPARTURES					
		SQ	JAN		FEB		MAR	
ATA	SYSTEM	ALERT	NO.	RATE	NO.	RATE	NO.	RATE
21	AIRCOND & PRESSN	16.6	13	7.6	19	12.0	20	11.1
22	AUTO FLIGHT	10.0	7	4.1	8	5.1	5	2.8
23	COMMUNICATION	27.0	17	10.0	20	12.6	39	21.7
24	ELECTRICAL POWER	13.4	10	5.9	16	10.1	24	13.4
25	EQUIPT & FURNISHING	10.0	6	3.5	4	2.5	5	2.8
26	FIRE PROTECTION	10.0	2	1.2	6	3.8	14	7.8
27	FLIGHT CONTROL	11.0	8	4.7	3	1.9	4	2.2
28	FUEL	12.9	8	4.7	8	5.1	7	3.9
29	HYDRAULIC POWER	10.0	5	2.9	6	3.8	8	4.5
30	ANTI-ATMOSPHERICS	10.0	8	4.7	4	2.5	6	3.3
31	INSTRUMENTS	13.1	14	8.2	6	3.8	10	5.6
32	LANDING GEAR	10.0	5	2.9	10	6.3	9	5.0
32	WHEELS & BRAKES*	10.0	1	0.6	3	1.9	4	2.2
33	LIGHTING	29.9	43	25.2	39	24.6	51	28.4
34	NAVIGATION	26.9	41	24.0	31	19.6	28	15.6
35	OXYGEN	10.0	1	0.6	1	0.6	–	–
36	PNEUMATICS	16.3	10	5.9	13	8.2	25	13.9
38	WATER	10.0	–	–	1	0.6	1	0.6
45	CENTRAL MAINT SYS	10.0	1	0.6	3	1.9	1	0.6
49	APU	10.0	5	2.9	4	2.5	7	3.9
51	STRUCTURE	10.0	–	–	–	–	–	–
52	DOORS	10.0	–	–	–	–	2	1.1
53	FUSELAGE	10.0	–	–	–	–	1	0.6
54	NACELLES	10.0	–	–	–	–	–	–
55	STABILIZER	10.0	–	–	–	–	–	–
56	WINDOWS	10.0	–	–	1	0.6	–	–
57	WINGS	10.0	1	0.6	–	–	–	–
71	PWR PLANT GENERAL	10.0	–	–	–	–	–	–
72	ENGINE	10.0	1	0.6	–	–	1	0.6
73	FUEL CONTROL	12.7	18	10.6	19	12.0	10	5.6
74	IGNITION	10.0	9	5.3	6	3.8	5	2.8
75	AIR	10.0	–	–	1	0.6	1	0.6
76	ENGINE CONTROL	10.0	–	–	–	–	–	–
77	INDICATING	10.0	2	1.2	1	0.6	6	3.3
78	EXHAUST	10.0	1	0.6	2	1.3	1	0.6
79	OIL	10.0	6	3.5	3	1.9	5	2.8
80	STARTING	10.0	3	1.8	4	2.5	3	1.7

*EXCLUDING NORMAL WEAR

Appendix 13: Calculation of Reliability Alert Levels Based on Pireps

Example 1 - Pilot Reports (Pireps) by Aircraft System per 1,000 Flight Hours

Method: Alert Level per 1,000 flight hours = Mean of the three monthly Running Average 'Pirep' Rates per 1,000 flight hours (for past twelve months) plus three Standard Deviations.

System: Aircraft Fuel System

Month	Pireps (monthly)	Pireps (three months cumulative totals)	Flight Hours (monthly)	Flight Hours (three months cumulative totals)	Pirep Rate per 1,000 hr (three months running average) (x)
Nov	42	—	2,400	—	—
Dec	31	—	2,320	—	—
Jan	58	131	2,350	7,070	18
Feb	46	135	2,300	6,970	19
Mar	58	162	2,560	7,210	22
Apr	26	130	2,600	7,460	17
May	42	126	2,750	7,910	16
Jun	65	133	3,100	8,450	16
Jul	78	185	2,880	8,730	21
Aug	74	217	2,700	8,680	25
Sep	58	210	3,000	8,580	24
Oct	54	186	2,650	8,350	22
Nov	35	147	2,610	8,260	18
Dec	46	135	2,330	7,590	18

N(months) = 12
Σ = Totals

(x)		$(x - \bar{x})$	$(x - \bar{x})^2$
18		−2	4
19		−1	1
22		2	4
17	MEAN$(\bar{x}) = \dfrac{\Sigma x}{N}$	−3	9
16		−4	16
16		−4	16
21	$= \dfrac{236}{12}$	1	1
25		5	25
24		4	16
22	= 19.67 (rounded to 20)	2	4
18		−2	4
18		−2	4

$\Sigma x = \underline{236}$ $\qquad\qquad\qquad\qquad\qquad\qquad \Sigma(x - \bar{x})^2 = \underline{104}$

STANDARD DEVIATION (SD) = $\sqrt{\dfrac{\Sigma(x - \bar{x})^2}{N}} = \sqrt{\dfrac{104}{12}} = \sqrt{8.67} = 2.94$

3 SD = 8.82 (rounded to 9)

ALERT LEVEL = Mean + 3 SD = 20 + 9 = $\underline{29}$

Appendix 14: Calculation of Reliability Alert Levels Based on Pireps (Cont'd)

Example 2 - Pilot Reports (Pireps) by Aircraft System per 1,000 Flight Hours

Method: Alert Level per 1,000 flight hours = The Mean (as in Example 1), plus the Standard Deviation of the 'Mean of the Means', plus three Standard Deviations of the Mean.

System: Aircraft Fuel System

Pirep Rate Per:1,000 hr- 3 months running Av. (x)	Mean of x (X)	Difference of X from $\overline{X}$ (D)	(D²)
18	18.5	1.3	1.69
19	20.5	0.7	0.49
22	19.5	0.3	0.09
17	16.5	3.3	10.69
16	16.0	3.8	14.44
16	18.5	1.3	1.69
21	23.0	3.2	10.24
25	24.5	4.7	22.09
24	23.0	3.2	10.24
22	20.0	0.2	0.04
18	18.0	1.7	2.89
18			
	218.0 = ΣX	23.7 = ΣD	74.79 = Σ(D²)

N (months) now = 11 and thus $\overline{X}$ (the mean of the means) will

$$= \frac{\Sigma X}{N} = \frac{218}{11} = \underline{19.8}$$

Σ = Totals

STANDARD DEVIATION OF MEAN OF MEANS

$$= \sqrt{\frac{\Sigma(D^2)}{N} - \left(\frac{\Sigma D}{N}\right)^2} = \sqrt{\frac{74.79}{11} - \left(\frac{23.7}{11}\right)^2}$$

$$= \sqrt{6.80 - 4.64} \qquad = \underline{1.47}$$

Therefore ALERT LEVEL = MEAN (x) ÷ STANDARD DEVIATION OF MEANS OF MEANS ($\overline{X}$) ÷ 3 SD

$$= 19.67 \text{ (as in Example1)} ÷ 1.47 ÷ 8.82 \text{ (as in Example 1)}$$

$$= 29.96 \text{ (rounded to 30)}$$

Appendix 15a: Calculations of Reliability Alert Levels Based on Components Unscheduled Removals

Example 3 - Component Unscheduled Removals by Individual Components in a Three-Monthly Period

Method: Alert Level = 95% cumulative probability of the Poisson Distribution based on past twenty-one months experience* to provide an Alert Level for use as a three-monthly period of comparison.

(a) Component: Auto-pilot Pitch Amplifier

number of components per aircraft,	$n = 1$
number of unscheduled removals in past twenty-one months,	$N = 62$
fleet utilization hours in past twenty-one months,	$H = 36840$
number of component running hours in past twenty-one months,	$T = (n5H) = 36840$
fleet utilization hours in current three months,	$h = 5895$
number of component running hours in current three months,	$t = (n5h) = 5895$
number of unscheduled removals in current three months,	$x = 12$

Mean unscheduled removal rate, $\lambda = \dfrac{N}{T} = 0.00168$

Expected number of unscheduled removals in current three months

$$= \lambda t.$$
$$= 0.0016855895$$
$$= 9.9 \text{ (rounded to 10)}$$

Referring to Figure B1 by entering the graph at $\lambda t = 10$ the intersection with 0.95 (95%probability) gives the maximum acceptable number of unscheduled component removals (A value) for the three month period as fifteen.

By comparing the current value of $x = 12$ one can see that an 'alert' situation does not exist for this component.

(b) Component: Temperature Control Valve
$n = 3, N = 31, H = 36840, T = 3 \times 36840 = 110520, h = 5895,$
$t = 3 \times 5895 = 17685, x = 9$

$\lambda = \dfrac{31}{110520} = 0.00028, \lambda t = 0.00028 \times 17685 = 5.01$ (rounded to 5)

from graph, acceptable A value = 8. Current value of $x = 9$, therefore Alert Level is exceeded.

Appendix 15b: Calculations of Reliability Alert Levels Based on Components Unscheduled Removals (Cont'd)

PROBABILITY OF EXACT VALUE OF A, OR SMALLER

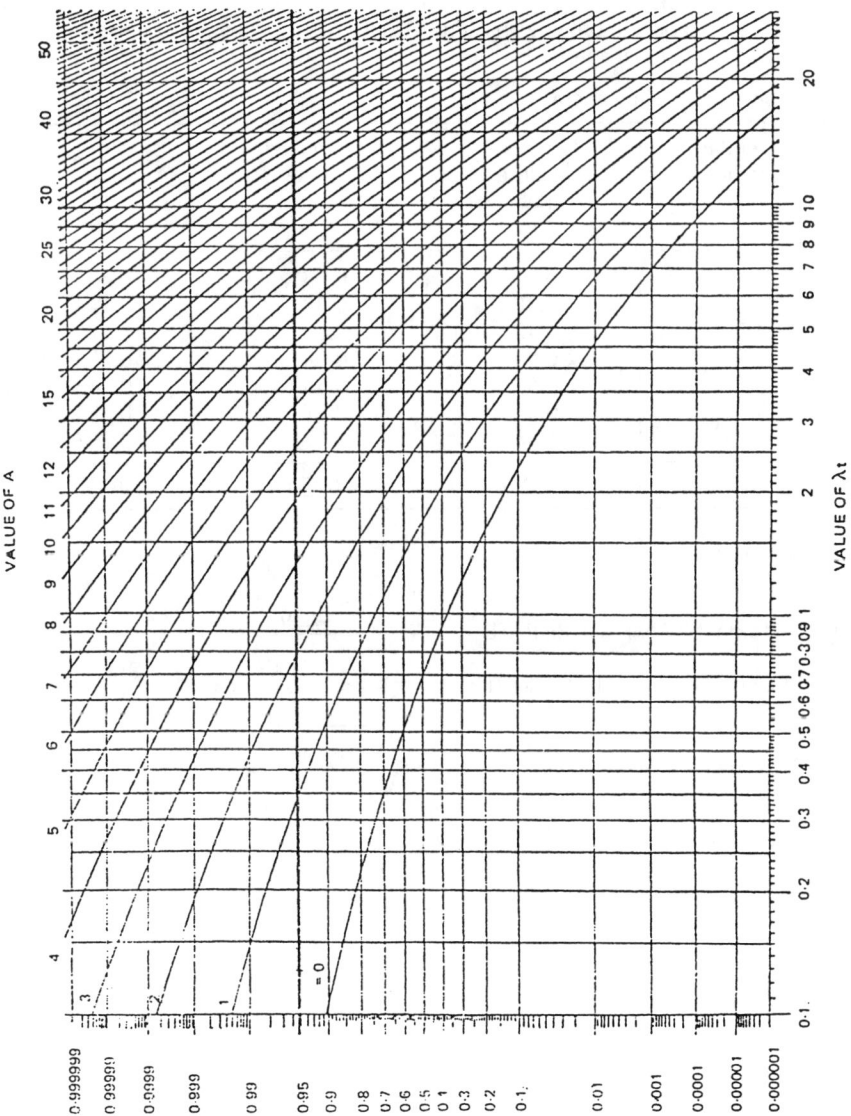

Appendix 16: Calculations of Reliability Alert Levels Based on Components Confirmed Failures

Example 4 -   Component Confirmed Failures by Individual Components in a Three-Monthly Period

Method: Alert Level = The 'corrected' Mean of the Quarterly Failure Rates plus 1 Standard Deviation of this mean, based on past seven calendar quarters of confirmed component failure rates per 1,000 hours to provide an Alert Level for use as a quarterly period of comparison.

Component: Main Generator

Calendar Quarter	Quarterly Failure Rate (u)	Corrected Rate (C)	(C²)
2/74	0.21	0.63*	0.397
3/74	3.38	0.38	0.144
4/74	0.42	0.42	0.176
1/75	0.84	0.84	0.706
2/75	0.59	0.59	0.348
3/75	0.57	0.57	0.325
4/75	1.38	0.63*	0.397
	4.39Σ(u)	4.06Σ(C)	2.493Σ(C²)

N (months) = 7
Σ = Totals

QUARTERLY MEAN FAILURE RATE $= \dfrac{\Sigma(u)}{N} = \dfrac{4.39}{7} = 0.63$

CORRECTED MEAN FAILURE RATE C $= \dfrac{\Sigma C}{N} = \dfrac{4.06}{7} = \underline{0.58}$

STANDARD DEVIATION, SD $= \sqrt{\dfrac{\Sigma(C^2) - \dfrac{(\Sigma C)^2}{N}}{N-1}}$

$= \sqrt{\dfrac{2.493 - \dfrac{(4.06)^2}{7}}{6}}$

$= \sqrt{\dfrac{2.493 - 2.355}{6}}$

$= \underline{0.15}$

ALERT LEVEL $= \bar{C} + 1\,SD = 0.58 \div 0.15 = \underline{0.73}$

---

*Where an individual Quaterly Failure Rate falls outside plus or minus 50% of the uncorrected Quarterly Mean Failure Rate (0.63 in this case), then this Mean is to be used as a Corrected Rate in place of the uncorrected Quarterly Failure Rate.

Appendix 17: A Sample of SIA Aircraft Fleet Reliability Summary

AIRCRAFT OPERATION REVIEW			
AIRCRAFT TYPE: B747-200/-300	**JAN**	**FEB**	**MAR**
AIRCRAFT IN FLEET	14	14	13
AIRCRAFT IN SERVICE	12.61	12.21	11.42
TOTAL HOURS FLOWN	4431	3931	4080
AVERAGE DAILY UTILIZATION PER AIRCRAFT	11.36	11.55	11.45
TOTAL NUMBER OF LANDINGS	1014	922	963
AVERAGE FLYING HOURS PER LANDING	4.37	4.26	4.24
NUMBER OF SYSTEMS DEFECTS	374	308	281
RATE PER 1,000 DEPARTURES	369	342	296
DELAYS > FIFTEEN MINS. INCLUDING CANCELATIONS:			
7Q AND 7R	19	21	29
FREIGHTER	10	7	4
TOTAL	29	28	33
RATE PER 100 REVENUE DEPARTURES	2.86	3.11	3.48
TOTAL NUMBER OF REVENUE DEPARTURES	1014	900	948

Appendix 18a: Name List of SIA Line Stations

SIA Engineering Company has its own engineering representatives at the following stations:

1. Bangkok (BKK)
2. Beijing (BJS)
3. Colombo (CMB)
4. Frankfurt (FRA)
5. Fukuoka (FUK)
6. Hong Kong (HKG)
7. Istanbul (IST)
8. Jakarta (GGK)
9. Los Angeles (LAX)
10. London (LHR)
11. Male (MLE)
12. Manila (MNL)
13. Narita (NRT)
14. Penang (PEN)
15. Seoul (SEL)
16. Sydney (SYD)
17. Taipei (TPE)
18. San Francisco (SFO)
19. New York (JFK)

The following ground handling agents are appointed to provide maintenance for Singapore Airlines aircraft at the following line stations.

STATION			HANDLING AGENT
ADL	-	Adelaide	Qantas
AKL	-	Auckland	Air New Zealand
ANC	-	Anchorage	Northwest
ATH	-	Athen	Olympic
BJS	-	Beijing	SIA Engineering Co.
BKK	-	Bangkok	Thai International/SIA Engineering Co.
BNE	-	Brisbane	Qantas
BOM	-	Bombay	British Airways/Swissair Air India
BSL	-	Basle	Balair
BRU	-	Brussels	Delta
BWN	-	Bandar Seri Begawan	Royal Brunei
CAI	-	Cairo	Swissair
CDG	-	Paris	UTA
CEB	-	Cebu	SIA Engineering Co.
CGK	-	Jakarta	SIA Engineering Co.
CHC	-	Christchurch	Air New Zealand
CPH	-	Copenhagen	Scandinavia
DEL	-	Delhi	Air India/Swissair
DHA	-	Dhahran	KLM
DRW	-	Darwin	Qantas

Appendix 18b: Name list of SIA Line Stations (Cont'd)

STATION			HANDLING AGENT
DUR	-	Durban	South African Airways
DXB	-	Dubai	Emirates/SIA Engineering Co.
FCO	-	Rome	KLM
FRA	-	Frankfurt	Lufthansa
FUK	-	Fukuoka	JAL/SIA Engineering Co.
HKG	-	Hong Kong	Haeco
HNL	-	Honolulu	Canadian
IST	-	Istanbul	SIA Engineering Co
JED	-	Jeddah	KLM
JFK	-	New York	United
JNB	-	Johannesburg	South African Airways
KHI	-	Karachi	Gulf Air
KUL	-	Kuala Lumpur	MAS
LAX	-	Los Angeles	Trans World/ SIA Engineering Co.
LGK	-	Langkawi	MAS/SIA Engineering Co.
LHR	-	London	British Airways
MAA	-	Madras	British Airways
MAN	-	Manchester	British Airways
MEL	-	Melbourne	Qantas
MLE	-	Male	SIA Engineering Co.
MNL	-	Manila	Philippines/ SIA Engineering Co.
MRU	-	Mauritius	Air Mauritius
NGO	-	Nagoya	Japan Airlines
NRT	-	Narita	Japan Airlines
OSA	-	Osaka	Japan Airlines
PEK	-	Beijing	SIA Engineering Co.
PEN	-	Penang	MAS/SIA Engineering Co.
PER	-	Perth	Qantas
SEL	-	Seoul	Korean Air/ SIA Engineering Co.
SFO	-	San Franciso	United
SPL	-	Amsterdam	KLM
SXF	-	Berlin	Lufthansa
SYD	-	Sydney	Qantas
TPE	-	Taipei	China Airlines/ SIA Engineering Co.
VIE	-	Vienna	Olyimpic
YVR	-	Vancouver	Air Canada
YYZ	-	Toronto	Air Canada
ZRH	-	Zurich	Swissair/SIA Engineering Co.

Index

A

Abacus, 51, 106, 107, 136, 150, 241

Abu Dhabi 14, 246

Aerolineas Argentinas 51

Air Force and Navy Standard 78

Air France 104

Air India 48

Air Traffic Control (ACT) 159

Air Transport World 19, 59, 168, 242

Airbus 14, 48, 72, 78, 168, 183, 187, 224, 247

Airline Business 18

airline industry 4

Airplane Condition Monitoring System 85, 86

airport, see Singapore Changi International Airport

airworthiness 54, 77, 79, 82, 92

Alitalia 105

Allen, R.L. 45, 61

Amadeus 106

American Express 129

American Society for Quality Control (ASQC) 31,

Apollo 104, 105

Association of Southeast Asian Nations (ASEAN) 50, 235

Auckland 58

Australia 13, 72, 98, 197, 198

B

Bailes, C.V. 45, 61

Balmain 179

Bandar Seri Begawan 155

Bandung 224

Bangladesh 172

BBC 184

Beechcraft 97

Belgravia 172-176

benchmark 25, 52, 167, 168, 170

Best Airline Award 20,

Blue Lane 117, 143

BOAC 9,

Boeing 10, 14, 15, 20, 48, 58, 78, 247

Boeing Everett 20

Bounds, G., 1, 6, 237, 238

Britain, see United Kingdom, the

British Airways (BA) 13, 14, 105

Brussels 14, 173, 223

Brussels International Airport 172

business managers, 1

Business Times, The 28, 166

*Business Travel
    International* 20,

C

Cabin Management/
    Interactive Video System
    (CMIV) 181, 182
Canada 21,
Cathay Pacific Airways 105,
    106, 169
Celestel 75, 180
Cenkarang Airport, 143
Certificate of Maintenance
    Reviews (CMR) 89
Cessna 96
Cheok, C.H. 169
Cheong, Choong Kong, Dr. 8,
    28, 166,
China 69
China Airlines 105
Christopher, M. 35, 41, 48, 61,
    64, 65, 75, 130, 139
Civil Aviation Authority of
    Singapore (CAAS) 53, 54,
    57, 77, 78, 82-84, 86, 93,
    94, 116
Civil Aviation Department 12,
CNN International 180
Cohen, Steven 3, 4, 6,
Collins, B. 67, 73, 75
Combi 48
competence 34,
competitive strategies
Concorde 13, 14,
Conde Nast Traveler 19
Copenhagen 51, 206
corporate mission 38, 46,
    53, 173
critical quality factors 52, 54,
    130, 133, 134, 136

critical success factors 52
'Customer First' 23, 24
customer focus 22, 37, 39, 52,
    64, 176
customer needs 15
customer retention 131
customer satisfaction 4, 36, 40,
    43, 132
customer service 34, 37, 47,
    49, 53, 78, 129-131, 133-137,
    141, 142, 151, 193, 215, 216

D

Dale, B.G. 66, 75
Delaplane, G.W. 44, 61
Delta Air Lines 50
Departure Control System
    (DCS) 114, 115, 126, 147,
    154, 155
Dhahran 14
Dhaka, 172
Digital Equipment
    Corporation (DEC) 51
Dragonair 105
Drucker, Peter 51, 61, 64, 75
Dusseldorf 126

E

Ee, T.H. 171, 177
Emirates Airlines 168
Environmental Protection
    Agency 3,

F

Faro 126
Federal Express 36,
flight operations 39
flight simulator 97
Fong, W.P. 170
Frankfurt 117

Frenzel, C.W. 105, 127
fuel savings committee 13,

G
Garuda 51
Garvin, David 31, 41,
General Electric 45
General Motors
    Corporation 29,
Globalserve 106
Glueck, W.F. 43, 61
government 6, 9, 10, 11,
    33, 59
    British 13
    Malaysia 9, 13
    Singapore 9, 10, 11, 38, 49,
    59, 79
ground services 39, 49, 152,
    167, 170-172, 216, 218
Gryna, F.M. 44, 60, 61
Guam 12,

H
H. Alias 172
Hamilton, Keith 8,
Heathrow 143, 155
Higher Ground 57, 137, 227
Hong Kong 12, 106, 117, 169,
    198, 224
Honolulu 12, 14, 164
Humble, J. 65, 75

I
IBM 36,
Inflight Catering Center 59
inflight services 39, 49, 53,
    141, 142, 179-181, 193
International Air Transport
    Association (IATA) 19, 21,
    143, 170

International Organization for
    Standards (ISO) 3, 4, 30,
    36, 37
    International Standard
    ISO/DIS 8402 3, 31, 36
    ISO 9000 6, 41
    ISO 9002 203, 210
    ISO 9004 36, 37
INTRAMAR 53
ITN Worldvision News, 180

J
Jakarta 224
Japan 180, 201
Japan Airlines 48, 170
Jauch, L.R. 43, 61
Juran, J.M. 29, 44, 60, 61

K
KLM 59, 104, 105

L
Lai, Kwok Chiew Peter 14,
LaLonde, B.J. 133, 139
Learjet 97, 98
Lee, G. 198, 211
Lee, Kuan Yew 17, 50
Lim, Chin Beng 7,
Lim, E. 171
London 13, 155, 202, 203, 206
Los Angeles 115, 164, 184,
    201, 246
Lovelock, C. 166, 179, 195
Lufthansa 12,

M
Maintenance Planning
    Document (MRD) 88
Maintenance Review Board
    (MRB) 88

Maintenance Steering Group
(MSG) 87, 88
Malacca Straits, the 13,
Malay Mail, The 8,
Malaya Federation 7,
Malayan Airways Limited
(MAL) 7,
Malaysia 9, 98
Federation of 7, 8,
Malaysia Singapore Airline
(MSA) 9, 10,
Malaysian Airline System
(MAS) 9, 17, 48, 105, 106
Malaysian Airways Limited
(MAL) 7, 8,
Malcolm Baldrige National
Quality Award 36,
management 3, 4, 35, 37, 38,
39, 44, 45, 55, 77, 92, 93, 95,
99, 122, 127, 129, 130, 153,
170, 172, 174, 179, 185, 190,
194, 215, 216
approach 2, 5
commitment 38, 135, 215
concept viii,
leadership 38, 213
systems 38, 60
Management Development
Center (MDC) 229-234
Managing Director's Award
217, 218
market quality management
(MQM) 63
market research 66
Mega Ark 48
Megatop 48, 75, 48, 180, 181,
183, 247
Mercury Singapore Airlines
Ltd 9,
Meurrens, L.F. 177

Military Standard 78
Motorola 51, 52, 62,
133, 129

N
Narita 117
National Aerospace Standard
7, 155, 1648
National Productivity Board
(NPB) 234
National University of
Singapore x
Faculty of Business
Administration x
Naumes, W. 47, 62
New York 223
New Zealand 72

O
Oakland, J.S. 66, 75,
222, 227
Ocean Steam Ship 9,
Oporto 126
Outlook 55, 62, 75, 166,
227, 235
'Outstanding Service on the
Ground' program 49

P
Paine, F.T. 47, 62
Paris 179
Passages 106
Passenger Name Record
(PNR) 147, 149, 150, 153
Passenger Transfer Manifest
(PTM) 156
people-focused management
system 2,
performance measures 51,
52, 54

Perspectives 38, 41, 62, 94, 195
Perth 58, 96
Philippine Airlines 105
PHOENIX 101, 102
Pillay, J.Y. 8, 10, 15, 166
pilot reports, see pireps
pireps 85, 86, 254-256
Portugal 126
Priority Passenger Service (PPS) 73, 79
process oriented approach 1,
Puri, S.C. 3, 4, 6, 37, 41,

Q

quality 1, 24, 29, 30, 31, 32, 43, 55, 64, 65, 78, 79, 129, 173, 174, 200, 221
    achievement 57
    assurance 43, 81
    audit 78
    control 43, 56, 79-81, 89, 93, 208
    council 55, 60
    definition 29, 30, 31, 32, 81. 82
    expert 29
    improvement 43
    improvement program 4
    management 2, 4, 30, 175, 207, 222
    objective 4, 51, 52
    policies 57
    program 4
Quantas 9, 20,

R

Rakowski, J. P. 133, 139
Recurring Defect Committee 91

reliability 34, 53, 54, 77, 79, 84, 85, 87, 88, 90
    definition 88
reliability control board (RCB) 57, 84
Rosander, A.C. 118, 127
Ross, J.E. 28, 29, 41, 166
Royal Brunei Airlines 105

S

safety 53, 77, 79, 176
San Francisco 14
Saudi Arabia 14
Scandinavian Airlines 51
Semi-Automated Business Research Environment (SABRE) 104
service and performance index (SPI) 23, 53, 118, 119, 135, 170, 219
service leader 35
service performance 35,
service quality 25, 32, 34, 35, 36,
Service Quality Center 234, 235
service recovery 145
SIA Properties (SIAP) 216, 241
SIA Training Center 230
SilkAir 20, 69, 70, 241
Singapore 7-13, 15, 17, 32, 46, 70, 72, 96, 111, 146, 155, 169, 184, 201-203, 232, 246
Singapore Air Navigation Order 53
Singapore Airlines (SIA) viii, ix, x, 1, 4, 5, 7-28, 38, 39, 46-51, 53, 55-59, 69-75, 77-81, 87, 89, 92-95, 97-102, 105-115,

117-123, 126, 129, 132-139, 141-149, 151-156, 159, 161-163, 166-173, 177, 179-181, 183-189, 191, 193, 195, 197-200, 202-204, 211, 213-225, 227, 229-233, 235, 237-241, 246-256, 260
Engineering Company (SIAEC) 80-82, 92, 216, 241, 248
Engineering Division (SIAED) 80-82, 248
    Engineering Planning Department (SIAED-EPD) 80, 81, 91, 248
    Quality Control Department (SIAED-QC) 80, 81, 248
    Technical Services Department (SIAED-TSD) 80, 81, 83, 92, 248
Singapore Airport Terminal Services (SATS) 25, 126, 134, 135, 168, 203, 211, 222, 241
    SATS Inflight Catering Center 199, 203-210, 241
Singapore Airworthiness Requirements 53, 82
Singapore Business 51, 62
Singapore Changi International Airport 49, 51, 59, 70, 111, 115, 150, 165, 166, 203
Singapore Flying College 96-98, 241
Singapore Tourist Promotion Board (STPB) 74
Staff-Ideas-in-Action (S-I-A) scheme 220

Stempel, Robert C. 29,
Straits Steamship 9
strategic alignment references
strategic quality management (SQM) 43-46, 60, 61
    approach 44
    brainstorming 45
    cycle 60
    definition 43, 44
    profit-quality approach 45
Sunday Times, The 181, 184, 195
Swissair 20, 50, 51, 59, 105, 114, 115, 223
Sydney 155, 246

T
Taipei 117
Taiwan 106
Taylor, Frederick 29,
Teheran 126
Temasek Holdings 14, 241
Tenner, A.R. 32,
Thailand 98
time-oriented program 2,
Toh, G.M. 168, 177
Tokyo 115, 201
Toro, I.J.
Toronto 223
Total quality management (TQM) viii, ix, 1-6, 22, 25, 27, 28, 30, 32, 36-41, 171, 222, 237, 238
    approach 4, 5, 29, 38, 39
    definition 3, 4, 36
    experts 1
    initiatives 25
    model 4
    practitioners 1
    product-centered aspects 4

service-related areas 4
system 36, 37, 40
theorists 1
Tradewinds 105
Training Award 235
Travel Industry Globe
    Awards 20,
Travel Weekly 20,
Turner inflight
    programming 184

U
United Airlines 164
United Kingdom, the 20, 197
United States of America, the
    12, 17, 72, 105, 117, 197
    Department of
    Transportation 118
    Federal Aviation Authority
    77, 78

Federal Aviation Regulation
    145 53
USAir 105
Utzig, L. 45, 62

V
Vandermerwe, S. 166,
    179, 195

W
Winning Ways Award 191
Wiseman, C. 103, 127
World Marketing
    Conference 22,
Worldspan 106

Z
Zeithaml, V.A. 34, 35,
Zinszer, P.H. 133, 139
Zurich 51